IN ALL RESPECTS READY

For Paul Scambler,
who justified my intuition
Gratefully
Ted Watt
Victoria '89

IN ALL RESPECTS READY

THE MERCHANT NAVY AND THE BATTLE OF THE ATLANTIC, 1940~1945

COMMANDER FREDERICK B. WATT,
RCN (R) RETD.

Frederick B. Watt

Prentice-Hall Canada Inc., Scarborough, Ontario

Canadian Cataloguing in Publication Data

Watt, Frederick B., 1901-
In all respects ready

ISBN 0-13-453630-4 (Case) 0-13-453648-7 (Paper)

1. World War, 1939-1945—Transportation. 2. World War, 1939-1945—Personal narratives, Canadian. 3. Merchant marine—Canada—History—20th century. 4. Canada. Naval Boarding Service. 5. Watt, Frederick B., 1901- I. Title.

D779.C2W37 1985 940.54′5971 C85-099145-5

Every reasonable attempt has been made to find copyright holders. The publishers would be pleased to have any errors or omissions brought to their attention.

Cover: *Convoy, Afternoon,* by Donald Cameron MacKay. Courtesy Canadian War Museum/National Museum of Man/National Museums of Canada.

Prentice-Hall Canada Inc., Scarborough, Ontario
Prentice-Hall Inc., Englewood Cliffs, New Jersey
Prentice-Hall International, Inc., London
Prentice-Hall of Australia Pty. Limited, Sydney
Editora Prentice-Hall do Brasil, Ltda., Rio de Janeiro
Prentice-Hall of India Private Limited, New Delhi
Prentice-Hall of Japan, Inc., Tokyo
Prentice-Hall of Southeast Asia Pte. Ltd., Singapore
Prentice-Hall Hispanoamericana, S.A., Mexico
Whitehall Books Limited, Wellington, New Zealand

ISBN: 0-13-453630-4 (Case) 0-13-453648-7 (Paper)

Production Editor: Bruce Erskine
Design: Gail Ferreira Ng-A-Kien
Production: Joanne Matthews
Composition: CompuScreen Typesetting Ltd.
Printed and bound in Canada by T.H. Best Printing Co. Ltd.
1 2 3 4 5 89 88 87 86 85

Contents

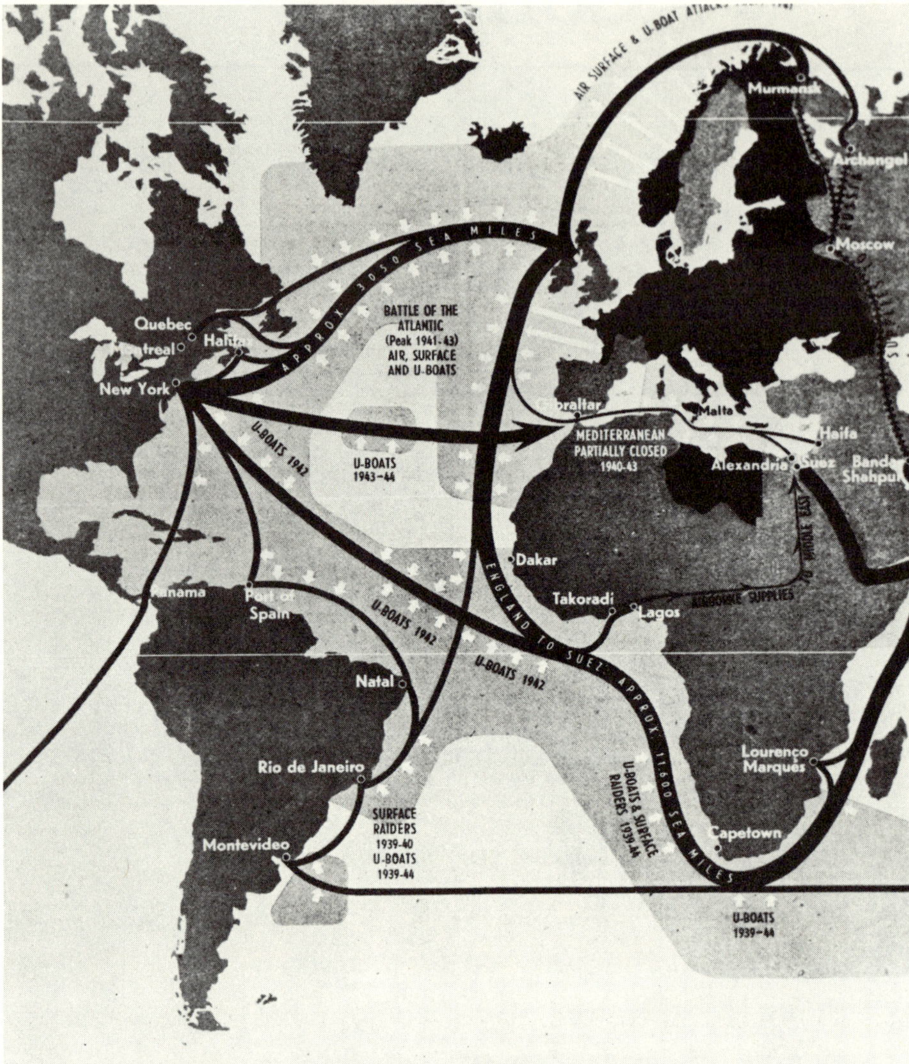

Maritime Command Museum

The routes and the risks. This map indicates the range of the convoys that plied the North Atlantic during WW II—and the range of the German U-Boats and surface raiders that inflicted so much damage on the convoys.

Preface

The Battle of the Atlantic was the longest, most unremitting campaign of World War II. It is arguable that it was the most crucial contest of all, for it was fought to keep Britain from falling to a Nazi machine that overran Europe with fearsome ease. Had England been lost, in President Roosevelt's words, "all America would be living at the point of a gun." England's stubborn stand, fuelled by the resources of the New World, created the first crack in the iron will of Hitler's Reich, and led the way to victory by the Allies.

This book does not attempt a full treatment of the war at sea. Rather, it is a personal history, set against the blackest days of the struggle. It tells, in human terms, of the little-known contribution of a handful of Canadians to the winning of the Battle. In the perspective of history, that contribution takes on a special significance. For these Canadians fought their war on a psychological front, one which has meaning today in a society which rejects the sense of duty that enabled ordinary men to sacrifice their lives for a cause that was not always clear.

The strategists, the men, and the ships of the Fighting Navy have dominated most histories of the Battle of the Atlantic. Accounts of the savage clashes between warships and Nazi marauders often acknowledge only in passing the heroism of those who manned the merchant convoys the Navy fought so hard to defend.

Those convoys formed the fragile lifeline without which Britain could not have survived. They carried vital supplies of food, munitions, and fuel through waters prowled by an enemy bent on cutting the slender thread. U-boats and surface raiders attacked the convoys mercilessly, in full knowledge that England would be more easily conquered by strangulation than invasion. In the early years of the war, vessels in the North Atlantic convoys were being sunk faster than shipyards could replace them. The cost in precious materials was huge, the loss of human life devastating.

Merchant seamen from many nations—all of them civilians—laboured anonymously aboard such ships. Down in the heat of a tanker's stokehold, you could not know if your vessel would be the next one torpedoed. You had no gun with which to fight: you fought by doing your job in spite of the danger. Death by fire, explosion, or drowning in the frigid sea could very well be your reward. Indeed, fewer than fifty percent of merchant crews survived the sinking of their ships.

Such odds provided fertile ground for psychological warfare by the enemy. German propagandists broadcast a potent message: such sacrifice was futile in a war already lost. Most vulnerable to this subversion were Dutch, French, Belgian and Norwegian seamen, whose homelands had fallen. The argument was cynically put. Yes, Britain was willing to fight to the last—the last Dutchman, Dane, Free Frenchman or Pole. Enemy agents in the ports worked methodically on the fears, suspicions, and grievances of the crews.

As a result, significant numbers of cargo carriers were paralyzed in harbour by something called, in wartime euphemism, "crew trouble". The term covered all manner of disturbances and delays, from sitdown strikes, to damaging of engines, to desertions. In essence it meant that crews were refusing duty—defying orders to sail and cutting off the vital supply lines at source.

The convoys faced a threat potentially even greater than that of enemy raiders on the high seas: they faced inner collapse.

In the beginning, the Allied nations had no coherent or effective means of countering the attacks on crew morale. As the problem worsened, some explored forceful expedients; it was argued, for example, that British merchant seamen refusing to sail should be pressed into service with the infantry. Canada passed Orders in Council that would allow even foreign seamen to be prosecuted and detained.

But a solution of another kind was developing, a product of the initiative and insight of a half dozen Naval Reserve ratings in Halifax, Nova Scotia.

These men worked under the command of the harbour's Naval Control officer, boarding and searching the merchant ships funnelled through the major port on their way to join overseas convoys. Many had been loaded in the still-neutral United States, and there was a strong threat that enemy saboteurs would take advantage of the situation, as they had in World War I, to place time bombs in ships' cargoes. The boarding party found no bombs, but they were quick to detect explosive attitudes among members of the ships' crews.

Themselves peacetime merchant seamen, the Reservists readily identified with the crews of the ships they examined. Their insights into the causes of low morale made them valuable intelligence sources to the senior officers wrestling with the crisis. They also offered practical ideas for meeting the danger. These, passed along the chain of command to Ottawa, helped formulate a full-scale plan to neutralize the enemy's psychological offensive.

Ottawa's methods—rooted in man-to-man contact between members of the Naval Boarding Service and the merchant crews—combined the practice of seeking out and correcting genuine injustice or negligence by shipowners with the passing on of information that would counter dangerous rumours. The boarders became the crewmen's advocates and friends; they were scrupulous about telling the truth, even if it were hard truth, for they realized that total credibility was crucial to their effectiveness.

And effective they were. Their accomplishments were less tangible, perhaps, than those of corvette sailors who scored kills on enemy submarines; but in the context of serious threats to convoy morale, they had remarkably far-reaching effects.

Boarding Services were established in nine Canadian ports, based on this record of success. And the commanders of Britain's navy took a sharp interest. In 1942 Admiralty's Director of Trade Division Captain (later Vice Admiral) B.B. Schofield wrote Ottawa: "I feel that nothing is done over here to bolster the morale of our Allied seamen—or even our own—and that MI 5 provide the wrong sort of security officers. They aren't sailors and the masters resent them. Your Naval Boarding Service is a much better show altogether."

At war's end, records of 50,000 boardings told the story

in terse, practical terms. The reports add rich texture and human interest to the history of the war. Many of these incidents are recounted in the pages of this book; they illustrate the progressive philosophy of the Service as its role was worked out in "hands on" fashion. Some are highly dramatic and have not till now been public knowledge.

The writer was directly responsible for the Naval Boarding Service from its beginnings until its last member was demobilized. As such he was one of the four basic links in the chain of command from the men in the boarding launches to the makers of policy in Ottawa.

The other three were:

Chief Petty Officer A.V. Oxner, B.E.M., who, as Able Seaman in the original party, handled the training of personnel.

Captain R.H. Oland, O.B.E., the Naval Control Service Officer responsible for the organizing and sailing of Halifax convoys.

Captain E.S. Brand, O.B.E., Director of Naval Intelligence and Trade, who was the primary mover of corrective action taken at many levels of government to meet the morale crisis.

This book is the five-year record of the lessons taught by the lives—and frequently the deaths—of the most courageous men I would ever know: The men who took the supply vessels to sea. During the war, I wrote a tribute to them, a narrative poem titled *Who Dare to Live*. It said a good deal about the attributes needed to win a war; but, across the intervening years, it has become apparent to me that I had another story to tell, that of the boarding service and the working philosophy it developed. The standards of conduct among those men were, it seems to me, of the highest order. They are among the few positives which can be drawn out of the experience of war, and they serve as a model of what is imperative to a society that wishes to avoid repeat of such wars.

A number of those who shared the experiences I have set down are still living, and they, along with members of the Directorate of History, Department of National Defence, and the National Archives of Canada have been invaluable in my quest for accuracy. The point of view is, naturally, my own; but, where possible, I have used the words of others to expand the dimensions of the narrative.

My particular gratitude is due Dr. Gerald Morgan for the Introduction which follows. We first met four decades ago, when Morgan was a young Master Mariner who had served on the bridges of cargo carriers under three allied flags, and survived the Battle of the Atlantic.

F.B. Watt
Victoria, B.C. 1985

Introduction

It seems characteristic of our time to kick at "the system" and swear our world's in a mess. And it's true that our society produces plenty of wrongs. But those of us who experienced World War II can say with truth, "It could have been a lot worse."

Forty years ago the hopes of the people of the "free world"—and of millions held captive—rested with a many-flagged mob of merchant seamen whose part in the system was simply: do or die. Had they failed, our world could have been a vast prison where there'd be no complaining at all.

Sometimes during that crisis the merchant seamen faltered. They had good cause to distrust the system which relied on them; most were underpaid, and few were appreciated. Still they sailed into the certain dangers of the Battle of the Atlantic. Their ships were the lifeline of Europe's last stand against Hitler. Without the petroleum, the munitions, the food and the troops carried by Atlantic convoys, the Nazis would have undoubtedly have taken Britain. It is arguable that Hitler would next have turned his machine against the North American nations so committed to preventing her fall.

Commander Fredrick B. Watt knew hundreds of these seamen; their moments of decision, the difference between success and failure, are the substance of this memoir. The events in this book speak for themselves. Yet a look at the historical background seems in order, to give fuller meaning to the tragedy of this war, and to the vital part played in it by the merchantmen and their escorts.

Events in Halifax under Mackenzie King's government owed much to Admiral Sir John Fisher and Kaiser Wilhelm II, who between them floated many a corpse. Theirs was a contest begun in the 1890s, between the old strategies of seapower which had made Britain imperial, and new notions which threatened to make her totally vulnerable. "Jacky"

Fisher (whose genius framed the "battleship mentality") prevailed, at horrendous cost.

Among six empires crippled or destroyed by the first World War was the 48-year-old Second Reich of "Kaiser Bill", whose naval and merchant fleets were seized as spoils in 1918. But the German sea-challenge was renewed by the power that rose from the ashes of a malignant peace to replace the Second Reich: the vaster, more brutal Third Reich of Adolf Hitler, aimed at a thousand years of world control. Hitler's grasping empire swallowed ten maritime nations in the early stages of the second World War.

At first the sea war was eerily familiar. The nations allied against Hitler often fought with the same sailors and the same ships as those used against the Kaiser a generation before. Sometimes the same old guns were mounted in newer ships. Sometimes (it was said) the same rats and cockroaches were chased in the old ships. For seasoned mariners the new war was, at first, a repeat of the old.

Merchant officers and men signed into the navy again to sail warships, although thousands were needed for usual seafaring, and some who had commanded destroyers in the first World War stayed in their merchant craft for the second. But in 1939-45 there were many merchant sailors new to war. They were part of a younger generation; some came from countries that had been neutral in World War I.

For all these seamen, old salts as well as new hands, the new sea-war developed a ferocity which none could have expected. In the end, it was far more terrible than the first one.

In both wars, each foe tried to starve the other. In World War I, British naval strategists baulked at a close-blockage of the German coast, counting instead on a distant-blockade. As a result, the Germans were able to freely send out submarines to sink scores of merchant ships; in fact they almost managed to blockade the British Isles. Britain was saved in the nick of time by the ancient practice of convoy-sailing, revived in 1917 on the insistence, apparently, of the U.S. Navy. The merchantmen, reprieved by the practice, supplied the fuel and armaments of victory.

Insensible to the lessons of history, World War II leaders followed the same pattern. Their distant-blockade of

Germany allowed U-boats to prowl freely while Allied convoys were weakly escorted to Britain, daring disaster with every trip. The Germans, quicker to learn the lessons of 1914-18, sent powerful U-boats thousands of miles past Britain, from Germany and the victim lands of Europe. Again the world's greatest merchant fleets became war's easiest targets, with deadly effect. In the face of these devastating odds, Allied merchant seamen were urged to "Do it again!"

In Canada, drastic measures were taken to preserve the ocean-link with Britain. The Dominion's navy was strengthened many times over as a "small ship" navy, designed to fight submarines. Hundreds of naval and merchant ships were built as quickly as possible, regardless of cost. The government, unable to conscript Canadians for service beyond its shores, made plans to force unwilling Allied merchant seamen back to sea.

Only those who have known both can appreciate the true differences of ocean life in peace and war. A death in battle is not the worst way of going; it's often a swift end, the soul ready. But there's no zest for combat when the sailor, trained to cope with hurricane or iceberg, with reef or traffic or fire, must endure his ship's crawling on imposed course in a drab huddle of strangers. All the while there is the suspense of waiting to see which vessel will be the next to burst into flame or a soaring cloud of debris, leaving a gap in the ranks of floating steel. In convoy the active sea-rover must bind himself on voiceless, lightless, crowded passage to strange secret points. He must bear a strained passivity, week after week, entirely dependent on the competence of a thin escort. For the restive, there's the owner ashore to think of, his champagne-bills mounting along with freights or insurance, while the war solves his problems of old tonnage as peace never could.

For many sailors, all illusion was lost in the hazards brought by war to the cold North Atlantic. For many, it might have seemed better to kick down "the system" before their lives were uselessly lost. Let the shore folk, who never learn, find other fools to "do it again". But if a demoralized sailor realizes he is the hope of millions of people, if someone lets him know by tone or gesture that his work, his sacrifice, is known, then he cannot but choose to sail again. This is what happened in Halifax, where the convoys assembled. How it happened is Ted Watt's tale.

He writes of his work, with others, in the Naval Boarding Service, which ensured that each ship to join a convoy for the cruise among U-boats to the mines and bombs of Britain's home waters was "in all respects ready for sea". This meant it must be seaworthy in hull, engines, guns (if supplied), lifeboats and in the minds and hearts of its crew. Battleworthy, in short, and tallied as such by the Naval Boarding Service.

Having begun his naval life in the crucial year 1917 as a boy in the famous Dover Patrol, Watt too had lived on the sea in war and peace. Presenting himself as ready in all respects for sea in 1939, he helped make others ready as well.

He did so at a time when most Naval men hoped for honours in the Battle of the Atlantic. But some had to forgo sea action so as to bear the burden of sending new men to fight the skilled foe. Ted Watt sacrificed his own chance of a command at sea among his "death or glory" comrades for the task of sending other men toward death without glory. He transformed the task, giving the seafarers a sense of purpose and meaning. He spent most of his war in Halifax, boarding thousands of ships, finding common cause with old salts, convincing querulous minds to sail again.

Many of the war's unwritten dramas can be glimpsed in the pages of this book. It recounts from a unique perspective the story of the Merchant Navy's war effort, too often seen only as a sidelight to actions involving regular armed forces.

★ ★ ★

The battle for Britain was the longest and most doubtful of the second World War. In its early months, casualties among merchant seamen exceeded those of all British armed forces together. At its end, 35,000 British merchant seamen had been lost; to their numbers must be added the thousands of sailors in exile from conquered lands who died on the explosive sea. One thousand Canadian merchant seamen were also lost. They paid this price in spite of the fact that in their own country Canadian merchant mariners were sometimes called "zombies"—the epithet applied to able-bodied men who shirked war-service; some of their cargoes were looted in the lading.

No one would have been surprised if the ocean life-line to Britain had failed. The odds were daunting as the U-boats roamed at will. But the sailors went to sea in spite of the risks; and their vital cargoes reached the United Kingdom, where planes were fueled and armies fed, and where invasion never came.

The events in this book vividly recall the merchant navy's war. Some engagements are justly famous. The sacrifice of *Jervis Bay*, sunk while defending her convoy, has won her an honoured place in naval history. She put up her famous challenge in the early days, before well armed escort vessels were widely available. After *Jervis Bay* went down, the freighter *Beaverford*, in the same convoy, defied the German raider with only two guns for five hours before being sunk with all hands.

There were terrible ironies. When the old Swedish vessel, *Stureholm*, refused to sail in convoy, after returning alone into Halifax with *Jervis Bay* survivors picked up at sea, a number of the prudent neutrals among her crew were replaced by British survivors. The *Stureholm* sailed in the next convoy and was sunk with all hands.

Whatever the statistics (and these were kept secret) might reveal about the concept of safety in numbers, no one supposed that a British convoy was any sort of guarantee; sailing this way was a calculated risk, known to be only somewhat effective. In addition, it was a risk shared. Norwegians suffered heavily, losing 54 ships in British convoys while Norway was still neutral. After Norway was invaded, this writer picked up Norwegian survivors from a ship sunk in convoy HX 133. The men were desolate as they huddled on our deck: they had no home to go to, even if we did reach port. The Norwegian experience is vividly set down in Per Hansson's tale, *Hver Tiende Mann Matte Dø*, (translated as *One In Ten Had To Die*). It's little wonder that

Meinerth Wick, a Norwegian, was such a valuable member of Ted Watt's team.

Sometimes the bombed British ports were too battered to receive convoys; instead of urging ships to run the gauntlet, the Canadians had to hold them back in Halifax. There have always been prime seamen who rove from flag to flag, from trade to trade, looking for decent pay. They chafe at restriction; and in wartime they are all the more choosy when part of the wage is death. However, few of the men in control on-shore were sailors, and few knew sailors well. As a result, officials often found themselves involved with complicated and longstanding crew problems.

The Greek ship *Michael J. Embiricos*, like many others a relic of the first World War, had, after a year of the second war at sea, lost twenty deserters in Halifax. Freelancers of the marine world, the Greeks had, on the outbreak of war, found their vessels so prized by rival British and Canadian shippers that their neutral government had raised a seaman's pay from a pittance of $30 a month to the U.S. level of $210; and still the owners profited. Later, when Greece fell to the Axis, the now-exiled government was persuaded to cut pay back to the British level of $30 a month.

Small wonder that many Greek seamen deserted. In the vast new U.S. merchant fleet a seaman could earn $1,000 for the same job, at the same risk, on a single voyage to a bombed British port. No small part of the Canadian task was to keep Greek merchant sailors facing the sea war in their own ships rather than choosing better ones or simply vanishing into a safe job ashore.

So it was with all the Allied fleets routed through Halifax. It was a major part of the battle to get the right crews aboard the right ships, to keep the seamen at their posts with, necessarily, the same spirit as that possessed by enlisted personnel.

★ ★ ★

The Battle of the Atlantic was an avoidable waste. But when flawed statecraft and strategy made it inevitable, the contest was fought magnificently by both sides. The great chain of convoys was kept moving by Canadians: by Captain Eric Brand in Ottawa, who directed convoys and tracked all vessels on the Atlantic; by control-officers like Captain Richard Oland in Halifax; by Commander Watt and his crew, boarding ship after ship, year after year. Their achievement prompted Britain's Admiralty to copy them. More than that, it saved Canadian jails from being crowded with merchant seamen. If unwilling seamen had widely preferred jail to seagoing, it would have meant a war lost.

As it happened, their sacrifice allowed "the system" to survive. Victory was celebrated with a wild exuberance which produced the Halifax riots on May 8, 1945: many Navy men joined in wholeheartedly. On May 12, 1945, Ottawa dismissed Admiral Leonard Murray, who had commanded battle in The Northwest Atlantic since 1943. Admiral Murray retired in a dignified silence, except for one memorable pronouncement:

> "The Battle of the Atlantic was not won by any Navy or Air Force, it was won by the courage, fortitude and determination of the British and Allied Merchant Navy."

Ted Watt is included in that company because of the work he details in these pages. The Commander-in-Chief's verdict is a fitting accolade to the fellowship of marine professionals Watt encountered in his career, which began in the First World War when, as gunner on H.M. armed trawler *Imperia*, he was on the Forth-Bergen patrol. It is noteworthy that another seaman-author, Joseph Conrad (aged sixty), went U-boat hunting on that same patrol with merchantmen in Navy uniform aboard the antique brigatine, H.M.S. *Ready*, which was used as a gunboat while masked as a Norse trader.

Watt and his Boarding Service performed difficult duties well, and by doing so helped bring the day of victory closer.

Gerald A. Morgan M.N.I.
Victoria, B.C.

1

"a city that watched and waited..."

It was the summer of 1940. The "Ocean Limited" discharged another wave of the human tide already overflowing Halifax. Carried by it, I was one of several middle-aged Prairie Canadians so abruptly summoned we had yet to be fitted for the uniforms that would identify us as naval officers.

The old port city had endured many wars. I had known another here a generation before. At fifteen, filled with a landsman's romantic conception of the sea and a boy's unquestioning patriotism, I had lied my way into the Navy and sailed overseas "to fight the Hun". Two years later, a Leading Seaman, I had been mustered out when the War to End All Wars exhausted itself.

Now there was another one and I was pushing forty. Between the wars, however, I had qualified on the West Coast as a lieutenant in the Royal Canadian Navy Volunteer Reserve and had every expectation of a quick berth in a fighting craft.

Halifax was much as I remembered it in 1918. The North End, flattened in December, 1917, by the *Mont Blanc* explosion, had been partially rebuilt, but the Citadel and St. Mary's spire still dominated the skyline. Rising from the waterfront were the same cobbled streets, salt-weathered commercial buildings, and tenements. And populating them were the same restless clusters of merchant sailors, servicemen and their women.

The swagger of the new generation, the over-loud laughter drifting from cafes in fleeting escapes from ship or barracks, were equally familiar. I, too, had loafed down Barrington Street seeking somewhere to spend an overnight leave and an Ordinary Seaman's dollar-a-day. I could still feel the toughed-out loneliness, the underlying boredom and the one certainty—the ordeal waiting beyond Sambro Head.

That summer the city was frantically re-gearing for its wartime role as a key Allied base. Construction cranes dotted the waterfront, Off-Limits signs were everywhere, new guns and submarine nets guarded the harbour approaches and military planes roared in and out of extended Dartmouth runways. At night the entire shore gloomed in a semi-blackout; offshore, the deeper darkness was occasionally pierced by the probing fingers of searchlights. Warships constantly slipped in or out of the Naval Dockyard. Merchant ships laden with munitions, supplies, fuel or troops crowded the commercial wharves or anchored in the broad waters of Bedford Basin to await convoy.

As far as many people were concerned, the war was turning Halifax into an overcrowded hellhole. It was jammed with people from all over the country. Every scrap of living space was filled—the hotels, the private homes, the boarding houses, the tenements and the slum rooms. Some enterprising newcomers resorted to makeshift shacks thrown up on the city's fringes and on into the woods.

I was luckier than most. I had friends in town, and found comfortable quarters in a home steeped in the tradition of Maritime hospitality. But the problem of living space, while acute, wasn't the only one encountered by the thousands war had brought to town. Everyone seemed to complain constantly about insolent cabbies, bored shopkeepers, indifferent waitresses. Many of the newcomers were sick of combing the slums looking for a place to live, tired of eating bad food in bad restaurants, fed up with being exploited by landlords and other profiteers who took advantage of shortages of food, clothing and building materials.

Most Haligonians were doing their best to cope with the overcrowding, and their anger at often unfair criticism added to the tension.

But if anyone worried about difficult conditions ashore, there was always the presence of the Atlantic itself to remind them of a greater battle, one that was being fought at sea. Halifax was first and always a sea port. The moods of the cold North Atlantic waters beat strongly in the city's pulse, and she was aware of herself as the final gateway to the European passage. For a city that watched and waited and lived by the ships of war, the summer of 1940 was a black time.

The Germans called that summer The Happy Time. Their U-boats were enjoying a bountiful hunt, attacking poorly guarded merchant convoys almost at will. They destroyed four million tons of shipping in 1940.

In the Dunkirk evacuation Britain had lost the entire equipment of her Expeditionary Force, many of her best soldiers and some precious units of her Fleet. Worse, she had lost France as an ally and the substantial contribution to the protection of her seaborne supply lines which the French fleet had provided vanished overnight. The heightened dependence on the merchant convoys bringing arms, fuel, food and troops from North America coincided precisely with the moment when the Allied navies were least equipped to defend them.

★ ★ ★

A German Naval War Staff memorandum dated October 1939 is revealing: "Germany's principal enemy in this war is Britain. Her most vulnerable spot is her maritime trade ... The principal target of our Naval Strategy is the merchant ship, not only the enemy's but every merchantman which sails the seas in order to supply the enemy's war interests. Military success can most confidently be expected if we attack British sea communications where they are most accessible to us with the greatest ruthlessness. The final aim of such attacks is to cut off all imports into and exports from Britain."[1]

This strategy was brutally obvious in 1940. The Germans had abandoned all gallantries, attacking even passenger ships without warning. In an attempt to even the odds, some merchant vessels had been armed, and this gave the Nazi raiders further excuse to exploit the savage strategy of sudden, sneak attack. Hitler's long-range submarines prowled the convoy routes in an all-out campaign to totally destroy the merchantmen and their life-sustaining supplies for Britain.

Of this time, Winston Churchill wrote: "Battles might be won or lost, enterprises succeed or miscarry, territories might be gained or quitted, but dominating all our power to carry on the war, or even keep ourselves alive, was our mastery of the ocean routes and the free approach and entry to our ports ... the only thing that ever frightened me during the war was the U-boat peril."[2]

The availability of escorts to defend the supply lines further dwindled as summer went on. By July, with Hitler poised to invade Britain, there was even greater demand for warships to protect the Islands themselves. That meant even thinner protection for the flotillas of thirty to forty merchantmen formed up over twenty square miles of ocean. From July to October, 1940, 217 cargo carriers were sunk. The price to Germany was two U-boats.

In Halifax, where the major convoys were assembled, the cost was counted in more than tonnage. The toll in human life was mounting steadily, and the harbour city knew only too well the harsh realities of such casualty figures. Seamen whose vessels were hit hard had only a 50 per cent chance of survival. Death by explosion or fire or scalding steam, or by drowning in the malevolent grey

---

1. Quoted in *The Battle of the Atlantic*, by John Costello and Terry Hughes (London: Collins, 1977).

2. *Ibid.*

waters as a ship was sucked under—all were horrific enough. Harshest of all, floundering men from fatally hit vessels had frequently to be left behind so as not to make sitting ducks of the ships still under way. Drowning sailors had to be abandoned to the cold Atlantic so that the greater number would survive.

The harbour was a daily witness to this grim war at sea. Stricken vessels limped back to port, their open wounds slicking the sea with oil. Men who had seen the battle told their appalling stories while the pace of activity in the shipyards and recruiting stations took on ever-greater urgency.

Canada was committed to building cargo vessels that would begin to replace those lost. She would make giant steps in expanding her navy from a token pre-war force to the sophisticated fleet that became one of the largest in the world—capable of a major role in winning the Battle of the Atlantic. Officers and men, many of them Reservists like myself, poured into Halifax, eager to man the new corvettes and mine-sweepers being built in Canadian yards.

For all that I had initiated my own arrival I was still gripped by mixed emotions. Any glamour war had held for me was long gone. For several years while World War II had been moving inexorably towards detonation I had worked passionately for its prevention. Yet, while I had been inactive in the Navy for a decade, its centuries of tradition, the seagoing friendships it had brought me, and the sea itself, were a constant part of my life, refreshed by frequent visits to the West Coast. They had launched me on a successful freelance career, providing many of the subjects of my short stories in American and British magazines. They had remained a vital part of me.

When the Nazi devastation of Poland in 1939 inevitably brought the violent confrontation of Europe's dictatorships and democracies, there had been no escaping the sense of where I belonged. I sent a message to National Defence Headquarters saying where I could be located if needed. There was no acknowledgement until the summer of 1940 brought the blitzkreig and the unbelievable loss of

France. My answer came in a terse signal ordering me to Halifax.

Idealism aside, I was like a host of other Canadians, grateful to be offered a full-time, paid job again. Ten years of the Great Depression had brought desperate times and paralyzing discouragement. My family—wife Ernestine and three young sons—had stuck it out in a drafty old house on the outskirts of Edmonton while I had clawed for anything in the way of a skimpily paid writing assignment. The feeling of worthlessness had been made no easier because it had been shared by hundreds of thousands of my countrymen. Materialistic through it might be, the thought of a monthly check to keep food on my family's table was a positive among the positives and negatives that went with me to Halifax.

★ ★ ★

My arrival in Halifax was followed by several weeks of a disciplinary course in the gunnery school. Nearly every man in my class was a World War I retread and the blaze of our service ribbons got us a nickname: "the Rainbow Division".

In a straight-faced speech of welcome our petty officer instructor remarked that we looked like people who thought they knew what the Navy was all about. In case we had forgotten, he added dryly, it would be his privilege to see that we remembered.

The unaccustomed effort of the drill square and the gun battery was hard on middle-aged bones. Officially referred to as a "refresher", the course had us physically and mentally exhausted by bedtime. We rediscovered that a perfect response to a command was humanly impossible but relentlessly expected, and it offended every sense of civil justice we had developed between the wars.

But at last it was over. By the time our drill instructor ceased his daily torments and began addressing us as "Sir", we had developed a full appreciation of the Navy's wisdom in putting us through our paces. We thanked the petty officer and began the anxious wait for our active service appointments.

Two of our number departed immediately to join a destroyer. The rest suffered twenty-four hours of suspense, while making the most of the Admiralty House wardroom. Them my chit arrived. It read: "Appointed to NCSO."

"Who or what is NCSO?" I inquired anxiously.

A Volunteer Reserve lieutenant with enough shine on his monkeyjacket to suggest he had gone active at the start of hostilities the previous year volunteered that he'd seen "NCSO" on the door in the dockyard administration building—just up the corridor from "Commanding Officer, Atlantic Coast".

On the strength of this lead, I set out across the dockyards to find out who or what my destiny was.

★ ★ ★

The Commodore's broad pennant was conspicuous on a tall staff stabbing above the Yard roofs. It guided me to a venerable two-storey structure which had so far escaped the frenzied destruction and reconstruction going on around it. The sudden need to replace ancient buildings and installations with new ones for the frantically expanding Royal Canadian Navy had set dynamite banging and jackhammers ringing. They were at a crescendo when I entered the bleak lobby of the Administration building, but the noise failed to drown out the decrepit creaking of the wooden stairs leading to the second floor.

At the top, I found a frosted glass door marked *NCSO.* It led to an office occupied by a scattering of deskbound officers and three pretty secretaries. One of the young women looked up inquiringly, but before either of us could speak a huge man whose sleeve bore commander's stripes burst from a glassed-in section of the room.

I recognized him instantly. In 1923, Richard Hibbert Oland had been captain of the trawler-minesweeper *Armentieres*, one third of the Royal Canadian Navy's then miniscule West Coast fleet. I had stood my first watch at sea as a recently commissioned Volunteer Reserve sub-lieutenant under Oland; now my old captain was evidently the mysterious NCSO in person.

"Splendid! Splendid!" he roared as he bore down on me. He shook my hand vigorously and drew me into his cubicle.

Oland's staff seemed unruffled by his exuberance. Standing six feet four as he did, with the well-proportioned girth that had once made him the heart of the Navy's rugby team, the Commander naturally dominated this or any other room he occupied. Sheer enthusiasm made him seem to loom even larger.

His handsome, open features and youthful eyes had changed little in the two decades since we had become friends in our early twenties.

"I wondered when you were going to show," he grinned. "Your course finished two days ago."

"I was expected, then?" I managed.

"You're bloody right you were—from the time I spotted your name on a signal." Oland looked pleased with himself.

"You asked for me?" I asked; I confess I was still a bit disoriented.

"Any objections?" Oland's gaze sharpened.

I recovered myself. "Not if it gets me to sea quickly."

The commander frowned.

"That would get you full marks almost anywhere but here. This isn't a seagoing appointment."

"I see," I said after a pause.

He read me instantly.

"You're thirty nine, and you're afraid that if you don't catch one of the new corvettes when they commission you won't get a second chance. Right?"

I nodded.

"O.K.," he said briskly. "If you're determined to go to the glory road I can help. The Commodore and I are old friends." He beamed at me, and I doubtless looked suddenly more cheerful. "But," he said after a moment, "Let's do it my way first. Why not take a run at what we have for you here for a couple of weeks? After that, if you still feel you have to fight your war at sea, well then—fair enough."

I nodded. It seemed the least I could do for a friend. But I was embarrassed.

"I'm really sorry. There's no one I would sooner have served with," I said.

Oland seemed unperturbed. "Take it easy. You're two weeks ahead of yourself." He stood up. "Come and meet the rest of the crew. They'll give you the lay of what we do here. Tomorrow you can join the boarding party and get the feel of the harbour."

I still had no idea what kind of unit Richard Oland commanded—but I took my cue and followed him.

He introduced me to two Volunteer Reserve lieutenant commanders, John Mitchell and George Buntain, and to a mixed bag of other volunteers and officers wearing the chain stripes of Naval Reserve professionals. All, explained the commander, were veterans of merchant shipping; most had their mercantile tickets as well as their naval watchkeeping certificates. Oland left me in the competent hands of his lieutenants for briefing.

NCS, I discovered, stood for Naval Control Service. NCSO was of course Oland's title—Naval Control Service Officer. What Naval Control controlled was all merchant shipping in and out of Halifax harbour. Oland's people plotted each vessel's movements: they were responsible for every detail of convoy assembly and routing.

The nondescript room in which I stood was the nerve centre of convoy organization. Across its desks passed secret information which determined the makeup and destination of each carefully planned ship movement. Across its threshold passed the captains of each liner, freighter, tanker and escort involved.

This then was one end of the lifeline on which Britain totally depended. Each of the officers I met that day explained his job to me, and I was able to grasp the outlines of a global operation under the aegis of the British Admiralty's Trade Division. On August 26, 1939, the merchant fleets of the British Empire had come under Trade Division's careful control. This was of course a move to protect the merchant shipping and to co-ordinate procedures developed by generations of maritime traders with the defensive measures of the Fighting Navy.

The convoy system, a time-honoured Naval method of

defence, was being used in this war without significant controversy. In World War I, some strategists had rejected the convoy idea, only to find that ships going it alone were even more vulnerable. In that war, too, England had been on the verge of starvation because of attacks on supply lines by German U-boats. Apparently, this time, the lesson had been learned. Admiral Sir Eldon Manesty, organizer of the convoys that saved England in the first war, had been reactivated in 1937, when the emerging Nazi threat was becoming too starkly apparent to be ignored. He had toured the seaports of Britain's Empire, organizing a system that could be put into motion when it was needed.

When the storm broke two years later, the flash of a code word integrated the merchant and fighting fleets. Each cargo carrier was immediately requisitioned for use as needed by the Supply authorities: it would be operated by its original managers where possible. Where and when each ship would sail was dictated in a Destination Room in London.

Convoys were intricately organized. A typical movement might consist of thirty to forty ships, ranged in a dozen parallel ranks six to seven miles across. It would be headed by a flagship, carrying the convoy commodore, and, ideally, escorted by warships patrolling its outer flanks. The most vulnerable ranks, the outer ones, would be made up of ships carrying raw materials. Vessels with more precious cargoes of troops, munitions, or oil would be positioned in the protected inner ranks.

The amount of intelligence required by those making convoy decisions was enormous. The ordered schedules of peacetime had become impossible because of heavy, unpredictable casualties and the frequent changes of course made in attempts to avoid them. Word of where each vessel was at a given moment was supplied by Naval Intelligence Centres, of which Ottawa was one. These were crossroads of information sent by Naval Control Service Officers in each Allied port; Consular Shipping Officers in foreign harbours; and by customs officials at smaller points of loading and discharge.

In London, at Admiralty's Intelligence Centre, the reports were analyzed, transmitted to ports of destination and distilled to meet the requirements of the ship's managers. Messages in turn went out to each Intelligence Centre, telling of vessels heading towards its area and giving their routes and expected times of arrival—information that had to be passed to both civilian and naval authorities whose numbers were limited, for security reasons, to those with a "need to know"—based on their involvement in the phases of each ship's movement.

Apart from this intelligence-gathering role, each NCSO was responsible for the expected time of departure (E.T.D.) of every merchantman passing through his port. Not only did he issue the sailing orders and organize the convoy in which the ship left; he had to be satisfied that it was "in all respects ready" for sea.

Agents and other civilian authorities were answerable for cargoes, supplies, repairs and personnel, but NCSO was the whip that guaranteed that requirements for sailing be met in the shortest possible time. Delay meant disruption of the convoy in which the ship was to have been included. It was also up to NCSO to supply each master with updated confidential books and last-minute reports on conditions expected during the hazardous voyage ahead. Each Canadian NCSO was himself a qualified master mariner and this ensured the understanding and cooperation of the merchant captains.

The convoy system proved effective for Commonwealth ships, and was adopted by its allies, including the governments-in-exile of conquered countries. Even neutrals like the Swedes, while requiring special consideration at the security level, were seeking such shelter as might be found behind the guarded flanks of the "floating cities".

Along with every Haligonian, military or civil, I had already become well acquainted with the physical shape of the convoys. We saw them nearly every day from the drill square where the Rainbow Division suffered and endured. A freighter would materialize where our view of the Narrows and Bedford Basin was blocked by the buildings of the Shipyard. Bulking large in the confined waters, it would approach in a silence as dramatic as a roll of drums. There was purposefulness in the way it slid down harbour, a flutter of pennants at its yard. Two or three minutes later it would be followed by a second ship, then a third.

Once under way, the convoy might move past for an hour or more, vessel after vessel thrusting into view like the units of a gigantic tow. Seen from the parade ground, three ships from the Basin were visible at a time—one rounding the Shipyard's corner, one showing its beam against the green hills of the Dartmouth shore, one drifting into the smoke haze down harbour as it altered course to clear George's Island and head for the open sea.

At first I was aware of details of each passing ship: peculiarities of its paintwork, off-duty crewmen lounging along the rail, washing flapping from an after-cargo boom, heat haze slithering from a funnel. But as the movement from the Basin went on, drawing in other vessels that had been waiting at docks or anchored in the stream, the convoys became single organisms.

In the Naval Control office, the concrete dimensions of the convoys were translated onto paper. Ships not yet cleared from their loading ports or individually making their way through the still submarine-free American waters were taking shape on Jack Mitchell's paper.

Typed signals gave each ship's present position, what it was carrying and when it could be expected to identify itself at the Halifax examination vessel. Data was included on where it would be bound, whether it needed to bunker, have crewmen replaced, or would require repair. These and other details were painstakingly worked out until the pattern of a specific convoy became discernable.

An almost completed plan lay before Jack Mitchell. It was a rectangular sheet divided into squares, a pattern which, two days hence, would be redrawn on the North Atlantic by actual keels. Each printed square held a slip on which was entered the name of a ship, its nationality, speed and cargo—all information that would be of vital interest to the convoy commodore and the commander of the escorting warships. Some of these slips would be juggled into new positions in light of last-minute intelligence: a tanker originally routed for the Mersey might be replaced in that section of the formation which would break off for the Clyde when the convoy dispersed off Ireland.

The final stencilled plan would show dependable station keepers at the heads of columns, more vulnerable ships tucked into inner lines for such protection as their outer sisters afforded, and other allocations governed by reasons ranging from critical speed to past reputation.

While Mitchell furrowed his brow over the plot, several of its human elements appeared at intervals through the frosted glass door—masters whose vessels would be in the next movement. Three who had just made port were checking in for the first time. Another was back to discuss mine-swept channels and newly laid fields with Lieutenant Freddy Day, the chart expert. Another had dropped in to reassure himself about corrections to his confidential books with Lieutenant Strous—a Free Frenchman now in Canadian uniform. Yet another, with a magnificent brass hat and florid features, wanted to talk about his crew with NCSO himself.

With the exception of the last arrival, all were unremarkable men in business suits. Each carried a large brief-case. Apart from their weathered faces and the way they set their feet on the deck they might have been prosperous salesmen. Different officers attended to their specific needs but Oland acknowledged them all, at least to the extent of a handshake. Some he drew into his cubicle for further conversation.

At last I'd been filled in by each staff member, and returned to NCSO's office myself.

"Well, what do you think of our set up?" he enquired.

"Very impressive," I answered. "Everything's so orderly it's difficult to believe there's a war on."

"It's on all right," Oland said, his voice suddenly grim.

He slid a signal across the desk. It was less than an hour old; listed on it were the names of five freighters just sunk in Britain's Western Approaches.

"A couple of weeks ago," said Dick, "the captain of each of those ships sat where you're sitting."

"I'm sorry," I mumbled.

He went on, speaking almost to himself.

"It hurts personally, but the big picture's worse. We're losing more ships than the yards can replace. You can work out for yourself where that sort of mathematics is carrying us. It can't go on indefinitely. The question is whether we can hold on until a crash ship-building program can tip the balance our way."

"We'll hang on," I said with the lame assurance of the ignorant.

"Of course we will." He was his customary confident self again.

"You spoke of my seeing the harbour tomorrow," I reminded him. "What should I be looking for?"

"Time bombs." Oland was obviously amused by the effect of his words. "Do you remember a fellow named von Rintellin in the First War?"

"I've read about him—if you mean the German naval attaché in Washington who engineered the Black Tom munitions explosion on the Jersey waterfront."

"Same man. He also had a way of slipping bombs into the cargoes of British ships loading in American ports. They were timed to go off at sea."

"I don't remember that."

"Admiralty did," said Oland, "particularly after Intelligence came up with the word early this year that the Germans had invested six million dollars in a sabotage program for America. The situation on the U.S. waterfront is much like it was in 1914. The Yanks being neutral again, there's nothing to prevent another von Rintellin from taking advantage of sabotage opportunities."

"You mean bombs in cargoes?" The thought was a chilling one. Oland's reminder of von Rintellin's exploits brought home to me that the threat was far from remote. Loading procedures in North American ports had changed little since World War I, but technology *had* changed. A saboteur with updated methods could be expected to use devices that would explode not on the open sea, but in the vital British ports themselves.

Oland was explaining the security system relied upon by the British in the early days, after Hitler's conquest of

Poland during the time known as the Phoney War.

"The British consular shipping officers are largely responsible for security on our ships loading in the States, but our Canadian Chief of Naval Staff has been put in charge of the whole business. There was little he could do when he got the word of the German sabotage program except to encourage the consular shipping boys to be doubly alert. He had nothing in his manpower bag with which to help them. In fact he was having the devil's own time to crew the warships that are his primary responsibility.

"But after Dunkirk, when it became apparent that England would be fighting the Nazis alone, the real pressure was on. Every resource Hitler had would be brought to bear on the problem of strangling Britain's lifeline. Submarines and surface raiders are one thing. You can get a handle on them. But sabotage—well, those American ports are still fertile and tempting places to try it.

"But those ships all come our way to join up with convoys, so Admiralty has asked Ottawa to arrange searches of every ship headed for the U.K."

Oland glanced sharply my way. "Since almost everything going to the United Kingdom passes through Halifax, that means *us*.

"It's obvious to Ottawa that we're the logical ones, because we've been boarding every ship bound for convoy anyway, to deliver official papers and generally just to prod the merchant captains into moving on time."

It seemed like a pretty large responsibility. Even I could calculate without much thought the time it would take to adequately search each outbound ship for saboteur's devices. I wondered how many men Oland had on hand for the job.

The work itself would be repetitive and routine. And no matter how concerned Admiralty was about sabotage, it seemed to me that the greater need was to counter the more obvious danger, that of the U-boats on the open sea. I couldn't imagine myself serving in a capacity that I saw as essentially shore duty. But I'd given Oland my word that I'd at least try it his way.

I tried to look keen. "I'll look forward to seeing the ways things are run, then."

"Good stuff, Watto," Oland beamed. He was his usual energetic, breezy self again. "Maybe you'll even be intrigued, who knows?"

He got up from his desk and shook my hand.

I beamed back at Oland, masking a certain regret. I was feeling a wrench at the thought that I was unlikely to serve under this valued old friend's command. Oland, busy and already preoccupied with his next interview, did not seem to notice.

He passed me back to Mitchell to make room for another shipmaster.

Shortly before the civilian staff and most of the officers called it a day, a grizzled man in shaggy tweeds arrived. He looked-for all the world like a retired admiral, which was exactly what he was—and a distinguished one at that. In two days, as Convoy Commodore, he would inherit the convoy Mitchell was putting together on paper.

Oland introduced the newcomer to the merchant captain still in his office. The cameraderie between the gray-haired commodore, the dynamic commander and the stolid shipmaster was plain to see. Then Oland, shouting "Good-night all!", departed with the war-activated admiral.

"If Sir George is lucky," offered Mitchell, "Dick will drive him to Blue Wing—that's his place down the shore—for the night. Even one evening there is a blessed breather. Otherwise it will have to be dinner with a couple of friends at the Oland suite in the Nova Scotian hotel—with the clatter from the docks below and the party hounds whooping it up in the corridor outside."

"They appeared to be old friends," I suggested.

"The commodores are all Dick's old friends from the day they take their first convoy out of here," said Jack, smiling. "It's fortunate he's got more than his naval pay to go on. He looks after them as he would his own family. Saved more than one from a nervous breakdown. It's pretty tough out there, you know, if you're seventy or so and bossing half a hundred ship's captains accustomed to doing things their own way."

2

"a world of grinding engines, raised voices, and the reek of gasoline..."

It was to be my duty to lead the search parties that checked out all the ships scheduled to leave Halifax harbour. If I had misgivings about the prospect, they were very quickly heightened when I reported in next morning.

Lieutenant Vincent, into whose hands I was delivered, was a personable Naval Reservist who had served on tankers before his military induction.

"Am I glad to see you!" he exclaimed. "I'm up for duty on a destroyer and I've been living in terror the appointment would come before my relief did."

"I'm only here for two weeks," I warned. I still had my own hoped-for transfer to active sea duty firmly in mind. He mustered a desperate cheerfulness.

"Two weeks will do it. The chit is bound to come while you're still about. Then you and the Commander can worry about who's to catch this case of sleeping sickness."

"Is boarding that bad?" I asked with apprehension.

Vincent snorted. "Going through the motions of the search is a joke. Even if there was something to find, no decent saboteur would leave it exposed enough for any examination we can make." He sighed. "But let's show you the ropes."

He checked with the office to see if there were any documents needing delivery to the ships he would be visiting, then led the way through the clamoring dockyard to Number Three Camber. This was a small and obviously very old tidal basin set into the Yard rim. Within its slimy wooden walls lay rows of harbour craft. Uniform only in their "crab fat" gray paintwork, they had a bewildering variety of origins.

None was strictly Navy. There were a couple of Cape Islanders, squat in the water, with graceful lines; but the rest were clearly odds and ends hurriedly mustered along the coast of the Maritimes. They ranged from sportsmen's cockle-shell speed boats to prosaic ten- or fifteen-ton diesel ferries. Some had wheelhouses forward, some aft. Some had commodious cabins, some were open-decked. Their most notable similarity apart from their colour was that all seemed to be manned by garrulous seamen who were either very good-tempered or very bad-tempered—depending on the success with which they manoeuvered in and out of the rows of tethered boats.

There was a constant turmoil of arrivals and departures at the narrow camber entrance, each bringing a convulsion to the close-packed ranks inside. It was low tide and the deepened pit compressed everything into a world of grinding engines, raised voices and the reek of gasoline, diesel oil and polluted brine.

Three young Volunteer Reserve sub-lieutenants were standing at the camber's edge, adding their shouts to those of the coxswains. One was yelling "*Breda*!", another "*Marmot*!", another "*Lucy G.*", in an increasingly irritated litany. No one in the boats or the surrounding dock seemed to be paying them the slightest attention.

"Who decides the winner?" I jokingly asked Vincent.

"The first coxswain who recognizes his boat's name and decides to acknowledge it," he laughed. "Subbies wanting to get back to their ships don't do so well here unless they come off in their own boats and manage to hang on to them. The harbour craft are pooled. If you apply at the Yard office and they like your looks you'll be told which boat you can have. The problem starts down here. I'm not saying the coxswains deliberately duck identification but most of them are peacetime small-craft men and it does something to their egos when they realize they no longer have to go looking for business."

He led me down a precarious ladder on the barnacle-encrusted wall, across two inshore boats and into the shallow cockpit of the *Grebe*. Her leading seaman stuck his face out the wheelhouse window and, with a salute more fitted to a London cabbie, inquired, "Where to, sir?"

Vincent consulted a list of ships that had entered since the previous evening and named a berth in the stream. A chart, with the entire sweep of the harbour and Bedford Basin marked in numbered squares, helped the coxswain to quickly identify our destination. He shouted to his two-man deck crew, the lines were expertly slipped, a bell signalled slow astern in the tiny engineroom and the screw began to grind. The propeller made a huge racket; it sounded exactly as if a huge drill were boring a hole in our stern.

"Don't be alarmed, sir," said a gruff voice at my elbow. "He's been trying to drive that engine through the bottom for a month now. But he hasn't got a hope. We're stuck with her for the duration."

I found myself facing a sailor with penetrating eyes under a jutting brow that made it difficult to decide whether he was smiling or scowling.

"This is Able Seaman Al Oxner, our senior hand," said Vincent. "If there is anything you want to know about difficult ships or difficult women, he's your man. There's nothing he's missed either way."

"Nothing, sir," admitted Oxner solemnly, "except for peace of soul."

The engine, now thrown into Full Ahead, showed a pleasing reversal of form as it carried us through the camber entrance into the gentle chop of the harbour. A steady breeze from the Atlantic swept away the mugginess of the land and the stench of the basin. Oxner, having moved to the extremity of the stern, stretched his arms dramatically and sucked in a mighty breath of salt air. He was obviously about to give voice when three of his six fellow seamen, mimicking his rolling tones, beat him to it.

"Ah—h!" they declaimed in unison, "this is the sort of weather we signed on for!"

Oxner gave them a deadpan look.

"You'll very quickly notice, sir," he said apologetically, "that there are men in this boarding party who find it impossible to think for themselves. In fact, you might say some of them are ignorates."

"How's that?" I couldn't help but ask.

"Ignorates, sir, absolute ignorates."

The objects of his scorn appeared unperturbed.

We were now well into the fairway and the full sweep of the harbour opened out. Seaward lay the containing jaws of land—beetling York Redoubt to starboard and the gentler wooded hills of McNab's Island across the gap. The old fortress of George's Island squatted like a bottle-stopper in the neck of the inner harbour. The outer forts and their long-range guns had rendered it obsolete, but the toothless fort still looked formidable. Under the light, sunny sky, the laneway between the island and the ocean terminals was marine blue, shading to metallic gray where the distant gate-ships framed the gap in the mine nets and, beyond it, the unbroken sea-path to Europe.

To port, on the Dartmouth shore, pockets of wartime activity focused around docks and marine slips, but the town, backed by a green pattern of hills, meadows and woods, seemed as unhurried and pleasant as I remembered it from the First War.

Halifax itself was a sharp contrast. The August sunshine did nothing to soften the lines of the Citadel on its naked hill, although the eighteenth-century spires below it conveyed the warmth and romance of the old city. The waterfront was solid with shipping, and busy streets ran upward from it until they were snubbed abruptly by the upper slopes of the all-dominating hill.

Astern, Bedford Basin could be glimpsed through the Narrows dividing it from the lower harbour—as though through a slightly opened door. The fine visibility allowed a view of Bedford Village, seven miles distant, a scattering of white houses against an emerald background. In between lay a mast-tipped maze of anchored ships, distance giving them the appearance of so many miniature models.

Oxner, following my silent survey, offered, "Fine anchorage, sir—if you forget about the stink from the fish plant."

We were pointed towards a group of vessels anchored between George's Island and the Eastern Passage—a well-found Furness-Withy package liner, two stolid British tramps, a Greek with a cumbersome deckload of lumber, and two good-looking tankers, one Norwegian and the other Dutch. Vincent responded with some enthusiasm to my inquiries about the tankers. To him they seemed to be old friends with whom he had shared some rare adventures. On the whole, though, the routine day was evidently boring him. The only time his eye lighted up was when we swept close to a brace of destroyers due to take out the next convoy.

Manoeuvering alongside one of the tramps, we secured to her boat rope. I determined to imitate Vincent's casualness, but curiosity gripped me. My past seafaring had been almost entirely aboard warships; this was my first touch with the Merchant Navy, as symbolized by the rust-flaked flank of the freighter.

Vincent surveyed a white line and the letter "S", painted in white on the ship's plates, eighteen inches above the wash of the light swell.

"Still not down to her summer marks," he commented. "She must have been short-changed when she loaded."

I hated to show my ignorance, but his observation was beyond me.

"Explain, please. This is all new to me."

Vincent smiled tolerantly. "It's simple," he said. "Each of those lines indicates the safe depth to which a ship can be loaded. The W—that's her Atlantic Winter—allows for less cargo and more freeboard. God knows she'll need it when that nasty piece of water kicks up. Then there's her Freshwater mark, for when the buoyancy is less. And her Tropical. Not that they're likely to mean much to you."

Not mean much! Already my mind had carried me to the seas and rivers that had washed that scabrous hull. T for Tropical! That probably meant the East Indies, the Gold Coast, the Amazon—

"Let's get on with it," said Vincent resignedly, starting up the side-ladder.

He left the ratings by the gangway and, discovering that the captain was ashore, sought out the chief officer.

"Contraband control," he announced.

"Whatever for?" exclaimed the sweatered mate, a sallow man with three days' growth of beard. "Has Canada declared a blockade against Britain?"

"Good question," admitted Vincent, obviously weary of similar queries. "I'll try to explain. Until Norway and Denmark were occupied certain cargoes shipped there kept right on going until they landed in Germany. Things Germany badly needed, what with her own ports sealed off. That was the contraband that needed controlling. A Contraband Control outfit was being set up over here when Hitler took over those countries. End of Contraband Control—all except for the name. Some genius decided"—he extended his hand towards Oxner and his party—"that it should be tagged on these fellows."

"Brilliant," sneered the other. "So what do *you* do?"

"We're supposed to search you and make sure no one has mucked you up while you were loading."

The mate's voice was heavy with sarcasm.

"How many days will that take?"

"We can spare you half an hour," said Vincent lightly. "Let's start with your cargo plan and crew list."

The chief officer took his time finding the papers. Finally the boarding officer was able to run his eye over the indicated contents of the holds.

"'General cargo' covers a multitude of sins," he observed. "We'll let the ratings look around a bit—long enough to entitle you your search certificate." He walked to where the party was waiting at the foot of the ladder to the superstructure. "No need to open anything up, Oxner. Just a quick look-see."

The party dispersed, some forward, some aft, and we returned to the mate's cabin.

"A little something?" he asked.

"The hair of the dog," accepted Vincent. "As I remember, it was Scotch last night."

The ship's officer rang for the steward, then looked in my direction. I told him I was on the wagon.

Conversation was desultory, even after the mate had joined Vincent in a large whisky. The steward, the physical surroundings, and the atmosphere were charged with surliness.

"Man," commented one of the ratings as we steered towards the next ship, "I've shipped on some scruffy ones but spare me that sort of rustbucket."

"We've seen worse," pronounced Oxner. "A bit of scrubbing, a bit of chipping, a bit of caring, and she'd pass. Not like that cripple we checked last week. They didn't dare chip *her* for fear of the hammers going through the plates."

Down harbour we came alongside another freighter, anchored well away from any other ship and flying a red flag.

"If there's any point in the search," conceded Vincent, "it's these munitions ships. We at least keep the crews awake to what they're carrying."

"I'd think they'd have difficulty forgetting in *this* harbour," I said. "I was here in '18 shortly after the *Mont Blanc* blew up."[3]

The city would never forget that day—nor could the people charged with moving the fuels of war for the second time in a century. There still wasn't much left standing in the North End.

"Most of these men weren't born when the big bang happened," said Vincent.

Nevertheless we encountered an air of vigilance from the moment the second officer, who was on harbour watch, met us at the gangway. Basically little different in design, tonnage and construction from the tramp we had just left,

---

3. On December 6, 1917, *Mont Blanc*, a World War I munitions ship, collided with another vessel in Halifax harbour, exploding with a force that flattened two square miles of the city, killing 1650 and leaving thousands injured and homeless.

this ship had the mark of owners motivated by pride as well as the instinct for profit. The officer who greeted us was in uniform, white shirt and tie included. The crew had a well-scrubbed look and the upper works were freshly painted. Though the opening of a hold—a specific requirement with munitions carriers—meant extra work, the bos'n and deckhands did it as though they saw sense in Vincent's demand. When the chocks had been knocked clear, the canvas rolled back and the hatch-covers lifted, the second officer accompanied us down the interior ladder.

The boxed bulk explosives reached to within a man's height from the deckhead except in one corner where a special wooden structure had been built to hold detonators—the most touchy element of the cargo. Flashlights were played on this, more to admire the carefulness of its construction than in any expectation of locating an enemy device. The cases occupied the hold from bulkhead to bulkhead, forming an unbroken wooden floor. We walked across it—and that was the search.

"O.K.," pronounced Vincent. "Thanks, mate. Nice stowage."

"It is, isn't it," agreed the second officer. "They're pretty good in Philadelphia and, even if they had inclined to be slack, the old man and the consular shipping boy wouldn't have let them get away with it. Nothing went into this ship that one of us wasn't on the spot to oversee every minute of the loading."

By the time the hatch covers were replaced, ratings had made a quick run through the engine room and accommodation. We received no offer to make the visit a social one.

Of the twenty or so vessels we boarded in the next two days, I remember the name of only one. *Frederick S. Failes* was registered in Hong Kong and had been recently redirected to the Atlantic to help make up for the heavy tanker losses there. Even Vincent made no attempt to conceal his admiration for this beauty from the Far East, still fresh in her peacetime paint.

Captain Ramsay had the frosted moustache of a man in his fifties but the eagerness of a youngster with his first command. It was not enough that we should be given a verbal description of the special fixtures of the *Failes* ; we must see for ourselves under her master's proud guidance. It was not enough to point out that the gyro compass and the depth finder were the latest models, there had to be full demonstrations.

Even wartime excressences like the plastic armour on the wheelhouse and the steel pillboxes on the wings of the bridge had been immaculately maintained. It was the same everywhere—there were no frayed or rusted guy-wires, no corroded surfaces slicked over with liberal doses of paint. Once, when he thought he was unobserved, I caught Captain Ramsay patting the engine room casing as one would caress something warm and living.

The *Failes* was lying in Bedford Basin, surrounded by more than a hundred other ships awaiting convoy. We had tea with the captain and his chief engineer, who commented on the extraordinary number of tankers.

"Looks as though the storage in the Old Country has taken about all it can handle," he said.

Vincent nodded. "I don't know how much of it has been knocked out by the Blitz," he said, "but some of these tankers have been lying here for two or three weeks waiting to be included in a movement. The Germans must have made a mess of the Thames and the Mersey." He pointed to a *Prince* cargo liner close by, her decks high with heavy wooden cases. "Maybe if they could get enough of those Yankee planes across to burn up some of the aviation fuel things would come back to normal in the Basin. Right now we've got more oil than water out here."

"The sooner we get going the better," remarked the Chief. "After the East the North Atlantic isn't my cup of tea, but it has the Clyde at the other end."

Next morning Vincent had the father of all hangovers. He had heard a buzz in the wardroom that it would be at least a month before his destroyer appointment came through. Flaked out on the settee in our little launch after directing the coxswain to a Basin anchorage, he made no move when we came alongside our first ship.

"Here's your chance to find a bomb," he drawled. "Don't be alarmed if you hear an explosion out here while you're searching. It'll only be my head blowing up."

Suddenly inheriting his responsibility didn't faze me, as it might well have done twenty-four hours earlier. The previous evening, assessing my position, I had concluded that as far as anti-sabotage skills were concerned, my feeling of inadequacy had been unwarranted. I was clearly a learner among learners.

There was no question that the search was an urgent necessity. Dick had told me that the unceasing Blitz by the Luftwaffe on Britain's major waterways might well be supplemented by time bombs such as von Rintellin had used, this time set to explode after the ships carrying them had docked. The devastation this would wreak on the U.K. waterfront could have very serious effects on the war effort.

Our security search might be a deterrent to saboteurs, but it was clear even to me that the undertaking, properly done, would require a good many counter-sabotage specialists and a good deal more time than the boarders had to cover the required ten or more ships every day. Unfortunately there were no security specialists as such in our party. These were in desperately short supply and were required in even more sensitive quarters.

But Oxner and his half dozen companions did possess experience of a kind. Their intimacy with merchantmen and their crews should, I reasoned, fit them to accomplish more than was being done at the time.

My ideas coalesced in the close quarters of the launch during the frequently long hops between the ships on our list. Oxner was a born inciter of debate and practically every boarding was followed by a vigourous discussion of the vessel we'd just inspected. Every member of the party would be drawn into it, recounting what he had learned while yarning with crew members during the lick-and-a-promise examination. Opinions on the ship's state of security were varying and amateurish but there was remarkable unanimity on such subjects as living conditions, wages, cultural idiosyncrasies and the general state of morale.

My curiosity drew me into these arguments, particularly after the debaters learned that inside my officer's uniform was an ex-Leading Seaman who, a generation earlier, had experienced the lower deck for a couple of years. As discussion warmed, rank was forgotten and the newspaperman in me found himself going after the human story of each vessel as revealed by the crew's reticence or openness; its discipline or lack of it; its optimism or cynicism.

This process, I began to realize, was not a digression from our appointed duty. On the contrary, the outlook and the attitude of a master or his officers, matched against the impressions of the crew brought back by Oxner and his mates, gave a fair picture of the internal security—or lack of it—which had attended the ship's loading. Men consistently on the spot, men whose lives were directly at stake, were likely to prove the most dependable observers and watchmen.

An overview of the ship's company also provided some idea of the level of vigilance that might be expected of them while they lay in Halifax. This assessment was no substitute for an adequate search, but it at least provided a basis of probabilities on which the least reassuring vessels could be given special scrutiny and more of our boarding party's limited time.

Even after such short experience I was finding it possible to anticipate what was likely to be found during a boarding. Certain nations and, within them, certain shipping lines, maintained standards of performance that made them the front line of the maritime community. They were served by "company men", a term of frank respect on the tongues of Oxner and his crew. With long service under a single house flag, their tradition of seamanship was as jealously guarded as that of any other long-established calling.

These were the elite, the men who could be expected to obey when ordered, to accept casualties unquestioningly, and to not only draw on their own inspiration, but to communicate it to others less convinced of the stakes. Their respect—even love—for the ships on which they sailed made them the instinctive guardians of their lives.

One's built-in radar picked this up as sharply as it did the warnings that flashed on many of the "hungry ships". Not that every scruffy vessel suffered from low morale or lack of discipline. There was a type of independent-minded seaman who seemed to prefer a berth lacking spit-and-polish or an ordered future, who yet had his own brand of grainy pride, competence and dependability. But beyond that category were the embittered, the slovenly, and the fearful—mariners to whom the sea was an economic fact of life, inescapable because there was nowhere else to turn. They were exploited by their masters on the basis of that hard truth.

So far I had encountered no unusual trouble among them but, according to Oxner, there was at least one vessel lying in the stream which had been there for over a month because men had been deserting her faster than her agents could find replacements. This was promising territory for anyone wishing to capitalize on a crew's ingrained resentment. I made a mental note to consolidate my observations for Oland before my two weeks were up.

But what I would have reported would have been understatement, for I had not yet fully grasped what I was encountering. There were, however, men much better equipped than I to evaluate how dangerously the Atlantic line of battle was approaching inner collapse.

Ten years later, Joseph Schull, writing the official history of the Royal Canadian Navy, put the buildup of crisis into a single sentence:

> "There would be times in the months and years ahead when the crews on the decks of waiting freighters and captains at the tables of convoy conferences would look at each other, wondering if a single, faltering word might lead to a general refusal of the odds against them."

3

"It's all yours..."

One day, Vincent arrived at the standby room with a gleam in his eye. Portentously, he drew from his pocket the small black notebook which, in that period of improvised procedures, contained the only log of Contraband Control activities.

"It's all yours," he exulted, "and this—" he flourished an appointment signal— "is all mine."

I had no difficulty sharing his happiness. His depression had been unbroken since the rumour first circulated about his new post being delayed. It was good to see the end of the gloom. Besides, the thought of having the boarding team to myself for a few days wasn't displeasing. I had started writing my final conclusions for Commander Oland, and realized that having total responsibility, however briefly, would be a valuable chance to garner new insights.

That night Oland invited me to dinner at the Nova Scotian Hotel. Afterwards we went upstairs to his suite for the first unhurried yarn since our reunion. Mrs. Oland, tiny but not overshadowed, waited until we were settled in our easy chairs, then remembered she had some phone calls to make.

There was a good deal of catching up to do. It had been fourteen years since Dick, as the Headquarters officer responsible for the Volunteer Reserve, had unsuccessfully tried to talk me out of resigning my commission.

"I meant every word of it," he recalled, "but I understood better when I headed for the beach myself shortly after."

Inevitably, the Royal Canadian Navy had seemed a dead end in the quiet after World War I, when its total strength sank to a low of under 500 men. Oland had been drawn to more challenging fields: as every Maritimer could attest, the large Oland clan was both extremely well-to-do and bristling with initiative.

Dick and his older brother, Eric, had both been members of a rare company—midshipmen graduated from the first two classes of the RCN College in Halifax. In the 1914-18 war Eric had brought to that short-lived institution its first Distinguished Service Cross. Dick acquired service ribbons as a gunnery officer in British cruisers. In subsequent years, he infused a generation of young Volunteer Reservists, myself included, with a lively mixture of Nelsonian tradition and Canadian inventiveness.

I knew he had done well in the insurance business after his retirement from the Navy; in the Nova Scotian that night, there was no mention of this, but I gathered that success had given him the opportunity to build Blue Wing, his seaside country house down the shore at Lawrencetown.

Blue Wing's delights were set aside for the duration after Oland was reactivated. The process was set in motion with the appointment of a new Director of Naval Intelligence in Ottawa. It had been customary in Canada's Navy for the intelligence director to be a senior officer on loan from the Royal Navy: there were advantages to having someone familiar with Admiralty and its global outreaches. When Captain E.S. Brand arrived in Ottawa in the late Thirties, he brought with him a sense of urgency based on the knowledge that war with Germany was inevitable.

Although Neville Chamberlain was still publicly optimistic about avoiding such a war, and Canada was abandoning herself to the nervous celebrations of a Royal Visit, the realists in Whitehall were grimly preparing to resist an avalanche of naked might. They knew that only weeks remained to correct the lassitude of years.

Among immediate priorities was the development of an organizational framework for a North Atlantic convoy system, plus a communications network to make it function. Captain Brand, intensively briefed before leaving London, was well aware that the greatest point of wartime strain in the Western world would be Halifax. Among his major requirements had been a competent NCSO in the strategic port.

Both the Vice Chief of Naval Staff and the Commanding Officer, Atlantic Coast, had assured Brand that among the retired officers being hastily reactivated, Richard Oland was his man. He took their word for it, arranged the appointment, and moved swiftly on. The race with time became steadily more demanding as the Trade and Plans divisions came under the Intelligence Director's aegis.

Brand and Oland did not meet face to face before the war began, but signal log and correspondence allowed them to take each other's measure. What they discovered had a profound bearing on all that followed: their personalities differed greatly, but in basic instinct and ability they were a matched pair. Implicit in all Dick Oland said that night at the Nova Scotian was his confidence in Brand.

★ ★ ★

The race to prepare Canada's Navy and the merchant vessels passing through Halifax for the coming conflict was terribly close, but on September 16, 1939, two weeks after the outbreak of World War II, the first convoy had passed Sambro Head on its way to the United Kingdom. By 1940 the system was well established, though haunted by staggering losses. Enemy submarine production was still outstripping the Allies' ability to counter it with new escort vessels.

Oland volunteered nothing that night about a peril that loomed even closer to home. Thirty years passed before I was to read a letter he had written Brand on August 16, 1940 that described the dangerous problem of crew trouble.

> "The Norwegian *Belita* is hung up with desertions. Although there are hundreds of Norwegians in the Basin and a hundred seamen of various nationalities in Immigration, not one will sign on as replacement. Another ship needs 16 men."

Nor did he mention that he had recently had a notice from Harry Mathers, agent for many of the ships in port, which warned:

> "The *Michael L. Embiricos* has already missed two convoys and will miss the next. There is no steam to load her cargo of steel. Twenty-one of her crew walked ashore last night."

Mathers added that his frustration and concern were shared by the other agents, all of whom were experiencing similar setbacks.

The nearest Dick came that night to expressing concern about desertions was when he said somberly: "A time will come when the pendulum will swing if we can tough it out long enough. We can build the ships and train the men if the convoys will keep us in business until we get our second wind. Sometimes, though, I have to talk to myself severely after two or three long-faced shipmasters have been in to tell me their troubles. If I scared easily, I'd be scared."

"Are you talking about the merchant seaman's beefs?" I asked.

He regarded me intently, then nodded. "They say a ship with a few beefs is healthier for it. I think that's generally true. But the times aren't normal and the beefs aren't all healthy ones."

"You're right," I said.

He concentrated on his pipe, as though he had only half heard me, so I kept on talking. Before I had finished I'd gone further than I'd intended. I didn't stop with my assessment of morale aboard the "hungry" ships. Instead I plunged on, listing some of the things Oxner and his seamen had told me they would improve if *they* were running things. Pay, food, accommodation, basic seaworthiness—the works.

Oland smiled ruefully. "I'd like to see the faces of some of the owners and agents if you presented them with a program like that. *Their* idea is that it's time to bring back the press gangs."

"The Oxner plan would take some doing," I agreed. "One thing I do know, after a few days of boarding ships, is that even the least admirable sailors seem to respond to being treated like human beings. Three ships, none of them too prepossessing, were full of goodwill just because some outfit in Upper Canada had sent them a gift of maple sugar. About two small cakes a man. Most were saving them for their families on the other side. It wasn't just something to ease the British sugar shortage. It was something that suggested they'd been appreciated."

We talked late. Oland's response to the boarders' lower deck impressions quickened. When I finally left he said, "We've got a good deal to think about." His eyes were still bright but the weight of physical weariness was beginning to show in the lines on his face. A convoy sailing day made demands enough without his taking on a maritime revolution the same evening.

It didn't occur to me until I was walking to my quarters that he hadn't mentioned our agreement about the length of my stay in the Naval Control Service.

4

"Eyes front!"

I woke before daylight, acutely aware that I'd talked myself into a corner. I'd pointed out some problems on the harbour, and even suggested first steps toward their solution. I'd have to put up or shut up. If what I had unloaded on Dick was worth pursuing, it was going to take a good deal more than a week.

Harbour craft extricating themselves from the camber did less backing and filling than did the emotions that accompanied me down North Street hill and into the Yard. A simple course towards the coveted corvette appointment lay open: I could put in the next week as uneventfully as possible. The alternative was an indefinite commitment to NCSO. As the sentry checked me through the hole-in-the-wall Centre Gate it seemed the appropriate moment to decide. "All hope abandon, ye who enter here," I muttered, and felt better.

The boarders were in the cubbyhole on the first floor of the Administration building that served as their standby room. They jumped to their feet as I came through the door.

"You're early, sir," said Oxner half accusingly. "We're usually not in the boat until—"

"I realized that," I said. "Sit down, please. I'd like to discuss a few things."

A single chair, a table, a couple of benches and a cupboard for the men's heavy weather gear made up the room's furnishings. Oxner offered me the chair with the air of sharing a prized personal privilege, then joined the others on the benches facing me. Seven pairs of eyes regarded me with caution.

"As I told you yesterday," I began, "Lieutenant Vincent has gone as navigator in a destroyer. You're likely to be seeing a good deal of me for a while."

The caution was still there.

"I'm the new boy," I went on, "and you've been boarding ever since someone topsides decided it ought to be done. If anyone knows the score on the harbour, you do."

"Yes, sir," said Oxner. It was difficult to detect whether he agreed with my statement or was simply giving it consideration.

"I had a long talk with Commander Oland last night," I continued, "and passed along a number of the ideas I've heard you tossing around in the launch—like what would happen if *you* were running the show. He was very interested. So am I. I'd like to know how I can do my end of it better."

Everyone looked towards Oxner. As an A.B. like themselves, senior only because he had been the first man drafted to the boarding party, he was not immune to off-duty kidding. Yet he had established his own brand of authority. This was an occasion when his leadership was expected.

"Well, sir," he said ponderously, "I always say the best place to start anything is at the beginning. The place *we* start is when we come over the side of a ship. If we don't expect very much to happen we don't fool anybody that we do. We just look like a bunch of clods in sailor suits come to pester the men who are carrying the mean side of the war. I think you should expect more of us than that, sir."

"You mean we should have more spit-and-polish?" I demanded incredulously, having overheard more than once Oxner's distaste for what had happened to him in gunnery school.

"Exactly, sir—much as I hate to admit it."

"You don't think too much 'Hearts of Oak' will antagonize the crews we call on?"

"No, sir," came another voice. "The more pusser we are the better they'll appreciate it. There's enough beefing about the thin protection they're getting from the Navy at sea without us slopping over the side as though we couldn't care less."

The speaker had in peacetime been a quartermaster in one of the passenger-carrying *Lady* boats on the West Indies run. A week's acquaintance with Alan Williams had convinced me that lesser men were being given officers' commissions. Tall and spare, with evenly drawn features, he had both intelligence and presence. His sense of humour, though leaning towards the sardonic, was not malicious. Above all, he was a seagoing professional, obviously high in the regard of his shipmates.

"Anyone like to challenge Williams?" I invited.

Bill Coffey, Williams' closest companion, said, "I never thought I'd see the day when I would vote for 'by numbers' or 'at the double'—not after what I went through in basic training—but Al's right. One day we're going to run into trouble out there. It'll come faster and be worse if we've wandered aboard like sleepwalkers."

Levin Gould, until recently a New Brunswick fisherman, said nothing but nodded agreement. He and Oxner had been the first two men drafted to the party. The sea which had invested the Lunenburger with its thunder had left the French-speaking Gould with the silence of its depths. Oxner, officially assessing him several years later, would write, "An old hand, a good, obedient seaman, but an extremely quiet fellow who never speaks a word unless actually called on to do so."

Meinerth Wick's agreement with a smartening-up campaign was practically automatic. Norwegian-born and another *Lady* boat quartermaster, he had the carriage of the expert skier he became when winter and geography permitted. He possessed a natural keenness even when cynicism about the limitations of the search procedure was strongest.

This was also the case with Clarence Charters, in his mid-twenties but with the cherubic face of a teenager. He wore his uniform well, was conscious of it, and the prospect of being seen at his sartorial best appealed to him.

Only Young, a Great Lakes sailor with a weight problem and a dubious bill of health, had reservations about how our clients would react to a crisper approach.

"Of course," he compromised, "if they don't like it we could tone it down."

"Cheer up, old son," rumbled Oxner. "If swarming smartly up the side becomes too much for you we can always heave you up in a cargo sling."

Having agreed to project a new image, the party worked out a drill for it. Instead of drifting casually down to the launch, someone suggested, they should fall in for inspection before the Administration building, march to the camber and maintain gunnery school discipline as long as they were in the eye of the public.

Coffey, who prided himself on his realism, asked me if I honestly thought the search did any good.

"I'm sure it does, as far as it goes," I replied. "Obviously we haven't the men or the time to make it what it should be. However, if we tackle the things you fellows seem to believe are possible, they may be even more important."

The knitting of Oxner's eyebrows was almost audible in the silence that followed. Finally he suggested, "Maybe all the boys aren't as clear as might be on what we think is possible. Would you mind pulling it together for them, sir?"

I was still feeling my way. "If there *is* sabotage, we're certainly more likely to uncover it if we're on our toes. What the Commander has in mind, though, is that saboteurs are likeliest to have things made easy for them where there's crew trouble. Crew trouble itself can put a ship out of action, for that matter. You men have been quick to spot where it's coming from, quick to identify *why* it is coming."

"That's true enough," said Williams, "but what we see

has always been there—always will be."

"Maybe," I conceded. "However, if it becomes the difference between winning the war or losing it, there must be people in high places who have the authority to correct what creates it."

"You mean those starvation wages, crummy accommodation, cheating owners—?"

Carried away by a mounting enthusiasm, I answered, "Yes. Everything."

"People up top have known about conditions for a long time," said Coffey.

"The Commander's the man to remind them of it," I persisted, "and I think he will. After all, it's his business to see that every merchantman leaving this harbour is in all respects ready for sea."

"All respects ready has meant one thing on the bridge, another in the fo'c's'le," said Coffey with feeling.

"That's what I'm getting at. What you men feel or hear below decks is as important as what a captain reports when he checks in at NCS. If it's accurate, it's relevant intelligence. It could result in some of the things you say are wrong in the ships being put right."

There was a considerable pause which I saw no reason to interrupt.

"There's a lot we pick up that's accurate, right enough," said Oxner finally, "but there's a lot that's just plain scuttlebutt—stuff like you hear on German broadcasts. Sometimes it's hard to know what to believe."

I was more certain of myself now. "That's more like my line on civvy street. My editors weren't always ready to take as gospel what I'd written. What we can do—as far as I've figured it out—is measure what we hear against what we know. I'll do what I can to get and give you the facts—even the hard ones. It will leave you chaps better equipped to spot the holes in the yarn some sea lawyer is spinning in the fo'c's'le—maybe put him straight. Killing a rumour with the truth, that sort of thing."

"You've given us a lot to think about, sir," said Oxner as the team filed out.

When I came back from checking the overnight arrivals the men were drawn up in front of the Administration building. Oxner called them to attention and raised an oversized arm in salute.

"Boarding party present and correct, sir."

"Thank you. Carry on to the launch."

They stepped off with a stride and bearing that brought heads up as they traversed the Yard. Had it been in the gunnery school area the martial display would have passed unnoticed, but casualness was the norm around the jetties and machine shops. The measured formation was momentarily threatened when a piratical character from one of the tugs, recognizing a former shipmate, hailed him derisively from the roadside. "Eyes right, Charters!"

Oxner was on top of it instantly: "Eyes front!" he roared, with sufficient force to steady Charters and blow his tormentor into the shadows.

We moved briskly out of the camber. Even the coxswain was affected. His bowman, cap slapped on the back of his head with an air of permanence, suddenly heard himself ordered to square it away and be smart about it. He was a big, blonde ex-fisherman and the eyes he turned towards the man in the wheelhouse were filled with hurt and disbelief. Slowly it dawned on him, though, that the coxswain meant business. Resignedly he pulled his cap squarely between his ears. The result was uninspiring, but he did look slightly less slap-happy.

A newly arrived munitions ship that had been ordered to await search outside the harbour demanded our initial attention. It was my first foray beyond the gate ships. The weather helped make our hour's run in the launch a memorable one. The long silken swell and the ebbing tide carried us along at what seemed twice our regular speed.

The big freighter, its red explosives flag bright against the blue, was rocking at anchor. Not until we were alongside did I realize that the swell, though smooth, was taller than it had seemed without a point of reference. The launch rose and fell half the height of the dangling Jacob's ladder.

Unhesitatingly the coxswain eased in, allowing the bowman to catch the boat rope with his hook. Teamwork between the man at the helm and the sailors at bow and stern was instinctive. The only sound was the occasional clanging of the engineroom telegraph, the resulting thrust or reversal of the screw and the slap of water between the steep black hull and the heaving launch. The three bred-in-the-bone small-craft men made it look wonderfully easy.

But transferring from the launch to the ladder was far from simple for an apprentice boarder. I managed to catch a rung at the highest point to which the boat's upsurging fo'c's'le head lifted me, but the follow-through of my feet was poorly coordinated. The second's miscalculation saw the launch drop at express elevator speed. I was jerked to the ladder with a minimum of grace and maximum punishment to my arms. Once my foot found a rung all was well but I had a sense of having let down the side; following me, each well-practised boarder swung from launch to ladder in a single motion.

Whatever their reaction to my performance, they concealed it. Even Coffey's nearly perpetual glint of worldly disillusionment was lacking as the line of stone-faced sailors formed up at the gangway.

The master, a dour Yorkshireman, was deep in paperwork in his cabin. He was probably in his early forties, but chin stubble and a scowl of resentful weariness added another twenty years to his appearance. Barely civil when he gave permission for the search, he glanced at my two wavy Volunteer Reserve stripes the way a racing driver might have regarded a learner's license. Brusquely he turned me over to his chief officer.

The latter eased my discomfort. His Hebridean lilt gave him the boyishness so frequently found in Stornoway seafarers. "Pay no heed to the old man," he advised. "He's shaking down a new ship after cutting his survivor's leave from the vessel he started the war with. Lost two thirds of his crew."

He glanced approvingly at the party as they came to attention. "Any particular hatch?" he inquired.

"Whichever one would leave you feeling more secure," I said. "We're a service, not an imposition."

The mate smiled. "Ask Chips to open up No 3," he ordered one of the deckhands, then turned to me. "You'll be wanting to get on with the search."

At Oxner's command, the party moved to predetermined parts of the ship. Two stood by to inspect the opened hold, two went forward, one aft, and one amidships. The senior hand retained a roving commission.

It was no surprise to find excellent stowage. Wherever any unavoidable space remained between the munitions cases there had been painstaking shoring up and the whole effect suggested highly responsible supervision. As the party reboarded the launch I held back, filled with a sense that I had unfinished business aboard the munitions vessel. In his cabin back of the bridge was a man who had tested my patience, yet aroused my compassion. It was all very well to remind myself that I had been there to conduct a mandatory search, and that neither the captain's feelings nor mine were at issue. Yet, when you got right down to it, the problem of morale that was haunting Oland and his superiors was inextricably related to what lonely men were experiencing behind closed doors marked "Captain".

I decided to return to the upper works.

I wasn't sure that I wouldn't do more harm than good, but the impulse couldn't be resisted. When I knocked, the captain's "Come in" was unwelcoming and his lined face, as he looked up from his paperwork, was resentful.

"We're through, Captain," I said. "Sorry to have troubled you but it's been good to check so well-found a ship. Perhaps I could drop back some time when you're anchored inside."

He regarded me in silence. Suspicion gave way to curiosity, then to uncertainty. "Could you stand a nip?" he offered.

"Thanks, no. We've at least ten more ships to check before the day's out." I paused in the door. "Now that you're flying our 'C' flag the examination vessel will be signalling you to head in."

The master rose and accompanied me as far as the ladder. He extended his hand and looked a little less tired.

"Come on board again if you can," he invited.

A long day followed. It was well after dark when we tied up at the camber—and only the watchkeeper was in the office when I made a final check on what the next twenty-four hours were likely to bring. I knew I'd made my decision to stay by that time, and it was a disappointment to have missed Dick Oland and the opportunity to tell him of it. At any rate, I was no longer in doubt. Boarding ship after ship that day, with my party demonstrating its fresh sense of purpose, had given me a new insight into the potential of our operation.

When I caught Oland in his cubicle next morning, however, he headed off my announcement.

"Just the man I'm looking for," he burst out. "You bought yourself a packet, Watto, when you started throwing around ideas the other night."

"Really," I said uncertainly.

"You were on target when you said the better ships are getting preferred treatment, while the lousy ones—the ones with real needs—are most often overlooked. Item: At Pickford and Black's wharf there's a magazine exchange run by a group of Halifax women. They've developed a country-wide collection system that brings in bales of used publications that are as good as new if you've been at sea for a month. An agent or master has only to lay a boat alongside the wharf and load up with as much reading matter as his people can use. The ones who bother to do it are the ships already looking after their crews, of course."

"And you'd like the boarding party to deliver some material to those who miss out?" I guessed.

"Good as far as it goes," grinned Dick, "but you're thinking small. Why not all the ships? Then you can't be charged with favouritism. You'll have a point of friendly entry to everything on the harbour. Do you realize how much hangs on the welcome you receive? Every little thing we do to make things easier helps the security process, as I see it. If you're right about the importance of morale among the men, this is one solid way to boost it. It shows how useful our talk was, the other night. You brought along valuable intelligence—valuable enough for me to pass it to Headquarters. The more of that the better."

"When would you like us to start?" I asked.

"This morning," said Dick promptly. "I spoke last night to Elsie Little, who runs the exchange. She'll be expecting you at ten o'clock."

I answered "Oh?" in a voice that drew me a quizzical glance.

"Any reason you shouldn't?" Oland wanted to know.

"I'm not concerned so much about today as I am about what's likely to follow," I explained. "If we are going to cover each ship to the best of our ability, taking on a magazine distribution might be the last straw. There's just so much time to fit it all in."

"We'll be able to justify a second boarding party if we can demonstrate enough need for it," Oland countered. "The magazines as morale boosters will be a good talking point."

"That's true," I admitted.

The sense of fun which so often saved Dick from being a hard task-master brought a sparkle to his eyes.

"You're beginning to act as though some corvette is going to be short a watchkeeper," he said.

I nodded reluctantly. He'd cheated me out of my big announcement.

"I knew it all along," he said placidly. "Now then, what other bright ideas have you come up with?"

I told him about the bull session in the standby room with the ratings and explained our decision to smarten our drill.

"Excellent!" he cried. "Where to from there?"

"As quickly as we can, we want to get the people in the ships to consider us trustworthy. I believe that trust will rest on two things—whether corrective action follows our interest in their working conditions and whether or not the information we give them to counter rumours turns out to be the truth."

"If they knew *half* the truth," said Dick grimly, "they couldn't be blamed if they downed tools tomorrow."

"As far as bad news is concerned," I countered, "there isn't much we could tell them they don't already know. They're living most of the bad news and the enemy broadcasts anything they may have missed. There's a lot of positive stuff, though, that gets lost in the fog. The boys can remind them of it."

"Such as?"

"Such as what's happening in our shipyards, the sort of help we're beginning to get from the States, the buildup of our armed forces that'll come if the convoys sweat it out a while longer."

"You don't have to sell me on the general principle," commented Dick, "but aren't you expecting too much from your crew? They're sailors, not propagandists. Most of them would look pretty silly making patriotic speeches."

I suggested he'd missed the point.

"They're already propagandists. A lot of what they hear in the ships bugs them and we spend a good deal of time between boardings discussing the rumours and the actual bad news they bring back. They're keen for honest answers themselves, because they obviously want to put their mates straight where they're being sold a bill of goods."

"Fine," said Oland more easily. "All you have to do, then, is let nature take its course. You keep telling your men the party line and they keep retelling it."

"It's not going to be quite as simple as that," I warned, "particularly on the local news front. When a coughing seaman shows a boarder his damp blankets and the weeping plate alongside his bunk he's a poor candidate for *any* party line. What he wants to hear is that the plate is going to be replaced next refit—as it should have been five years before. A small matter, but what we tell him can have a good deal of bearing on how he behaves on sailing day."

The Commander was unsmiling now.

"I suppose you're asking me what he should be told?"

"I didn't set out to," I said, "but that's where the conversation seems to have carried us."

He regarded me narrowly.

"Was that a hypothetical case?"

"No. It was reported to me yesterday."

"What did you do about it?"

"I went to the fo'c's'le and had a look for myself."

"Was it bad?"

"Yes."

"What did you tell the man?"

"I said I'd see that a responsible officer spoke with the

ship's agent and that something would be done about the plate—if not here, at least when the ship next docked."

"Did that satisfy him?"

"Not entirely. I think he was pleased he'd been able to sound off to someone who seemed to listen, but he was obviously cynical about anything happening—assuming the ship stays afloat long enough for refit."

"In a word," said Oland, "he didn't believe you?"

"He didn't have much chance," I replied. "I had a pretty good idea I was feeding him a pious hope. One of our men had put in a voyage with that company before the war and he said the best any one could do for the fellow was offer him condolence. He didn't put it quite that politely, but that was the gist."

"Your rating wouldn't be much use trying to raise that particular man's morale?"

"Not much."

"Would it be a mistake for him to try?"

"Probably—as things stand now."

"But you think the situation can change?"

"It's got to," I said with some heat. "Multiply that ship by the number of similar or worse ships and remember how little time we have."

"Agreed," admitted Oland. He sat for a long time, his eyes on the section of the harbour visible from his window. A convoy had been assembling for the next day's sailing and the anchorages over towards the Dartmouth shore were well filled. His glance went slowly from one vessel to the next. Finally he gave me his attention again.

"What you told that man was the truth," he said. "Something *will* be done about the weeping plate—though if the ship's to catch tomorrow's movement it may have to wait until she gets to the other side. And the 'Hungry Fleet' is going to change, too. It will take time; you don't sweep out the garbage of centuries overnight—even with a war pushing you. But, by God, it's going to be different. There are enough people with enough weight to make it different."

An officer came to his door with a signal.

"Will it keep five minutes?" Oland asked.

The other nodded.

Dick picked up the phone and called the agent for the

ship with the wet fo'c's'le. When he suggested that something could be done to alleviate the condition in question—even before the plate could be replaced—he began to get an argument. It was short-lived. Oland's temper seldom got the better of him, but when it did it was volcanic. His voice shook the glass of his cubicle. It was plain when he hung up that he had reached an understanding with the agent.

"Well," he announced, his colour gradually returning, "next time anyone suggests that Naval Control isn't the sailor's friend, you'll have an anecdote to spin."

I felt the need for levity.

"That would mean trusting your reputation to a propagandist," I warned.

He reacted in kind.

"I knew before you were through your first watch in the Straits of Georgia seventeen years ago that the old *Armentieres* was in peril. When I left you alone on the bridge and flaked out on the other side of the bulkhead, I'll admit I looked out the scuttle a few times to be sure you weren't running down any CPR ferries. You didn't—and you know more now than you did then. Run the boarding party your own way and let me know when I can help."

He forestalled my thanks by adding sternly, "And don't forget to pick up those magazines. They're more important now than they were ten minutes ago."

5

"desperate gallantry..."

On October 28, 1940, I attended my first convoy conference. This was one detail of the NCS operation I had previously missed because tensions on the harbour always multiplied on the eve of a sailing, when the conferences were invariably timed. (Malingerers usually saved their complaints until then, knowing that if a medical decision on their actual physical condition couldn't be immediately obtained their ship would be compelled to leave without them. Deliberate mechanical damage was most prevalent, too, at an hour when it would be impossible to make it good in time for a scheduled departure.) The boarding party was most heavily occupied when the ships' masters and escort commanders, with the convoy commodore and NCSO, met to discuss sailings. Oland decided nevertheless that my education must include an experience of the quietly dramatic gathering that preceded each setting-forth.

"It's the climax of everything we work for," he explained, "the end result for each man-jack who carries final responsibility for getting the cargoes across. You need to actually feel it to realize how much you're a part of it. Line up your day so you can be spared for a couple of hours. If anything critical breaks while we're meeting, you can always be hauled out."

As it turned out, I participated in a meeting which no one who was there would ever forget. The convoy was HX 84, whose mid-ocean escort would be the Royal Navy's armed merchant cruiser *Jervis Bay*, until recently a liner on the Australian run. Canadian destroyers, the local escort, would accompany the convoy out into the Atlantic, and other fast anti-submarine protection would be waiting for it when it came into the U-boat hunting ground of Britain's Western Approaches. In the broad sweep of ocean between, where the danger was surface attack, *Jervis Bay's* six-inch guns would be the merchant convoy's security.

The conference might have been run in some efficient industrial boardroom. At the head of the T-shaped table, with Oland as chairman, were the senior executives. Around the shank of the T sat the merchant captains, twenty-nine seagoing branch managers. Each detail of the undertaking—navigation, station-keeping, communications, blackout, emergency routines—was dealt with by its corporate expert. The printed sailing orders lying before each ship's master included a chart that showed his vessel's position in the formation. Questions were asked freely, and their answering began the knitting-together of a human and mechanical entity which would take physical shape beyond the harbour approaches.

The Irish wit of the mid-ocean escort commander contributed a note of confidence to the gathering. I had heard of Captain Fogarty Fegen, RN, ashore, where his repartee over the bridge table had delighted some of my civilian friends.

Concluding his remarks to the masters, he said "I think I can assure you that if we run into any routine unpleasantness, such as one of the enemy's armed merchant cruisers, *Jervis Bay* will be able to attend to it. Should we have the unlikely bad luck to cross the path of a pocket battleship, I can only promise to do my best. Under those circumstances there will be a good deal you will want to do for yourselves."

Once again the group ran through the carefully worked-out strategies that would be put into motion by such an eventuality.

The conference dispersed with the commodore's final "Good sailing, gentlemen."

Little groups formed and reformed as old friends, either from peace-time or from previous convoys, paused for a few words here or a handshake there. If a single figure stood out among the ship's masters it was the large, hearty fellow who commanded the British tanker, *San Demetrio*. Captain George Waite's O.B.E. was a momento of the time a *San* vessel was blown in two under him; by a valiant effort he had very nearly saved half the doomed ship.

Richard Oland had been on target when he decided that sitting in on the conference would help me feel even more closely identified with the convoy when it passed down the harbour with the well-found *Cornish City* at its head. The commodore had chosen her in preference to the more comfortable liner, *Rangitiki*. She had both greater manoeuverability and excellent bridge accommodation for himself and his signals staff.

When the parade of ships faded into the haze off Sambro it was an unusually moving experience for me.

On the afternoon of November 5, the protective wireless silence into which the convoy had sailed was broken. I was in the office when the messenger hastily laid the signal on Oland's desk. The commander's great fist fell on the words before him as though they could be physically crushed. My feelings echoed his when the message was silently passed to me.

"Cornish City being gunned. Latitude 52 30 N, 32 W", it read. We stared at one another in dismay.

More messages trickled in, each one more painfully terse than the last. They told a devastating story: what Captain Fegen had described as unlikely bad luck had become brutal reality. A German pocket battleship was ravaging the convoy at will, her eleven-inch guns far outranging anything that could be brought to bear by the defensive escort.

Those of us ashore knew the plan the embattled convoy would try to follow. As protective radio silence fell once more, we could visualize the ships—those that were still afloat—breaking formation as *Jervis Bay* tried to divert the wolf from the sheep, Captain Fegen doing his best with what he had. The only thing that might possibly save Convoy HX 84 from complete disaster was the hour of the attack. Dusk would be falling in that section of the Atlantic; visual contact would soon be denied the raider, just as the stilled wireless impulses were denying him electronic bearings. Further protection would be sought behind smoke floats.

But it was flimsy at best. In the silence of that Halifax office we thought of the ships and men we had come to know as part of our harbour duties.

Naval Control people had learned by necessity to live with their losses. The previous year the speedy German raider *Graf Spee* had picked off many merchant ships routed independently out of Halifax to southern waters. But, devastating as they were, the surface attacks had at least occurred in waters where those who escaped sinking vessels could survive long enough to be taken prisoner aboard the pocket battleship.

The massacre of a North Atlantic convoy in November was another story. The toll in human lives could be expected to outstrip the losses, in kinder waters, to *Graf Spee*. The days of waiting to learn the cost cast a pall over the NCS office. It penetrated every detail of assembling the convoys due to follow in HX 84's wake. There was a chill in the eyes we met as we came over the gangways to inspect the ships anchored in the safety of Halifax harbour—the men aboard these vessels knew they'd be next to face the menace that struck HX 84.

Bits of intelligence and rumour at last came together in an accurate picture when the Swedish freighter *Stureholm*, which had escaped during the attack, put back into Halifax with survivors she had courageously waited to pluck from the sea. After *Stureholm* anchored in the Basin her captain was whisked ashore before I could board her. The second officer, haggard from the physical and mental battering of the past few days, gave me an eyewitness account.

He told of sighting the ominous silhouette of *Admiral Scheer* on the dimming horizon; of *Jervis Bay* steaming from the head of the convoy to draw the fire of the German's long-range turrets; and of how the convoy methodically scattered under a smoke screen in the time gained.

Captain Fegen, though hopelessly outgunned, kept *Jervis Bay* between *Scheer* and the convoy for twenty-two minutes. He and most of his crew met a fiery death just as *Jervis Bay* came within range of the battleship. As darkness fell, recurring flashes of gunfire and pillars of burning fuel oil marked the kills as *Scheer* hunted down those merchantmen she was able to overtake, illuminate and destroy. The valiant stand of *Jervis Bay* ensured that there were only five of thirty-seven merchantmen sunk, including *Cornish City*.

The *Stureholm*'s own story was in a way a direct contrast to *Jervis Bay*'s. It was concisely told in COAC's signal to Admiralty on November 19. The laconic dispatch told first of heroic rescue efforts, but later took on another kind of drama.

> "On convoy scattering *Stureholm* altered course, adjusting speed and courses as necessary to keep smoke cloud between himself and raider. This continued for four hours. At 2100 he observed SOS made by hand electric flashlight and headed for this. At 2300 he picked up 20 men from *Jervis Bay*, then his own crew manned the boat and took three men from one raft and ten men from another. Boat now unserviceable so that crew re-embarked and remaining 20 men taken off second raft by manoeuvering ship alongside at 0500. Meanwhile firing and starshells and searchlights had stopped about 2330.
>
> "Master then called consultation of crew and, thinking it not wise to proceed eastward, course was set for St. John's. Finding their charts were not suitable and as Halifax would offer better protection, course was altered for Halifax.
>
> "The morning after arrival the master and all officers except the second officer refused to sail, stating they

would prefer to be shot. Their example was followed by 14 of the crew. These officers and men are now being paid off and it is hoped to complete the crew from other survivors of ships in HX 84 and sail *Stureholm* perhaps in HX 91. No disciplinary action is now contemplated and no awards are recommended."

There were 13 Canadians from *Jervis Bay* among those *Stureholm* had rescued. When the Swedish vessel put to sea again under the command of her former second officer, some of the British survivors from HX 84 rounded out her crew. But when she faded over the eastern horizon it was for the final time. On the night of December 12, U-96 closed in mid-ocean and sent a torpedo into her. There were no survivors.

San Demetrio was one of the vessels reported lost from HX 84; some of her crew had been picked up after abandoning her to a holocaust of shell-ignited fuel. But eight days later she appeared in a lonely Irish bay, completely shorn of navigational instruments and with every means of communication—including her signal flags—incinerated. She was under her own power, however, and controlled by sixteen of her crew who had reboarded her after the fire subsided.

The raw courage of *Jervis Bay* and the posthumous Victoria Cross awarded Captain Fegen stirred pride in Naval hearts, but the need for such desperate gallantry heightened the fears of merchant sailors faced with crossing the waters where HX 84 was attacked. And German marauders were not the only enemy—winter gales intensified the hardships of the crossing. Even on the harbour and its approaches, wrapped in our winter duffles, we had a bitter taste of sailoring in the merciless North Atlantic.

Oxner's forecast that our launch would one day bore a hole in her own stern was very nearly fulfilled. At any rate our doughty inspection boat broke down. While she was on the slip, we went through a series of replacements, each one more incongruous than the last. It pointed up the need for boarding craft specifically built for the task.

The first of the makeshifts was a rakish, narrow-beamed affair which providentially vanished from the camber after our first day's use of her. Granted, she was harshly tested.

The night before there had been a near-hurricane. Pandemonium reigned in the Basin when the Dutch liner *Nieuw Amsterdam*, serving as a trooper, dragged her hooks. Picking up two nearby freighters by their anchor chains and clasping one to either bow, she had driven downwind and almost ground herself into the spiked shore. Several frantically mustered tugs plunged to her rescue just in time. Next morning, in the gusty aftermath of this blow, we rode to our business amid high swells. While our temporary launch was reasonably dry with everything battened down, she rolled badly with the wind on the beam. She offered poor foothold even on our first boarding—a ship chosen because her berth offered better shelter than anything else in the Basin.

Heading for our next call, the violence of the launch's movement gave me pause.

"How about it?" I asked her coxswain, "Is she up to taking it?"

The man at the wheel assured me she had taken worse. I should have realized that this was not an objective opinion. A certain proprietorial defensiveness had been roused in the man by the caustic and indiscreet remarks of my crew of boarders. And perhaps I was over confident; after all, we were relatively sheltered here in the harbour.

"All right," I said, "we'll carry on, but keep her head to it and drift over to where we can get a straight run at the next ship."

When our destination was bows-on, the coxswain rang for increased speed. Clouds of spray burst over the stem and a crazy bucketing shook the hull. She galloped like a cayuse from wave to wave, filling us with exhilaration. Then we encountered a particularly steep swell and dug into the green of it. Instead of parting harmlessly like its predecessors, the wave hit the wheelhouse a solid blow and drove in two of its windows. Our comfortable insider's view was lost in a welter of salt water that carried on into the cabin and silenced the remarks which had so enraged the coxswain.

The engineer jerked the throttle to "Slow" as fast as the helmsman could ring for it. With just enough way on the launch to avoid being broached or pooped, we eased her out of the Basin like a punished dog with its tail between its legs. Not until we were past Turple Head and able to skulk along in the lee of the coaling tips and the Shipyard did the engine return to full power.

Trying its best to make amends, Harbour Craft alotted us its greatest pride next morning. We found ourselves aboard an imposing Chris Craft some millionaire had unloaded on the Navy. Built for deepsea cruising, it rode the swells beautifully and boasted a bridge which might have passed for the Crystal Palace. Established there, I had, for the first time, the feeling of having achieved a worthy command.

In the broad nose was a small cockpit from which the bow lines could be worked—a waist-high well accessible from below decks. On calm days it provided a handy approach to gangways and side ladders but, like the rest of the boat, it was too fancy for the rough-and-tumble of heavy weather boarding. At that, its greatest value was demonstrated on a day of lively wind and water.

We were bound for the harbour approaches and meeting the swell cleanly. The bow was lifting and falling rhythmically, breaking the backs of the oncoming waves and flinging graceful explosions of spume to either side. The wind, snatching spray from the crests, dashed it against the bridge and left the windscreen streaming between sweeps of the wipers.

As my view alternately misted and cleared I slowly realized that the bow cockpit was occupied. A set of broad shoulders and a head shrouded by the hood of a duffel coat showed above the coaming. Having seen no need for an exposed lookout—and having ordered none—I sent a hand forward to summon my mysterious volunteer. When he reported to the bridge, it was none other than Oxner. He was, to say the least, moist.

"I'm curious," I said. "Are you standing lookout or taking soundings?"

The senior hand was imperturbable.

"It's this way, sir. Most winters about this time, I get a touch of rheumatism. This year, though, I've been trying an emulsion they claim will handle that sort of thing. Been taking quite a ride from the boys but, by thunder, I haven't had a twinge."

"Congratulations." I said. "But what has that got to do with pretending you're a figurehead?"

"I reckoned," he replied, without a change of expression, "that a spell up there in the eyes of her would give the emulsion a proper test."

There was, perhaps, the suggestion of a twinkle in his eye—but with Oxner you were never quite sure.

On a less amusing occasion, we went to the wide reach above McNab's Island to check a tramp that had just anchored after a rough passage up the coast. She was riding unusually light, her propeller half out of the water. Freezing weather had sheathed her twenty-five feet of free-board in ice. No attempt had been made to haul in the side ladder by which the pilot had boarded her, and it, too, was heavily glazed.

We hailed, but no one appeared above. We assumed the anchor watch had sought shelter in the galley or some other island of warmth. There was a moderate swell coming in from the Atlantic, but it wasn't too steep to prevent our securing a bow line to the ladder so I could transfer to it. I hadn't mounted a dozen rungs, however, before I realized this would be no ordinary climb. Clinging to the molded ice with mittened hands and feeling for a precarious foothold made every upward step a severe physical test. Though I was in good shape from several unbroken months of boarding, I knew I'd better be careful indeed. I glanced down and saw Oxner on the point of following me.

"Hold everything until I'm on deck," I called.

It was a long, laborious struggle. I completed the climb out of sheer perversity—that, and the fact that the upper terminus of the ladder was closer than the lower when I realized how much it was taking out of me. I was shaking when I reached the deserted deck. Waiting for the fit to pass, I shouted to Oxner, "Stay where you are. The ladder's murder. We'll leave this one till she comes alongside."

I glanced seaward. Chebucto Head was disappearing in a black wall of driven snow which was bringing violent winds our way.

I ducked into the officer's quarters, located the mate and told him I wasn't impressed by his welcoming arrangements. What I saw of the ship before announcing I'd return when she'd docked did nothing to raise my estimate of her.

The squall was very close when I started inching my way, rung by treacherous rung, back to the launch. Already the sea was uneasy. Oxner and the bowman were having difficulty steadying the lower end of the ladder. I could hear the wind coming. I had reached the second last rung when it struck.

It came with full force, and it hit like a fist. In an instant the launch swung broadside to the blast and the bow line jerked the free end of the ladder out from the ship's side. Then the line snapped. The launch lurched downwind and I thumped back against the freighter's hull. I was facing outward: in its writhing the ladder had twisted completely around.

If clinging to the ladder had been difficult before, it was doubly so now. My legs, outstretched at a forty-five degree angle, forced the ladder away from the hull. The only support I had was the pressure of my back against the glassy steel plates and my hands with their tenuous grip on the slippery rungs. I hooked my arms around the rungs, knowing my fingers would soon be completely numbed by the cold—and then I would have no grip at all.

I saw the launch rolling into the downwind smother. The engine had been balky that morning and I realized that it had chosen this moment for a repeat performance. There went my hopes of a quick rescue.

In the next interminable minutes I had ample opportunity to contemplate sins past and present. The furious sea kicked at my feet and the wind gnawed at my weakening arms. With the strength draining from me I heard at last the faint sound of Oxner's voice and the restored rumbling of the launch's engine. Through the roar of the wind came the vicious slapping of waves against the launch's bow. Then strong hands snatched me back to the land of the living.

I was not alone in such adventures. In 50,000 boardings, many under difficult conditions, several officers and ratings were injured or cast into the drink. None died, though. Doubtless we had a guardian angel; but alert, highly disciplined men played the major role in creating this record.

★ ★ ★

Well before the boarding service carried any official authority other than the right of search, we found ourselves regarded as representatives of law and order. The impression may have been fostered by situations like the one which arose on a tanker from the Far East. Her chief officer had drawn the wrath of one of his Chinese crewmen. The berserk seaman had chased the mate around the ship, all the while unsuccessfully attempting to drive a knife into him, then had holed up in the fo'c's'le. His mates had seen fit to grant him exclusive occupancy.

All this had happened just before we came over the side. We found ourselves confronted by an agitated company of Chinese crewmen on deck, and a perplexed group of officers in consultation on the bridge. Our providential arrival was instantly hailed as the solution to the crisis. To these people we were the law.

Had I given the situation any thought, I would immediately have sent ashore for the real thing. Violence in ships alongside was a city police matter; what happened aboard ships in the stream fell under the jurisdiction of the RCMP. I could quite easily have brushed aside the assumption that we would intervene: instead, I allowed myself to be guided by the expectations of the ship's officers, and undertook to talk to the knife wielder.

The fo'c's'le was illuminated only by the meagre daylight that filtered through its open entrance and the scuttles. It took a while for my eyes to adjust to the gloom after the glare outside. I could only stand and peer into the shadows, uncomfortably aware of the possibility that my quarry might easily by stealing up behind me, his blade at the ready. There was no sign of him, and I could hear no sound. I stood frozen, every nerve taut, every sense alert.

Then, very gradually, I made out his motionless silhouette. He was partly concealed by a stanchion, and standing as still as I was. The silence dragged on for several seconds while I pondered what move to make. My command of Chinese was limited to a few words acquired in a boyhood friendship with a laundryman in Edmonton's East End. But out of this memory pool came a phrase that proved useful. I said sternly, "You bad boy."

The motionless shadow thought it over, then replied in equally simplified Chinese: "No, no. No bad boy."

"You come with me," I suggested. "We talk."

For several long moments he did not reply. I waited. Then something flashed in a shard of sunlight that had penetrated the darkness of the fo'c's'le. I braced myself. Moving into the clear, the fellow extended a small metal case.

"Have cigalette?" he invited.

There was no sign of his knife. The murderous rage had completely subsided. A man in his sixties, the sailor shuffled along with me in the direction of the bridge like a penitent youth anxious to make amends. There was considerable palaver, with a Chinese bos'n interpreting, then the chief officer said everything had been settled, thanked me and suggested we go ahead with the search.

Word of the incident spread and, with it, the assumption that the boarding party offered a handy substitute when the police weren't available. The impression took firmer hold when a couple of wartime Orders in Council invested us, under certain circumstances, with the power of arrest.

6

"new loyalties..."

The magazine depot on Pickford and Black's wharf run by the society matrons of Halifax was a regular port of call for members of the boarding service. For five years Oxner and his cohorts became almost as much at home in the exchange as in their standby room.

At first there were formalities. Oxner would pull up in the launch at a set hour, take on board a cargo of baled magazines, then head out into the harbour to deliver them during the searches. Oxner's visits were a colourful break for the women involved in the monotonous work of sorting and baling the magazines.

Some time after the distribution of reading material had become an accepted morale-builder for merchant seamen waiting in Halifax for their convoys to assemble, the departure of an unusually large movement made impossible demands on the exchange's personnel. A tired, near-tearful voice on my phone announced that the next day's requirements couldn't be met.

"The girls are coming back tonight and there will be *something* for you tomorrow but it won't be all you've asked for."

I passed the bad news to Oxner, who had just requested permission to dismiss the men for the night. It had been a long and demanding day, with an exceptional inflow of ships, and Oxner was unusually tired. He raked the black stubble on his chin.

"That's too bad, sir. The men out there are beginning to notice such things and you can lay to it the ships we have to miss will sound off. Of course, we could cut down on the number of bales we give each."

I agreed with the suggestion and told him to carry on ashore. He made no move, however, and the rasp of calloused fingers on his whiskers grew louder in the otherwise silent office.

"There's another angle," he offered finally. "I've watched those women work. They'll take it hard if they can't make a job of it. Even if they come back tonight, there'll be no one on the wharf to give them a hand with those big boxes . . ." He paused, awaiting my comment. I looked at him expectantly. Oxner frowned and went on.

"You might say it's *us* they're working for. Maybe some of the boys—"

I dismissed him with a wave and a grin. If I knew "the boys", they'd have reserves of energy available for such gallant duties, no matter how exhausting their day had been.

Other matters kept me in the Yard late that evening. When at last I could, I dropped down to the magazine exchange. The ancient buildings along the dark waterfront brooded in the rain, but windows were aglow at the end of Pickford and Black's wharf.

Inside the shed, three sailors and half-a-dozen women in smocks were drinking coffee around a sorting table. They seemed weary but good-humoured, while Oxner buoyed everyone's spirits with one of his dead-pan anecdotes. The nub of this heartening tale was, I gathered, the enthusiasm with which, that very day, sailors aboard an Indiaman had received their bale of magazines. The women listened raptly, and some sipped their coffee with modest pleasure.

The spell was broken when I was spotted in the doorway.

"Well, there you are," said the woman in charge, pointing proudly to a wall of stacked bales. "We've got the material you asked for, after all. And we wouldn't have missed tonight for the Lieutenant Governor's ball."

"That's right," seconded another of the volunteers. "We really had no way of knowing, till now, whether our work counted or not. The boys have convinced us just how important the magazines are to the sailors."

A foundation was laid that night: much was built on it as the war dragged on. Volunteers from the boarding service were never lacking when similar emergencies arose; and Oxner always insisted on giving matters his personal touch, even when he could have passed the torch to others. The stories with which he regaled the women gave them the feeling that they were active participants in the Battle. This they were, and their continued high morale made their work useful to many others over the years.

★ ★ ★

The winter of 1940-41 was a time of crisis in the battle to defend Britain's Atlantic lifeline. As the decimated Nazi air legions faltered in their effort to open England to invasion, the U-boat fleet redoubled its effort to starve her. Waves of long-range submarines fanned out towards America, attacking the convoys with new ruthlessness. Casualties rose, and the bitterly cold Atlantic added to the toll of those who ran the gauntlet.

I had recurring doubts about the decision that had kept me ashore as an adjunct to the Merchant Navy. I craved action on a warship.

The first of the Canadian-built corvettes were arriving from the St. Lawrence; the need of them had been underscored by increased casualties among the Navy's destroyers. My old ambition to serve on one of the speedy escorts resurfaced. The feeling was sometimes one of helplessness, like the time most of the *Margaree's* crew went down with her. The gunnery petty officer who had whipped the Rainbow Division into shape was among them. With the loss, I felt a sense of displacement, an urge to *act*, and to act directly, in the seagoing role I had visualized when I re-enlisted.

Equally painful, however, was my awareness of new loyalties. A freighter's master I interviewed told me how thankful he was that he wasn't skipper of a tanker. One had recently been "fished" abeam of him in convoy and had gone up like a bomb.

"Usually somebody gets away," he said, "but not this time. Just *bang*—and nothing but a great fireball. I knew her captain. You probably met him. He lay here in the Basin for quite a while, waiting for storage on the other side."

I'd boarded many such tankers, but a chill went through me as he added, "Ramsay, his name was—out of Hong Kong." The mention of that particular ship brought into perspective the importance of the work we were doing among the convoys.

There were other ships from the Far East and the southern runs joining the North Atlantic convoys. They were desperately needed; Allied losses could not, in many cases, have been otherwise replaced. But the malevolence of winter was almost as unsparing of their seamen as enemy torpedoes. Built for the tropics, many still with native crews, these ships were floating disaster areas. Their sleeping quarters hadn't been designed for sub-zero temperatures. Their galleys were cold in harbour, and much worse when they were being buried under heavy seas off Greenland and Iceland.

Oxner maintained that the only reason *all* the crews of such vessels didn't mutiny was that they never thawed out long enough to reach the decision.

Our concern for them had led us to further develop the rapport between ourselves and the ships' companies. We'd uncovered problems which worsened considerably an already bad situation.

Voluntary agencies like the Red Cross and the Navy League had been distributing bundles of woolens and other cold weather gear to the needy merchant vessels. They tended to trust chief stewards or other functionaries aboard to dole out the gifts to the sailors, but one of the most persistent beefs the boarders were encountering was that many bundles were being sidetracked. While the stewards were, in the main, men of integrity, there were exceptions. These petty chisellers not only denied the sailors gear they needed; they steered the undistributed donations onto the black market when their ships reached the U.K. and earned themselves a tidy profit.

More important than actual cases of this kind of thievery was the effect embittered accounts of them had on the morale of the crews. In the minds of the men, such practices were not the exception, but the rule.

Brand and Oland suggested to the volunteer agencies that our boarding group was in a position to ensure that the bundles went where they were intended to go—to the freezing sailors. In a very short time winter woolens were part of our cargo in the boarding launch.

Distributing the winter gear meant more work, but there was no complaint from those who did it. The sight of a Lascar sailor's eyes glistening with gratitude above the folds of a scarf knitted by some Saskatchewan farmwife was its own reward.

The process also won us friends. Information began to be volunteered, and complaints aired openly and accurately, as seamen were encouraged by the expectation that something would be done about them.

Not that all became sweetness and light overnight. The balance between the merchant crews' willingness to sail and their defiance of authority remained on knife-edge. It was kept there by the recurring ordeal of the Atlantic passage—and by a more elusive influence, that of ever-present agitators.

Of these, the Communists were the most worrisome. They were a presence in many of the ships, and most were above average at organizing mischief. Russia was still honouring its non-aggression pact with Germany and encouraged her agents to exploit low morale in the ships. Championing the fearful and the disgruntled was old hat to such practitioners of subversion; they were skilled at accomplishing their ends behind a screen of essentially loyal and patriotic dupes.

As long as defiance of authority existed only in small pockets, or malingering was confined to individuals, there was always the possibility of getting a threatened ship away by sailing time. But the supply of experienced sailors ashore in Halifax had dwindled almost to the vanishing point and it was sometimes necessary to rush replacements from other ports to complete crews.

It was true that plans were already well advanced to create manning pools and training schools for dependable reinforcements. Until they were operational, however, a threat hung over the personnel situation—the possibility that sitdowns would become too widespread to be successfully countered.

Trouble came in waves, some of them long-term. I had, for example, been conscious for some time of problems created by ethnic and cultural differences. The Greek crews we encountered were a case in point. Along with wit, gaiety and courage, they possessed an emotionalism beyond our Anglo-Saxon comprehension.

Some of us thought that their ships held more than an average number of Communists: ideological antagonisms certainly dominated many situations. But it seemed to my boggled mind that many problems arose from forces specifically and definably cultural.

Once we discovered that a Greek crew had downed tools the moment their vessel's anchor dropped. Since the ship wasn't due to convoy for a couple of weeks we left her to herself in the hope that the captain would manage to work out the impasse he had reached with his men.

A week later we found a dead, cold hulk. Though the crew had made no attempt to go over the side, the boilers were untended, there was no electric light and even the galley stove had been allowed to die. Hunkered in their fo'c's'le, the strikers were eating out of cans, creating a litter that was as offensive to the nose as to the eye. Nevertheless, they exhibited a sublime righteousness.

Attempting to get to the heart of things, I raised the question of the ship's articles. The captain told me with tears in his eyes that he had observed them to the letter. I asked the crew if this was so. With a smile and a shrug, their spokesman agreed that the master had told the truth.

"Then why in the world won't you obey his orders?" I demanded.

"He has no caring for us," replied the seaman, with a pained expression.

"How do you mean?"

"He gives us only what the articles demand."

"What else should he give you?" I demanded in exasperation.

"Oh," he shrugged, "some sort of present—a bottle of wine, a basket of fruit—"

Since the tie-up was costing the vessel thousands of dollars a day, it seemed to me that a five-dollar basket of fruit would be a very reasonable price to pay for getting her to sea again. When I advanced this thought to the master, I expected that he would at least give it serious consideration. Instead, his sobs gave way to roars of indignation. He was not going to be dictated to by unspeakable pirates. It was an outrage! It couldn't be done.

But it was done. A settlement was reached and the ship went her way. I can't be sure what influence my prodding had, nor what secret deal was made between master and men. It is reasonably certain, though, that negotiations involved an under-the-table cash bonus.

★ ★ ★

More widespread trouble followed Italy's declaration of war on Greece in October, 1940. The wages of Greek seamen had skyrocketed by about seven hundred per cent, mainly because neutral Greek shipowners had found the Allies desperate for shipping of any description and prepared to pay almost any price for it.

But the swift success of Axis forces in Greece changed matters drastically. The country's government-in-exile was urged to bring Greek seamen's wages back into line with those received by other Allied sailors. The suggestion received short shrift—particularly in vessels whose labour leaders flew the Communist banner. What happened was a demand for even higher pay, more commensurate with the ever-increasing hazards of the Atlantic crossing. When this was refused, a general strike hit the Greek ships in two of Britain's chief ports.

Such strikes were crippling to a war effort that depended for its lifeblood on the supply ships of the Atlantic convoys. Merchant seamen, while not enlisted as members of Allied armed forces, had to be persuaded to accept the pressures and risks of wartime duty. The persuasion took the necessary form of wartime law.

Canada's merchant shipping legislation, while generally adequate for its own vessels, was of little help when problems developed aboard foreign callers. The legal complications that arose when foreign sailors refused duty were immense. Canadian magistrates disliked hearing such cases and the captains of the ships involved found the expense of hiring lawyers scarcely worth the results achieved.

Alarmed by the Canada Shipping Act's ineffectiveness in such situations, Captain Brand took word of the threat to high places. With unusual speed Ottawa issued a drastic Order in Council. P.C. 4751 was aimed at crewmen in Allied cargo carriers using Canadian ports. Under it, refusal of duty became a misdemeanor outside the jurisdiction of the civil courts. Offenders would henceforth be whisked away to Immigration detention. Only by promising future obedience to ship-board authority could they regain their freedom.

A week before the Order came into force, Commander Oland encountered the sort of crisis for which it had been tailored. The agent for the *Michael J. Embericos* informed him that twenty-one of the ship's company, including junior officers, had refused to perform work of any kind. The ship was loading two thousand tons of steel urgently needed in London; but without steam for the winches everything had come to a dead stop.

Although the Order was still not law, Dick acted unhesitatingly. He sent the vessel's captain stern instructions:

"You are required to muster your crew forthwith. Tell them that under no consideration is any man to leave the ship or go ashore without a written order from you. Any officer or man disobeying this order is liable to summary conviction and imprisonment."

The captain sent back his reply by the same messenger. His men, he reported, had been cooped up in the ship for six months and were tired of working. They didn't want to make trouble and they were not holding out for a bonus. They were simply homesick and wanted to be shipped back to Greece.

Had their demand been met, they would have reached their native soil just in time to be conscripted for the defence of their homeland against Italian invaders. This, of course, was a situation they could not foresee. As it was, their stubborn sit-down created an impasse. Oland fumed in frustration during the week that had to pass before P.C. 4751 became official, and the *Embericos* had to be deleted from the outgoing convoy.

I visited the ship at its silent dock, taking along Williams and Coffey to yarn with the hands while I talked to the captain. The object of our visit was to make certain the crew fully understood what would happen when P.C. 4751 came into force. We wanted to be regarded as friendly advisors rather than wielders of the big stick, so the ratings brought along a couple of bales of magazines to lighten the strikers' boredom. The Greek seamen were more than ready to enter into debate with the boarders about their situation, but any sweet reason that showed signs of developing vanished whenever the captain's name was raised. The result was continued stalemate.

On September 11, Oland met with the government departments concerned and ironed out the details involved in enforcing the Order in Council. On the morning of the 12th he alerted me.

"This is the day. We'll wait until after dark, when there will be less happening on the waterfront and less likelihood of sympathetic onlookers."

We discussed the *modus operandi*—without entirely agreeing. Dick thought the boarders should take the strikers into custody; I had argued that the civilian police should be used.

"They're accustomed to arresting people," I argued. "Besides, we're still most useful as the sailor's friend."

Oland quickly let me know that I hadn't changed his mind.

"The best friend is held in firm respect," he said. "As the arm of the Order, you'll get it. Turn your prisoners over to Immigration and they'll do the rest."

At dusk Oxner mustered our full force and we set out to face three times our number in the form of a foreign crew of unpredictable temperament. In two station wagons and a truck we followed the cobbled waterfront road to the commercial dock where the *Embericos* lay. There was a certain tension among us as we bumped along.

The ship was badly lighted, but the sound of voices coming from the fo'c's'le relieved one concern, that the crew might have gone over the side and disappeared into the city. Putting Oxner on the untended gangway, I posted the other ratings along the wharf where, looming large in their duffel coats, they presented the best image of strength and authority.

Locating the captain, I made certain that he had laid the proper charges under the Order. He told me the number of strikers had now risen to thirty-two—practically the entire ship's company. After instructing the junior officers to take their gear ashore and wait there, I went forward to the fo'c's'le.

My appearance through the hatch cut all conversation short. I had an instant audience, the temper of which was difficult to read.

"I would like someone to translate for me," I announced.

A self-assured young seaman stepped forward. He spoke quick but intelligible English, and that was all that was needed for the job at hand.

"I'm sorry you have reached no agreement with your captain," I told him. "You were warned about the new Canadian law for this sort of disobedience. Did everyone understand it?"

The sailor answered for all.

"Yes, mister."

"And you are still refusing to work?"

"Yes, mister."

"Translate what I have just said, please."

He did so. There was a solid chorus of affirmatives.

"O.K.," I said. "I want everyone refusing duty to pack his gear."

"We are all packed," answered the amazing young man. "We knew your men spoke the truth when they warned us." He grinned mischievously. "Can we take our magazines with us or will your men bring us new ones to the jail?"

I couldn't help smiling.

"Better leave them here for your replacements," I told him, "or in case you decide to come back and sail the ship. All ashore that's going ashore."

There was a spate of obviously amused comment, then everyone began to dress for the raw night that awaited them outside. They passed their seabags and other personal gear to the deck.

"They're coming out," I called to Oxner, "and there isn't going to be any trouble. Pass the word to the lads to help them load the truck."

The prisoners seemed to find nothing strange in their captors giving them a hand. On the contrary, I had sense that our effort among the crew was having its desired effect: we were being accepted as friends in a bitter situation.

Checking the crew list to be certain no one had slipped unnoticed into the darkness, I asked the interpreter to have each man respond as I called his name, then fall in beside the station wagons.

In the light of a rating's torch, I found myself confronted by polysyllabic Greek names, all of which were beyond my powers of pronunciation. Undaunted, I called out my version of one.

"*Karageorghis*!"

The only response was a confused silence. I called the name again, more slowly. My audience went into a huddle. After some discussion, the interpreter emerged, shepherding one of his shipmates.

"This is him," he declared triumphantly, and spoke a name which obviously belonged to the man but had only a remote resemblance to the one I had ventured. Amusement rippled through the crowd; I could see that my own men weren't being entirely loyal. I showed Karageorghis where I wanted him to stand, then made an attempt to save my dignity.

"Xenophanes!" I shouted.

There was another conference, and again my interpreter produced a man who, he announced, was the party's choice. Realizing my dignity was beyond redemption, I gave into laughter. The laugh touched off a gale. When it had died I said to the interpreter, "Come here, please. When I point to a name I want you to sing it out."

It was a perfectly coordinated operation from there on. When every name had its tick after it, thirty-two prisoners and their escort embarked for the ride to Pier 22 and Immigration detention. On the way we were serenaded with spirited Greek songs.

Whether the bloodless coup and the beginning of our new duties turned the trick or not, the drafting office found the bodies to double our strength early in December.

In the beginning—the NSCO staff, Halifax, 1940. Front row officers (l-r) Cdr. Leslie Banyard, RCNR; Cdr. Richard Oland, RCN; Lt. Cdr. George Buntain, RCNVR; Lt. Cdr. John Mitchell, RCNVR. Top row, (l—r) Able Seaman Meinerth Wick; Able Seaman Al Oxner; Below Wick, Stoker First Class George Beaman—all RCNR. Banyard took over as NSCO Halifax following Oland's death in 1941. Public Archives Canada/neg. no. 2310-B

A convoy begins to take shape in harbour. Many convoys were delayed due to heavy German bombing of British ports. Delays were both costly in terms of time and in their potential for developing "crew trouble".
Canadian Forces Photograph/REA-391-5. Maritime Command Museum

Toronto Star reporter Fred Griffin interviews Commander Watt in Halifax during the winter of 1941. Griffin was the first newspaperman granted access to the story of what the NBS was trying to accomplish.

Public Archives Canada/DND/PA 104379

The Halifax Boarding Service, 1942— Officers (front row, l-r)—Tyrer, Browne, Conkey, Watt, Green, Noonan, McGee.
Second row, extreme left—Leading Seaman Oxner.
Back row, second from left—Beaman, Fourth from left—Williams.
Extreme right—Crossan. Public Archives Canada/DND/H-2517

An escort ship accompanies a merchant convoy through the bitter and treacherous North Atlantic, keeping a constant watch for the enemy above and below the waves. Maritime Command Museum/M-804-R

Commander Watt and crew boarding a freighter in Halifax Harbour, winter 1940. In these early days the single boarding crew climbed aboard as many as 20 ships in a day. By war's end, they had conducted 50,000 boardings. Public Archives Canada/DND/H-731

NBS Able Seaman Charters checks the shell locker of a merchantman during a search. The possibility of enemy sabotage made such inspections imperative. Public Archives Canada/DND/A-104377

Commander Watt, Senior Boarding Officer, Halifax, 1943. By this time the author, convinced of the importance of the Boarding Service, had put aside his earlier aspirations of sailing on a warship.

Public Archives Canada/DND/PA 106486

Saved to sail again. HMCS "Arvida" brings ashore survivors of a torpedoed merchantman. Some survivors refused to risk their lives repeatedly—part of the work of the NBS was to make sure enough sailors did return to the convoys. If they hadn't, defeat would have been imminent.

Public Archives Canada/DND/PA 136285

Able Seaman Smith, NBS Halifax, distributing magazines in the course of checking a freighter's fo'c'sle. Such activities by the NBS earned the trust and respect of merchant seamen and helped buoy their spirits during the worst days of war.

Public Archives Canada/DND

Public Archives of Canada/PA-105297/Maritime Command Museum

Commander Richard Oland (standing, centre) oversees a convoy conference in Halifax, 1941. Such meetings, in which orders were issued and destinations confirmed, were standard procedure prior to sailing.

Public Archives Canada/DND/X33

During a visit to England to discuss the role of the NBS with his British counterparts, the author met the Poet Laureate, John Masefield. Commander Watt holds his book, *Who Dare to Live*, published in 1943, which dramatized the trials faced by merchant seamen. *Who Dare to Live* went through two printings during the war.

Public Archives of Nova Scotia/E.A. Bollinger Collection/#270A

The influx of the military—army, navy, and airforce—meant overcrowding in Halifax during the war. This created problems that, along with other factors, culminated in the riots on VE Day.

Public Archives of Nova Scotia/E.A. Bollinger Collection/#602-B

The Allied Merchant Seaman's Club, Hollis St., Halifax, a place where military and merchant seamen could relax between the risks of convoy. Here, on VE Day, the NBS performed one of its last wartime duties—rounding up AWOL sailors during the Halifax riots.

7

"an education..."

While our attention was focused on the erosion of morale on the Greek ships in Halifax harbour, a potentially more serious breakdown was developing among the crews of two other major Allies.

Norway and the Netherlands had great merchant fleets spread across the globe. The bulk of these ships were at sea when Hitler overran their home ports. Liners, tramps and tankers, they became available for the Atlantic lifeline, and had been making a significant contribution to it. The boarders assessed them as unusually well-found and crewed by disciplined, professional seamen.

I was surprised when a worried Oland summoned me on one November morning to hear my opinion of the small Norwegian tanker, *Marit*.

"For a Scandinavian she's a bit grubby and the crew—like all those whose families are in enemy hands—are sensitive to the separation," I told him. "Considering her age, though, she's in pretty fair shape."

"No questions raised about her not being armed?"

"Oxner said there was some mention of it in the stokers' mess but you hear that on most of the ships that haven't been given at least a twelve-pounder. Which means almost any ship that moves out of here these days."

Oland sighed, "I suppose we had to expect it sooner or later. There's just been a message from *Marit's* captain. His crew has refused to sail, almost to a man, unless she's given a gun."

Thirty years later I read the correspondence that caused the furrow on Dick's brow. The discussion was between Sir Edward Beatty, Canadian representative for the British Ministry of War Transport, and Admiral Nelles, Chief of the Naval Staff in Ottawa. On August 24, 1940, Beatty mentioned the troubles being experienced with Norwegian and Dutch crews.

"It now seems to be resolving itself into the question of guns. The position taken by the Dutch seamen is that they flatly refuse to sail without a gun and the Norwegian attitude is that the crews will not assemble without the promise of one."

He went on to tell how the freighter *Ruth I* had arrived in Sydney with the assurance of the Norwegian Committee in New York that she would be armed on reaching the Cape Breton harbour. She had discovered no such weapon awaited her and the crew had immediately downed tools. Citing the acute shortage of such armament, Sir Edward urged the utmost tact in dealing with ships like the *Ruth I*, in order to reduce the chance of adverse reports reaching vessels already detained by crew trouble in American ports. He asked Admiral Nelles for a frank picture of what guns could be hoped for from Naval Armament.

Nelles replied that a certain number of guns had been promised for delivery in Halifax within the month. Six weeks later, however, Beatty was deploring the fact that none had shown up.

In the meantime, the sitdown in *Ruth I* had so seriously affected foreign ship morale in Sydney that the Navy's Commanding Officer for the Atlantic Coast had issued a peremptory order to the NCSO of that port:

"Masters, officers and crews are to be informed as necessary that we are determined that no consideration will stop our and their prosecution of the war. They are therefore ordered by their government, through you, to sail as ordered by you with such armament as you are able to provide at the moment."

If they refused, he added, they were to be prosecuted under P.C. 4751.

Ten days later a shipment of four-inch guns reached Halifax from England but instead of the thirty-two expected there were only three—just sufficient to raise further arguments as to who should get them. Meanwhile, in St. John, the Dutch *Boeklo* had become a centre of unrest similar to that caused by *Ruth I* in Sydney. On October 8 a harassed Director of Naval Ordinance urged Captain Brand to make certain that every Allied ship should be in possession of the true picture.

"Everyone concerned," he emphasized, "endeavors to arm Allied ships exactly as British ships, but when armament is not available they should agree to sail as do British ships."

Why such essential information had not got down to me or, for that matter, why it had escaped the boarding party's normal sweep for intelligence, was one of those wartime imponderables. The fact remained that when I set out to further investigate the *Marit* I was still under the impression that I'd find no more than a routine spot of bother. I took Williams and Wick with me.

"I'll be talking with the captain," I told them as we approached the tanker. "While I'm with him, drift on board and scrounge a cup of coffee while you're waiting for me. No poking around; just see what you can pick up on the galley wireless."

The master was congenial, cooperative and confused. Most of his crew had been with him since before the conquest of Norway and he had had no trouble with them until, during the present layover in the Basin, the question of the ship having no cannon had been raised.

"Do they realize that some British ships that *had* guns have had them taken off to defend the English south coast when the invasion comes?" I asked.

"Yes, I've told them," said the master. "I'm afraid they don't believe me. They refuse to sail without being able to fight back if attacked. It is in writing."

"All of them?"

"All except one Swedish fireman."

"What's his attitude?"

"He is neutral. He feels it is not his quarrel."

The irony was striking.

"There are no neutral torpedoes," I suggested.

"Perhaps you would like to have him explain himself?"

"Thank you. I would," I said.

I expected to meet some staunch individualist, instinctively opposed to any popular decision, but the man who presented himself was a quietly spoken, reasonable type who spoke meticulous English. Fair and trim, he told me his name was Emil Mystrom. The master made an excuse and left us alone.

"I understand you haven't signed the demand for a gun," I led off, "yet you have less reason to sail than the others. There must be an explanation."

"I have been at sea for twenty years and have sailed under many flags," said Mystrom. "As long as the captain has treated me honestly I have gone where he has decided to take his ship. This is the way it has always been with me."

"Why not a Swedish ship?"

"What difference would it make? The Germans are as quick to sink a Swedish ship as any other. Better a good Norwegian than a poor Swede."

"Are the crew angry because you haven't gone along with them?"

"They understand how I feel. They are seamen, too."

"Then why don't they feel as you do? They're no less accustomed to taking a ship where her master decides she should go."

He shrugged.

"They are angry at the British—feel they gave too little help when Norway was invaded. That is not a problem with me. I can go home when I wish. I am not emotional about the war."

"Do your shipmates ever consider that every cargo that

reaches Britain now will bring closer the day when they can sail into their home ports again?" I asked him.

"They should," said Mystrom. "I do."

"What do they say when you tell them so?" I demanded.

"I don't argue with them. It would leave me without friends," he replied.

"You are a reasoning man, and a professional among professionals," I said carefully. "I believe they would listen to you if you were to remind them that the Germans are the only ones who profit when a ship fails to sail where her master wants her to go."

"You are a reasoning man, too," he countered. "Why don't *you* speak to them?"

"Perhaps I will," I said, and left it at that. I felt better for having talked to a man with pride in his calling, and I wanted to consider my next move carefully. There was still time before the *Marit* was due to sail.

Williams and Wick confirmed the excellence of the ship's coffee and the solidarity of the crew's refusal to sail without a gun. They also reported that the cook was a person whose influence went well beyond the usual level.

"A good man," advised Wick, "but very stiff—like a teacher I once had. We did what he told us, but it wasn't much fun. When Norwegians stop laughing, they get very set in their ideas."

I considered talking with the cook but decided against it. I was full of optimism that Mystrom would respond to the seed I'd sown, and begin to talk reason among his shipmates. Oland shared my feeling when I brought him up to date.

"Not being too hard pressed by *Marit's* sailing date, I suppose we can afford the experiment," he said. "They sound like a basically decent crew and they won't be much use to anyone locked up."

Two days later, having given Mystrom what I thought was time to exert his influence, I returned to the *Marit* alone. The captain, to my disappointment, reported that nothing had changed. However, I asked him to muster his men on deck. Standing halfway up the ladder to the superstructure,

I was able to scrutinize the faces of the thirty or so seamen regarding me from below. I had particular eyes for Mystrom and the cook, but their expressions told me nothing.

When I spoke there was little I could say which they hadn't already heard, but I hoped that dealing with a new intermediary might make it easier for them to save face if they'd had second thoughts. I repeated the assurance that every avenue was being explored to find them a gun, but pointed out that the number of times a merchant ship had fought off an attacker was negligible. I emphasized that effective defence lay with the convoy escorts.

The austere middle-aged cook spoke for the entire company when I had finished. He was respectful, dispassionate, yet emphatic. No gun, no sailing.

As I moved towards the gangway I found Mystrom at my elbow.

"I'm sorry," he said in a low voice. "I tried."

Oland's disappointment was less for my failure than in the way I was taking it.

"You did your best," he said brusquely. "Stop looking as though you had personally lost the war. You'll need to be in authority when you gather in that gang under 4751."

I slept little that night. Tension kept me tossing, because I felt sure the true picture of the *Marit's* crew had escaped me. But the harder I tried to sort things out, the more paralyzed my reasoning powers became.

Mentally, I retraced the entire experience. The voices of Oland and Wick returned: Dick's half-humourous poke at my self-importance, and Wick's insight into what happened to his countrymen when they lost their sense of humour. That was it. The problem was that I was taking it all too seriously. I needed to take a different approach.

Next morning I was grateful that Oland was too busy to issue the expected order to take the Norwegian crew into custody. Locating a new arrival anchored close to the tanker, I made it the object of the day's first search. Then, leaving Oxner in charge, I signalled Wick to join me and headed for the *Marit*.

"I want to be sure they understand every word I say today." I told him. "They may miss some of the fine points in English. Translate me sentence by sentence."

No warm welcome awaited us, particularly when I announced I wanted to speak to the crew again. Even the master found it difficult to be civil. Finally, though, everyone was on deck and I had assumed my former perch on the ladder, with Wick positioned a step below.

"In order that you may fully understand me today," I began, "I have brought my Norwegian voice."

Wick translated. There was restrained acknowledgement.

"I have always admired the Norwegians as fighters," I declared.

Wick threw out his chest and his voice rang like a trumpet.

"Because I'm married to one," I added—truthfully.

Unbelieving, my translator whispered, "Do you want me to say that too?"

"With feeling," I answered.

Wick tried manfully to do my bidding.

At first, the attempt at humour had little apparent effect. The rows of set jaws shifted only slightly. For five seconds there was complete silence.

Then someone at the back of the group chuckled. Another voice joined in, more loudly. And then another. Once released, the swell of laughter moved swiftly, dissipating the frigid atmosphere of moments before. It was as though every last man had been waiting a long time to let go with an unrestrained belly laugh. The cook, slow to start, was the last to finish.

My follow-through was threadbare—the same facts they had been given from the time the question of armament had become an issue. But it was as though they were hearing them for the first time. Before Wick and I left they had decided to take the ship wherever the master directed. Two days before Christmas they honoured their undertaking.

I hadn't had an opportunity to thank my Swedish accomplice but, as the ship moved seaward, I felt sure he was experiencing the satisfactions of a worthy calling worthily served.

Six months later I encountered Mystrom for the second time when he returned to Halifax in the Norwegian *Braganza*. We met at the moment the freighter should have been departing in convoy HX 127.

Lieutenant Jack Conkey, a new addition to our boarding staff, had carried out the *Braganza* search, and had come across a problem. The crew was insisting that every man should have a gas mask before going overseas. There had been no such demand previously on any vessel. Conkey told the men the matter should be taken up with the ship's owners on its arrival in England, and left the freighter with the impression that his advice had been accepted.

However, Oland and I decided we should take no chances. He authorized the drawing of fifty masks from Naval stores. They were in the launch when I set out to help herd the convoy to sea on sailing day. As an extra precaution, Captain Johnson, the new Halifax representative of Norwegian shipping, was also on board.

At the appointed time convoy pennants fluttered on the dozens of vessels in the movement, announcing they were ready to heave in. No pennant rose on the *Braganza*, however. We were lying close, on the chance that this might happen, and we boarded her immediately.

"No gas masks, no sailing," was the word.

"Fine," I announced. "I have them in the launch. There will be one for every man when the hook is clear."

Word was passed to the crew, and for a few minutes there was much coming and going between those on deck and those whose duties lay below. Finally I was informed that another issue had arisen. A delegation from the engineroom insisted that the ship's machinery was in no shape for the Atlantic crossing. Despite the chief engineer's insistence that it was in excellent condition, they refused to sail.

Joining the master in his cabin, Captain Johnson and I sent for the two ship's delegates, spokesmen for the crew. The deck representative proved to be the carpenter, a belligerent fellow named Larsen. I was less interested in him, however, than in the delegate from the black gang. For an instant after he had come through the door he looked as if he planned to back out again. Then, a mask falling over his face, he stood there waiting.

"I've often wondered what happened to you, Mystrom," I said. "There was no opportunity to thank you when the *Marit* sailed."

"I don't understand," he said blankly.

"You don't understand English?"

"I understand English well enough. I just don't understand how I could have helped you. Your face is not familiar."

All I could get out of him was his scorn for the chief engineer's inability to assess the state of his own machinery. The ship's carpenter gave him arrogant support. It was clear that if we'd been able to supply new engines as readily as gas masks, still another complaint would emerge to justify the sitdown.

Two hours later, when the final unit of HX 127 had left the gate ships astern, the impasse continued. Captain Johnson urged the application of 4751 against every man refusing duty, which would include the bulk of the crew. I compromised by skimming off the leadership—Mystrom, Larsen, and a known troublemaker named Wiggin. That night they were locked ashore.

During the succeeding days I spent a lot of time with Bill Bryan, the RCMP Special Branch investigator, looking for the roots of Mystrom's obvious influence over the *Braganza* crew. We discovered that some were in his financial debt—but that could happen under any circumstances. All other leads turned to quicksilver as Bryan tried to pin them down.

A check of the Swede's background established that he and Larsen had signed on in Texas. Immigration officials there had marked them as troublemakers but had been unable to pin anything specific on them.

Eleven days after the sitdown, satisfied that they really didn't need gas masks and that the engines were as the Chief described, the crew of *Braganza*, with three replacements, departed in HX 129. Shortly after, Mystrom repented and asked to sign on another ship. There was nothing in 4751 that allowed his further detention.

We were to have a further meeting, though. A year or so later the boarding operation had been extended to all major Canadian ports, and P.C. 4751 had been replaced by the Merchant Seamen Order, a document with teeth in it. On a visit to Montreal's senior boarding officer, I asked how the legislation was working.

"There's a case this morning," he replied. "Why not sit in on it?"

In the dock was the man who had once so moved me with his apparent devotion to his calling. Time and the strains of troublemaking had not been kind to Mystrom. The features that twitched recognition when I entered the room were deeply lined and unshaven. Every surly word he spoke tightened the chain of evidence establishing a poorly executed attempt to tie up yet another ship. I didn't wait for the verdict, but in due time learned he had been convicted and put securely away—most likely for the rest of the war.

Whether Mystrom had been a trained, ideologically motivated agent, and whether he would have retained his grip if the long arm of coincidence hadn't brought about more than one meeting between us, were questions to which I could never find answers. But one thing was certain: he had been an education for a naive boarding officer.

8

"fighting on the right battleground..."

When the strength of our boarding party was doubled it was too much to expect that the proportion of Naval Reserve men would be maintained. Corvettes and other new warcraft were hungry for experienced seamen and had first call on them. Our reinforcements were V.R.s, all of whom hailed from Winnipeg, half a continent either way from salt water.

The prairies, however, had long been a prime recruiting ground for reservists. What the new ratings—Brownrigg, Kennedy, Ransome, and Tyne—lacked in briny background, they made up for in enthusiasm and adaptability. They had a healthy romanticism about the ocean which, from my own experience, could be a practical asset. It was good experience for the old hands to teach these eager pupils not only the skills of seamanship, but what they had learned about the subtleties of human nature as applied to the important question of ships' morale.

Rounding out the enlarged party were three inspired choices from the drafting office. Beaman, Stevens, and

Funge had been among the handful of Canadians plucked from the suffocating oil scum which marked the grave of *Jervis Bay*. With hospital and survivors' leave behind them, they were now recommended by the medical people for shore berths so their physical and emotional recovery could be further monitored.

Two were thoroughly experienced Naval Reservists and the other a young permanent service rating. With those qualifications alone, the three would have brought full value to our squad; but there was something more. The words *Jervis Bay* had a special ring wherever sailors went their ways. Although the newcomers were quiet about their part in *Jervis Bay*'s agonizing and heroic mid-Atlantic battle, the marine grapevine swiftly spread the word of their presence among us, and our image was embellished.

George Beaman, Stoker First Class, was still with the party at war's end. His Distinguished Service Medal, a souvenir of the *Jervis Bay* action, spoke of his courage in crisis, but it was an inadequate yardstick for the whole man. He brought us a thorough familiarity with engine rooms, and he carried out their search with a no-nonsense directness typical of everything he did.

He had a family ashore in Halifax to whom he was devoted, but he pointedly rejected this as a reason for special consideration on nights when the men had to be turfed out for emergency duty. Even Oxner held him a little in awe. As respected by hands in his charge as he was by officers who drew on his experience and judgement, Beaman quickly became one of the non-commissioned leaders who gave the boarding operation a firm framework for what lay ahead.

Just before Christmas, Officers Appointments came up with a commissioned leader for our second party. I found myself of two minds. Lieutenant Edmond St. John (pronounced Sinjun) Green, RCNVR, might have been very valuable to us because of his ability, thanks to his Danish mother, to converse with Scandinavian seamen in their own tongue. On the other hand, he was a man of marked fastidiousness, who wore a white handkerchief up his sleeve and was engaged to the niece of a recent Prime Minister. It occurred to me that he might be more at home at some diplomatic cocktail party than in the bowels of a freighter whose crew were protesting sanitary facilities paralyzed by a Canadian winter.

When I took him on an indoctrination tour of the harbour, our first ship was a freighter well fitted to put Lieutenant Green to the test. Half of her deck-level fo'c's'le had been assigned to livestock. In fact, it was not unusual to find cows, sheep or poultry sharing forward accommodation with the crews of certain nationals. It was a highly practical arrangement. Butchered periodically during a voyage, the livestock provided the seamen with fresh meat and saved the owners the cost of refrigeration.

One of the party informed me that this particular fo'c's'le had been experiencing very hard times on account of our severe Northern temperatures. Green and I set out to look conditions over. As we crossed the forward hatches, two of the crew emerged from the cavernous entrance to the living quarters. They were leading a calf which, with glazed eyes and stiffened legs, was resisting each forward step.

Sinjun, who I had learned was an animal lover, clucked with dismay and indignation at the rough handling the beast was receiving. On coming closer, however, we discovered that the men were being as gentle as necessary, for the poor calf could no longer feel anything. The sub-zero weather had frozen it solid as it stood in its stall. Sinjun, though temporarily shaken, was thereafter prepared for anything.

★ ★ ★

With two parties it became possible to give every vessel more than a nominal check, and the more sensitive ones were searched with relative thoroughness. Williams assumed his logical place as Green's senior hand. Wick and Beaman were capable of handling a party if Oxner were otherwise engaged. Nevertheless, the reinforcements had arrived none too soon.

Our recent arrest of an entire crew had, for the moment, a restraining effect on similar mass sitdowns. Oland happily wrote the Director that of three Greeks, five Swedes, two Norwegians, and one Dutch ship scheduled for HX75, all had sailed without incident. Of the thirty-two men from the

Embericos who had been sent to Rockhead Prison, five had already joined other vessels and, with the exception of the four ringleaders of the strike, the remainder were prepared to return to sea as called on.

Nevertheless, the long-range picture was an ominous one. In Ottawa, where an overall perspective was being maintained, the conviction was growing that patchwork methods were not enough. Naval Service Headquarters' *Outline History of Trade Division (1945)* provides a glimpse:

> "On 21st January, 1941, a meeting was held to discuss the position of foreign forces in Canada. The Judge Advocate General and Director of Intelligence and Trade were present. An opportunity arose for bringing up the pressing matter of merchant seamen of all nationalities in our ports. The meeting considered it too big to deal with on the spot and appointed a sub-committee to go into it. . . .
>
> "The Naval point of view, which had been brought out so clearly during the previous few months, was that the whole matter should be tackled comprehensively. Munitions, which were then coming into considerable production in this country, could never be removed from the country unless the merchant seamen situation was dealt with. For the sake of one or two crew members, ships were missing their convoys which, in many cases, involved delays of more than a week."

The Ottawa strategists, men who dealt with global charts, statistics, and graphs, were not as distant as I had thought from the very human immediacies we were attempting to deal with on the harbour. I learned this after Oland said one day, "Bring your toothbrush when you report in tomorrow. It looks as if we're in good enough shape for the moment to allow us a night at Blue Wing."

We got away shortly after lunch and, while the back-country gravel road to Lawrencetown did unkind things to Dick's roadster, we arrived at his rambling lodge with a couple of hours' daylight in hand. The log retreat was perched on a promontory from which the twin lighthouses of Devil's Island, halfway up the coast to Halifax, were visible.

The peace of the place was almost frightening. Broken only by distant smoke smudge of a patrol vessel, the vastness of the Atlantic had never seemed less troubled. I drank it in wordlessly.

"I came here as a boy," Dick said finally, "and from that day I promised myself that this point would be mine and that I would build the sort of house it deserved."

"I won't profane the moment by saying the obvious," I told him.

"Full marks!" he barked. Then, "How's your eye? There's a twelve gauge and some old hunting gear in your room. I wouldn't be surprised, if we wandered back into the salt marsh, to find a flight or two of greenheads coming over."

I was surprised to discover that his spare waders fitted me. They had clearly been bought with guests in mind. We started along the soggy margin of a tidal inlet a quarter of a mile from the house, Dick having decided on the blind which would best catch the evening flight. It was almost like being back in the Western sloughs I'd once haunted at this time of year. Again, I had an overwhelming sense of peace.

Halfway to the blind, Dick halted abruptly and a shadow crossed his face.

"Anything wrong?" I asked.

He didn't answer immediately, then he spoke in a taut voice. "No, I've just been thinking. There's really only room for a single gun in that blind. You take it. I'll wander back along the shore and pick off anything you miss. We can meet at the cottage."

"Look," I insisted, "there *is* something wrong." I was alarmed now, by the tension in his stance and by the tight lines at the corners of his mouth.

Again there was a pause before he spoke. He seemed to choose his words carefully. "O.K.," he said finally. "Just don't mention it to anyone. It's on the secret list." I was sharply aware of the impression of indestructibility he emanated, in spite of those deepened lines.

"Is it your heart?" I pressed.

He nodded.

"Nothing to go to panic stations about. The surgeon

spotted it when I came back into the Service and said he'd have to clear his yardarm with the Chief of Staff before he passed me. They decided between them that I was a fair risk if I looked after myself. It's always useful to have old shipmates in the right places."

"You certainly picked yourself a swell spot for a rest cure," I put in dryly.

"It was NCSO or nothing," shrugged Oland. He smiled thinly. "Let's say we reached an agreement. It was the appointment I really wanted." He became suddenly brusque. "All right, get along to your blind. The light's starting to go. I'll take my time walking back."

"If you're sure—?" I fumbled.

"A senior officer is always sure," he said.

I did what I was told but the squadron of mallards that flew past fifteen minutes later suffered no casualties. My eyes were too frequently on the tall figure walking slowly on the distant path to Blue Wing.

After dinner Mrs. Oland left us to talk shop. We sprawled before the great stone fireplace and the chill that had followed us from the marsh eased out of our bones. The flames provided as much light as we needed and painted fantastic shapes where the beams of the living room roof soared two storeys overhead.

That night at Blue Wing Dick moved from the generalities we had discussed at the Nova Scotian to the specifics he had since covered with Brand. Dick Oland's respect for our Headquarters chief was something I'd never known him to accord any other fellow officer. During the evening, the depth of his affection became apparent. Later I would learn that this was not the empathy of similar natures. Brand had a British reserve as marked as Oland's Canadian extroversion. Their common ground was a tireless commitment to their enterprise and to the men on whom its success rested.

What most directly affected me was their mutual conviction that while physical sabotage remained a danger to be guarded against, sabotage of the seamen's spirit had become the greater peril. They were also satisfied that whatever encouragement the boarding service might bring the merchant crews, its lasting value would be dependent on a transformation of the seamen's working, fighting and living conditions.

Those with the power to bring this about were in fact moving towards what the boarding ratings had envisioned in their natterings the previous summer. Justice at sea, recreation between voyages, training schools to replace casualties with worthy new hands, pools that would allow the seamen continuous employment and be a source of reinforcements—all were being studied and worked on. Moving from one Ottawa committee to the next, making full use of the ammunition supplied by Oland and others in the ports, Brand had been enlisting and stimulating action which would contribute heavily to a new day for the merchant sailor.

"We're almost there," declared Dick, gazing into the fire at Blue Wing. "A few more months and we'll have the machinery we need."

As it grew late Mrs. Oland and I urged Dick to turn in, but he insisted he'd never felt better in his life. Keeping under way, he argued, was the perfect answer to drift. I wondered if his wife had been told the reason for his early return from the marsh, and thought it doubtful.

★ ★ ★

My memory of the evening at Blue Wing—at least its reassuring side—was something to fall back on during the first very hard months of 1941. The customary midwinter malevolence of the North Atlantic intensified the already comfortless conditions in many of the fo'c's'les. Breakdown of morale and obedience increased in proportion. But my knowledge that the problem was being attacked at its heart gave me patience and hope. There was a feeling that we were fighting on the right battleground.

Besides, there was mounting evidence that the original reason for the search procedures had failed to materialize. U.S. loadings had shown no indication of saboteurs at work. Convoys originating overseas and heading for African and Far Eastern destinations sometimes were targets for bombs disguised as beer tins, or for pencil incendiaries and other tools of the saboteur's trade, but the only explosives we had unearthed had been planted in men.

An occasional vessel had been damaged by crew members intent on prolonging their stay in port, but the great majority of missed sailings had been attributable to either spontaneous combustion of the human variety or deliberately induced insubordination. Between intelligence received from U.S. ports and that picked up by Oxner & Co., a pattern of mischiefmaking was becoming clear.

Among the Americans anxious to extend hospitality to Allied seamen at their docks were many individuals, ranging from prostitutes to clergymen, whose "goodwill" resulted in desertions, malingering and "accidental" damage to enginerooms—all of which contributed to convoy disruption.

These same agents were also responsible for morale-sapping rumours and subversive propaganda along the theme, "Britain is willing to fight—to the last Norwegian, Dutchman, Belgian, Greek, Pole, Dane, or Free Frenchman." Slogans such as this could be traced to the machine of Dr. Goebbels himself.

Apart from enemy influence, there was always the unpredictable to contend with. One sailing day a large British freighter was steaming down harbour, holding her place in the column of ships pointed towards the sea, when she suddenly veered off course near the Dockyard. Coming within a breath of cutting down her next-in-line, she managed to drop her hook just in time to avoid piling up on the Dartmouth shore. We were close by in the launch, and I was able to board the runaway within two or three minutes.

Her agitated captain explained that the wheel had jammed while the helmsman was altering course. We investigated the steering engine house and immediately spotted several wooden wedges ground into the gears that controlled the ship's rudder.

Sabotage was a matter for the RCMP. An investigator joined us as speedily as the launch could bring him from King's Wharf. He had something to go on: the damage must have been done by someone still aboard the ship. The freighter had handled perfectly after leaving her Basin anchorage; therefore the wedges had obviously been introduced after she had cleared the Narrows.

Though restoring the steering engine to working order could have been done in a few hours—plenty of time for the ship to overtake the convoy—priority went to flushing out the saboteur. As it turned out, that took a bit longer.

Corporal Bill Bryan of the RCMP Special Branch was a companionable, comparatively young man, with little suggestion about him of the bloodhound. Discussing the mishap with the crew, he showed sympathetic concern, behaving more like an interested bystander than an aggressive lawman. He had to move cautiously, because there was no obvious direction to take. The master swore by his crew, and they gave every appearance of deserving his confidence in them.

"They're company men, mostly," the captain declared, "and a few new hands we've taken on have been well screened."

But Bryan's patient interrogation, deduction and applied psychology finally revealed the culprit. He proved to be a company man if ever there was one. The sea, which had been his living for thirty-five years, had put the mark of strength and dignity on him. He seemed at first to be the least likely of all the crew to commit an act of sabotage.

Our man talked readily enough, almost eagerly, in fact. He was proud of his country and his calling, he insisted, but the war had become too terrible to be allowed to continue—even if it meant losing it. Anything that would discourage its being further pressed would speed the day when the horror stopped.

What had started him feeling that way? asked his interrogator.

Three months before, the seaman explained—the life suddenly gone from his voice—there had been a direct bomb hit on one of London's dockside tenements. His wife and eight children had vanished that night.

There was compassion on the faces of the listeners. The saboteur was taken off to hospital ashore. Later he was sent home "D.B.S."—Distressed British Seaman.

Working with Bill Bryan, as I did more and more frequently, was an enlightening experience. The longer our association went on, the more I was impressed by his deceptively casual methods.

A high point was his investigation of the affair that reduced a large East Indian vessel to a state of silent terror.

It started when the ship was loading in Saint John. Two of her British gunners were rushed to hospital with apparent food poisoning. One died. NCSO Halifax was asked to make sure that replacements for the gunners were standing by when the ship arrived for convoy. It was assumed that the victims had shown poor judgement in their choice of eating places ashore; but that was not the end of the story.

The reign of fear began when the vessel was bucketing her way around from the Bay of Fundy. She signalled that two more gunners had been taken violently ill. Ambulances met the ship, and the sick men were whisked to the Naval Hospital. Their lives were saved, and in the process the laboratory established that the patients had been fed arsenic.

A check by the authorities in Saint John of the food poisoning diagnosis there revealed an error: the earlier victims had been felled by arsenic as well. The death of one of them could no longer be regarded as an accident. Instead, there was every possibility that it had been murder.

When Bryan and I reached the East Indiaman she had been moved to the Basin. With the exception of the officers and gunners, the crew was made up of Lascars and Goanese, the latter being the catering staff.

In our past experience of such ships we had learned something of the caste system that governed the lives of the easterners. At the top of the structure was the *tindal*, the Lascar equivalent of a bos'n. At the bottom were the sweepers. Should we make the mistake of distributing seaman's comforts to anyone low on the social register before those above, the latter would accept nothing. We had to learn these distinctions quickly, to avoid creating trouble.

But such ships were often free of run-of-the-mill crew disturbances. For example, since the religion of the crew forbade drinking, drunkenness (the cause of fifty percent of the problems on other ships) was eliminated as a source of trouble. On the other hand—at least from our point of view—the menagerie kept aboard for ritual slaughter according to the dictates of their faith was a definite complication of shipboard life.

Whatever inadequate knowledge we had acquired of these people, none of us deluded himself that he knew what was going on. We were aware that the Lascar seamen and the Goanese had traditional differences. We assumed that the barriers between the European and the Asian seamen would be even greater. In a ship where four Europeans had apparently been the objects of a death plot, there was strong temptation to jump to conclusions.

We learned that, unlike the ship's officers who were long familiar with Indian crews, the recently added British gunners had had everything to learn about the customs of their fellow crewmen. Bryan's interrogations repeatedly brought out the suggestion that the British gunners might have in some way offended the men who prepared their food.

Suspicion focused more sharply on the Goanese when we discovered that the gunners habitually dined apart from the rest of the ship's company. A mess had been built for them in one of the upper holds and here they had lived their private lives, a clear-cut target for the galley if that happened to be a seat of hostility.

The investigation took several days, long enough for the ship to miss her convoy. The tension on board reached a new pitch as the RCMP corporal carried out his unsparing search of the messdeck, the galley and other possible sources of clues. Interrogations went on and on.

One incident did brighten things a bit. The chief officer suggested one day that, instead of going ashore for lunch, we remain on board as his guests. As meal hour approached, I suddenly remembered pressing business ashore. The light of suspicion glinted in the Mountie's eye.

"Too bad," he said, straight-faced. "I had counted on your launch taking me somewhere just after lunch. Perhaps I'd better go along with you now."

The mate gave an understanding nod when we made

our excuses, but the offer of hospitality was never repeated.

One morning, after several days when it seemed the relentless tension would never end, Bill appeared at King's Wharf carrying a vacuum cleaner. When we reached the ship he headed purposefully for the messdeck and directed the nozzle into the crannies of the quarters from deck to deckhead. When he was through, he had labelled samples of dust from every area.

"Explain," I said.

"Oh, just an idea," replied Bill, with studied nonchalance.

I bristled with impatience, but no answers were forthcoming until twenty-four hours later, when the samples had been analyzed. They showed that dust taken from the flanges of the steel beams which supported the ceiling of the gunners' mess was heavily impregnated with arsenic.

Bill Bryan explained, "Once I got my head on straight, it was as simple as an old cargo plan. The last thing this hold carried before it was converted into a messdeck was sheep dip for Australia. It had a high arsenic content."

"And the dust accumulated on the flanges kept sifting down into the gunner's food?" I asked in some wonderment.

Bill nodded.

"If the chief officer asks us for lunch today," he said with a wink, "let's take him up on it."

★ ★ ★

That winter was unsparing. In the subzero dawns, the launch was an ice-glazed, labouring lump, and our bodies were numb and miserable inside our woolens.

Above the smoking water, the curdle of mist was frequently impenetrable. To reach the ships we had to board we relied on the compass, the sound of ships' bells, and sheer intuition. We had to quickly identify whichever befogged hull materialized ahead; then, by establishing its berth on our harbour diagram, we could establish the general direction toward the craft we sought.

Sometimes the launch would break free of the smother

and move into a pocket of clear air. Beyond you could see more fog, rising twenty or thirty feet above the sea. Projecting above this chill embankment there would be a thicket of mastheads, like the bayonets of infantrymen poised to leave the shelter of a trench to face the wind of death.

Sometimes I wondered if we were really getting anywhere.

Richard Oland was no longer in doubt. He wrote to Captain Brand in January.

> "Strong arm methods (of crew control) are of limited value. This was illustrated very pointedly recently when we had to place several naval guards on board two particular ships. These were not from our trained boarding party and the situations rapidly became worse. On relief by our trained men the situations became better in a very few hours.
>
> "During the same period we also had our trained parties in two other ships and both of these have now sailed, while neither of the original ones have yet done so. We now have one leading seaman, eleven A.B.'s and eight stokers but may find it necessary to increase the strength as, for the past two months, they have been working seven days a week with only an occasional afternoon off.
>
> "We would, I feel, inject a healthy serum into the most unhealthy areas of the Mercantile Marine anatomy—particularly in the non-British ships. The spots in which our men would work are, naturally, the most unpleasant, possibly the most dangerous, and by far the most challenging. Our boarding party is fully aware of this and, to a man, is eager to tackle this new and natural stage of boarding work which, as already stated, challenges their initiative, imagination and trustworthiness."

9

"To join the ragged band...who dare to live again."

Two of my experiences sharply illustrate the burden carried by a Naval Control Service officer and the way a boarding officer came to share it. The first concerned the most miserable ship I ever knew; the other, one of the proudest.

The winter of 1940 had just bared its teeth when I came over the side of a Free French tramp lying deep in the Basin. Darkness had fallen and the boarding party had climbed nearly twenty side ladders since morning, but the ship lay in the launch's path and we knew we would have to visit her sooner or later. A quick examination would save us the long trip back the next day.

We had noted her oil-burning anchor lights, so we were not surprised to find the rest of the ship similarly illuminated—if such a word could be used for the cheerless semi-darkness in which she lay. The half-light seemed fitting for the men who moved within it. All the shocked pride of fallen France was in their sullenness and the bedraggled appearance of even the officers. They spoke no English and, as Gould translated, the captain made no move to leave the foredeck where he had received us. There were two spiritless mongrels at his heels, one of which lifted its leg and urinated against a bollard in a symbolic gesture.

The vessel, we discovered, was electrically fitted after all, but the dynamo had failed. It was being worked over by ships' engineers who had limited expectation of success. The master at first was reluctant to permit a search. Whether this was due to the ship's condition or to his general defensiveness was difficult to say; while he was technically a supporter of de Gaulle and the Resistance, he was also a countryman of those sailors who had recently died in the destruction of the French fleet by the Royal Navy at Oran. The situation was not going well.

As we talked, however, a young Canadian naval gunner who had been assigned with his Lewis gun as anti-aircraft protection for the tramp, appeared from the fo'c's'le. He saluted me and his gesture seemed to remind the master that we were allies. He gave the word for the search.

His destination, the captain told us, was Martinique, that uneasy Caribbean outpost where France still ruled and where some of her fugitive warships were lying—neither submissive to Hitler nor whole-heartedly supporting those who resisted him. For all his hostility, I could feel nothing but a sadness for the master. The feeling deepened when I talked to the ratings later in the launch and heard their descriptions of what they had found below decks. It was a tale of dirt, decay and demoralization.

Next morning Oland told me there was a French ship in the Basin on which he would like an immediate report. He was impressed by just how immediately he received it.

"Would you say she was seaworthy?" he asked.

"I'm no maritime surveyor," I said, "but if you asked whether I'd care to sail in her—quite apart from her unhygienic quarters—I'd say no."

"You're sure?" he insisted. "What you're saying is going into a signal."

"Oxner and the others who looked at her below say they wonder how she's got this far. She's peeling rusted metal as though it were old paint."

Dick tapped a message form on his desk and muttered, "Others have reported as much, but that didn't prevent her being shoved along this far. I've got enough to worry about without being handed a political hot potato, but here she stays until there's at least a fighting chance of her lasting out any heavy weather."

He wrote a signal to Headquarters and asked me to read it. It stated that his boarding officer had reported the Free Frenchman as unseaworthy and that he proposed withholding her sailing orders until necessary repairs had been made.

"That means we're stuck with her for at least a month," he said resignedly, "but I'd prefer that to having her on my conscience."

But she was to remain on his conscience, despite anything he could do about it. The vessel's operators declined his proposal to hold her in Halifax and were able to make it stand up in those places where delicate political decisions were juggled. Instructions came for the ship to move south.

Oland reacted sharply, repeating his earlier judgement. This time he was mindless of the inconvenience the delay would cause. He was concerned only for the men who would sail the miserable ship. His protest changed nothing, however.

We watched her drift down harbour, and, though her sailing orders had been explicit enough, I had a sense that she was a ship going nowhere. Danger and uncertainty accompanied each of the hundreds of vessels I'd seen moving down that fairway, but clear-cut purpose had also gone with them. Nothing accompanied the little tramp except an oppressive melancholy. And, as it turned out, nothing awaited her except the hurricane that finished her suffering.

"I did my best," said Dick, repeating the words several times after telling me of her loss with all hands. I needed no convincing, but it seemed to help him to talk about it with someone who understood.

★ ★ ★

My experience with the Dutch liner *Columbia* in the final days of 1940 produced the only occasion where I found myself on the receiving end of Oland's bad temper. For a time I wondered if I might not end up in corvettes, after all.

"This is no ordinary sitdown," he explained. "Not only have the crew refused to sail, but the master agrees with them. Normally the *Columbia* belongs in the South American trade but she's wanted in the U.K. as a depot ship. The people over there are damned impatient about getting her, I might add."

"Which convoy is she supposed to catch?"

"She's got the speed to go independently," said Dick, "and that's the problem. They've got it into their heads they should have a destroyer escort—as though we weren't already staggering to give the slower ships minimal protection. There's not a thing we can do for her—even if she deserved it."

"Does the captain know that?"

"I told him personally, but he's a rum one. Stiff as a poker. Said he'd pass the word to the crew but warned it wouldn't do any good. Seeing he's already on their wavelength, that can be taken as official. I want you to go out and have him confirm it, though."

"Shall I take a party along?"

"No," said Oland impatiently. "It would be a waste of time. Eventually the Dutch authorities are going to have to straighten this out for themselves."

"Have you any idea what brought it on? We might be able to smoke out an agitator or two on board."

"It's simpler than that," he said, edgy as I had never before seen him. "The fact is they've been having it too easy down south and have gone soft. There was a report to that effect before they got here. My interview with the master confirmed it."

"You mean they're scared?"

"Exactly. That's what I've told Headquarters and that's why the Dutch are going to have to work this out for themselves. There's a lot of national pride involved. If the captain was prepared to lay a charge against the crew we might be able to help him change their minds but, if anything, he's encouraging their stand. That's what makes it so sticky."

"So all you want me to do is make certain he's passed the crew your statement about the escort situation?"

"That's all. Naturally, if he's had some second thoughts or if there has been a change of attitude in the crew, make the most of it. There won't be, though. Whatever the man's rating in courage, you can take my word for it they don't come any more stubborn."

"Absolutely no hope of an escort?" I pressed.

"Not a hope," rasped Oland.

The liner, still bright in her peacetime colours and anchored among the gray North Atlantic freighters and tankers, was like a beauty queen caught in a crowd of hard-bitten labourers. Not only did her size cause her to stand out, but all her passenger-carrying grace had been maintained with scrub brush and paint pot. A spotlessly uniformed junior officer met me at the companion ladder and, in perfect English, said, "The captain?" Yes, sir, Come with me, please."

Along our upward course to the master's cabin, I admired the ship. Sound and attractive workmanship had gone into her building and she had been honoured by those who served her. *Columbia* seemed to possess a disciplined reserve, the same as that of the seamen who, out of the corners of their eyes, followed my passing.

The captain's cabin was handsome but not ostentatious, a balanced setting for the precisely polite, middle-aged officer who received me. The stubbornness Oland had described was evident in his expression, but his pale eyes were expectant rather than hostile.

"I hope you have come to say we will have proper protection for our crossing?" he said by way of greeting me.

"I can only repeat what the Commander has already told you," I answered. "You have the most effective protection there is—your own speed."

His jaw set.

"It is not enough. We must have a destroyer."

"There is none available. I can assure you of that."

"Then we must remain here until there is one. I am sorry, but the crew is determined and I must support them—as they have always supported me when the ship has been endangered."

I wished then that I had a party of my own men circulating through the *Columbia*, to establish the crew's attitude at source. The master struck me as honest and straightforward, but he might be using his men as an excuse for his own unwillingness to sail. He caught the shadow of my suspicion.

"Perhaps you would like to discuss it with the men's representatives?" he suggested sharply.

"That would be helpful," I agreed.

There were four of them, impressive samples of the deck, engine room and catering staffs. The Chief Steward was their spokesman. Apart from the lines around his eyes which put him in the same age bracket as the master, he created an impression of youthfulness while carrying the dignity of a veteran company man. When the captain introduced me to the group it was, in a sense, like the sharing of a guest—though the fine line of respect that kept the ranks apart was never threatened.

My conversation with the crewmen was remarkably similar to the one I'd just had with their captain. It was plain the master had fully briefed them on his talk with Oland and that their decision had already been reached. They were not unmindful, said the Chief Steward, that they were inconveniencing those who awaited *Columbia*'s arrival overseas as well as those whose duty it was to forward her, but, until she could be adequately protected against the U-boats, it would be wrong to sail her. If the authorities chose to punish the crew it would be unfortunate, for they were loyal men, but the prospect would change nothing.

This was spoken quietly, but passion underlay every word. I was satisfied that there was no more hope of upsetting their decision than there was a toppling an iceberg with a .22 calibre bullet. I told them I would continue to explore any hope that might alter the situation. I knew there was none, but it seemed more sensible to leave the door open than to slam it shut.

When I returned to Oland's office he glanced up, almost belligerently, and said, "I was right, wasn't I?"

I nodded.

"Yes. The captain has repeated his conversation with you to the crew and he gave me the chance to confirm it. They still refuse to sail."

"What are the crew like? Have they got the wind up as badly as the old man?"

I knew my answer wasn't going to please him but I had thought about it a good deal in the half hour's launch trip back from the Basin. Part of me knew that there was nothing to be gained by further upsetting Dick. Yet my usefulness would only diminish if I started limiting myself to observations that did not threaten our personal friendship.

"They're not frightened for themselves," I said slowly. "They're like the master—frightened for the *ship*. Their weakness—if that's what it is—lies in their pride in her, their attachment to her. They're no more and no less concerned about risking their lives than any of us, but hazarding the *Columbia*—as they think, unnecessarily—is too much."

Oland regarded me as he might one of the rebellious crew.

"A hell of a chance we'd have of winning a war with that sort of sentimental crap," he roared. "Cowardice is cowardice, however cleverly you dress it up."

"They're not cowards," I shot back, his anger touching off my own.

Between expletives my white-faced commanding officer ordered me out of his office. His parting words were to the effect that I could delay my return until the unlikely event of a further invitation. Mercifully, I had a harbourful of ships to go to, with enough troubles of their own to prevent me from brooding over the disastrous course my naval career seemed to have taken.

Most of the staff had left when I returned ashore, but the light was still burning in the Commander's office. The watchkeeper, who had overheard the morning's explosion, nodded in the direction of Oland's door and said in a sepulchral voice, "You're wanted."

I was anxious to get it over with. My parting speech

was in pretty good shape, and my jaw was the first thing that came through Dick's doorway. Pen in hand he looked up as though it were just the end of any other day.

"Oh, there you are. Have a pew."

He went on writing long enough for my truculence to subside, then spoke casually. "We have an escort for *Columbia*."

"Good," I said, my guard still up. "Who is she?"

"*Revenge*."

"You're kidding."

"*H.M.S. Revenge*," he repeated.

"But you don't send a battleship as escort for a small liner! *Revenge* is no protection against submarines, in any case."

"Agreed," Oland said mildly. "She'd be handy if there was a commerce raider around, though."

"Have they bought it on the *Columbia*?"

"Not yet. They haven't heard about it. You're going out in the morning to sell them. You can do it, can't you?"

"I don't know. I can try."

Oland smiled with his eyes as he made his only reference to the morning's quarrel.

"You have more faith in them than some people. It should help."

"How did you shake *Revenge* loose?" I wanted to know.

"Oh," he replied, "I thought I'd better make another cast or two. Finally someone remembered that *Revenge* had been ordered back to Britain as quickly as she could be stored and was sailing alone day after tomorrow. Nobody seemed to object to *Columbia* tagging along with her. There's been considerable heart-burning in Ottawa over the possibility that the Flying Dutchman might not fly on schedule."

When I reached *Columbia* shortly after daylight the next morning, I had rehearsed my meeting with the captain as carefully as any actor faced by a major role. My attitude, I realized, was all important. I must appear relaxed and confident in those first critical seconds. Actually, I was neither, but that didn't prevent my creating the right effect. The master rose as I entered, his face alight.

"You got us an escort!" he exclaimed.

"It's almost too good to be true," I confirmed. "More than one could hope for. You will have a 30,000-ton battleship all the way across."

I held my breath, fearful that he might raise the objection I had raised with Oland—that a battleship was no quick-turning hunter of submarines. The captain's reaction, however, was uncritical.

"Good!" he declared. "I have worried a great deal about this. I hope the crew will be as pleased as I am."

"They should be, shouldn't they?" I demanded.

"Yes," he said tentatively, "but they themselves must decide, I cannot order them after what we have been through together."

Before I could comment he had pressed the bell for the bridge messenger.

"You must tell the crew what you have told me," he said. "Not just the delegates you met yesterday—all of them."

The gathering was in the ornate salon where first-class passengers had danced in happier times. The entire crew was there—the firemen, galley boys, deckhands, stewards, wireless operators—everyone except the few whose eyes had to remain on a gauge or the signal station at Turple Head. The captain and I took up positions on the stage in front of the grand piano, facing the sea of questioning Dutch faces.

"The lieutenant has a message for us," announced the master, "You will have a decision to make when he has finished."

As I explained what had happened he translated it sentence by sentence. The faces before us showed intense concentration. This was no group of chronic malcontents; it was a crew of self-respecting seamen who had risked their professional reputations for a reason they only half understood. As such, they were less predictable than if they had been outright troublemakers. When I had finished explaining the offer of *Revenge* as a shield for *Columbia*, there was no immediate response. The listeners stopped gazing at me, looked inquiringly at one another, then at the man beside me on the platform.

"What do *you* think, Captain?" the Chief Steward's voice rang out.

"I am one hundred per cent for it," said the master firmly.

There was another dramatic silence, then again the voice of the Steward.

"That is good enough for us."

Confirmation by the rest of the crew started with a murmur and rose to a low roar. The captain turned and shook my hand and the *Columbia* was on the first stage of her voyage to England. *Revenge*, as it turned out, had no occasion to defend her from submarines on the way.

★ ★ ★

These encounters with men who knew the loneliness of command stirred my impulses as a writer. As I had confessed to Dick, the impressions accompanying every boarding set me scribbling. The men I met were unconscious of the drama which went with their life-and-death business on the Atlantic. This, it seemed to me, was itself the essence of drama. For several months, though, my attempts at poetry that would express this missed the target.

Several writers, mainly newspapermen covering the war on Canada's doorstep, suffered no such difficulty. Fred Griffin, veteran feature writer for the *Toronto Star*, was the first to get clearance from Ottawa to accompany our boarding parties. His articles paid tribute to the merchant seamen, and encouraged other correspondents to continue their story.

My own difficulty lay in the fact that I was too personally involved in the subject to write about it objectively.

I probably wrote to relieve the emotional pressure built up in me by innumerable encounters with ships' masters and crews whose lives I briefly shared. My identification with them was intense, so much so that I seemed to be looking for a voice not my own. Perhaps it was that of a merchant captain, someone like the man I had interviewed when he dropped anchor with casualties awaiting disembarkation, or the one whose silences had been more eloquent than words when I delivered his sailing orders. So many unforgettable, quietly heroic figures crowded my mind that it was no wonder a single character had difficulty breaking free.

Then, one day, even as we talked for the first and last time in our lives, I knew I was listening to the voice that would flow naturally for me. The man was chief officer in a British freighter whose house flag spoke of fat dividends for her shareholders but thin grub and accommodation for her seamen.

His captain met me at the gangway and supplied all the standard information I required. Later, in the launch, Oxner asked, "Did you have a chance to talk to the mate, sir?"

"No," I replied. "Something special about him?"

"I would say so. You don't usually find a man who's commanded a cargo liner for a respectable company sailing as chief officer for an outfit of cut-throats."

"Too much of the bottle?" I suggested. It was usually a safe first guess.

"Too little sense of when he's been well off, according to the cook," said Oxner. "He shouldn't be at sea and, even if he had to be, he shouldn't be in that hooker. The old man's a proper bully-boy."

"I shouldn't be surprised," I agreed, recalling my own impression of the captain.

Oxner waited to be pressed for more of what he'd picked up in the galley but I gave him time to volunteer it.

"Like the cook tells it, the mate had a nervous breakdown last year after his command had been sunk under him. Only half a raft-full of crew got away. He was in hospital for quite a while. When he was sprung, his company offered him a good shore job. He wasn't interested. Said he wanted another ship. The company tried to be nice about it and kept putting him off but finally he realized they didn't want him back afloat. So he took what he could get—mate on this hooker. He couldn't have picked a better one if he wanted to go completely crackers."

"How do the crew feel about him?"

"They're jumpy."

"Would they make trouble because of it?"

"I raised that with the cook," said Oxner, "but he came up with his canvas flapping. Nobody wants to give the mate the first shove. In a way, he's the one who makes the ship bearable. But I know how I'd feel sailing with a second-in-command who was likely to spring his seams if the blow got rough enough."

This was something that had to go into my report on the ship. If the situation was as serious as it appeared, the wartime shipping people and the company concerned needed the opportunity to head it off. I had only written a sentence or two, however, before I realized that Oxner's information, while doubtless accurate, was insufficient when a man's future was at stake. Three days remained before the ship sailed. I boarded her, alone, next morning.

I knew that the master had gone ashore and that the chief officer would receive me. He was a sandy, unremarkable man in his forties, of medium height and build. The only striking thing about him was an almost childlike gentleness of speech and manner.

I had prepared myself with some additional questions about the ship and her cargo. He invited me to his cabin, ordered the inevitable tea, and answered my inquiries readily. He had the details of the vessel's operations at his fingertips.

On the desk in his small, sparsely furnished cabin there were photographs—one of a woman as plain as himself, the others of a boy and a girl in their teens. They were like their parents—commonplace, wholesome, suggesting quiet reserves of staying power. I nodded in their direction.

"How long since you last saw them?"

"Three months," he replied. "It seemed longer when we were hung up, half loaded, in Galveston."

"Where's the boy headed—seafaring?"

"If he chooses. It's a good life—even if it knocks a man about a bit."

"You've had your share of knocks?"

"I'm still alive," he said dispassionately. "There are better men who sailed with me who aren't. I once had my own ship, you know."

"Yes, I heard."

His eyes lighted, still defenseless but with a hard directness.

"I'm the reason you're back," he said.

"Yes. No one sent me, though."

"There's been no complaint about me?"

I shook my head.

"There shouldn't be," he declared with a flash of anger that was gone as quickly as it came. "The ship's in better shape than when I joined."

"I'd expect her to be," I said.

We sat for a long time wordlessly. Finally he said, "I don't hold it against my old company that they didn't trust me with another command. They couldn't be expected to be as sure as I am that I'm as good as new."

"They offered you a good shore job, didn't they?"

"Yes." He was thoughtful. "It was the sort of thing I'd have gone for in peacetime, I imagine. More time with the family, that sort of thing."

"You don't strike me as a man who enjoys danger for danger's sake."

"I don't," he said, his voice still steady and almost emotionless. "I hate it. I die each time a gun bangs or a depth-charge coughs. But I belong at sea as long as the war lasts. I'd go to pieces if I did anything else. Don't ask me how I know. I just know."

"No one would hold it against you if you went on the beach " I advanced. "There are plenty of men with masters' tickets ashore because they're irreplaceable there. We've got some in Naval Control."

"It's not what people think of me," he said patiently. "It's how I feel inside. This is where I'm secure and useful. The master's a bastard. I wouldn't have accepted him as third officer on my own ship. The men aren't sure I won't crack up some day when their lives may depend on me, but this is where I belong."

I understood him better than he knew. It didn't add up—a healthy man like me in a comparatively safe job, a half-mended one voluntarily back in the element that once had broken him. But then, the war itself didn't add up.

We yarned for another hour or so, each with his guard down in instinctive faith in the other's understanding.

There was no sentimentality in it. I knew when we

parted that it was possible the ship and her company faced a hazard with this man as First Officer. When I made out my report next morning, however, it contained no mention of the mate.

Later I instructed Oxner to go out with one of the hands to distribute a few more seaman's comforts to the ship.

"Have another yarn with your friend the cook," I told him. "Let him know your officer had occasion to meet with the mate yesterday and was impressed by what a sound fellow he is—that he's the sort of seaman that he'd be happy to sail under himself."

"Aye, aye, sir," Oxner responded, his gimlet eyes trained on mine. "I'm sure you wouldn't say so if you didn't feel that way."

"You're sure, eh?"

"Pardon, sir?"

"You don't think I may be postponing trouble that may break out in some other port—or at sea?"

Oxner rubbed his sandpaper chin.

"It's *your* conscience, sir, if I may say so."

"And yours," I amended. "Would you rather I send Williams out?"

For a moment Oxner obviously thought I was pulling his leg. Realizing he was wrong, he began to study the deck at his feet. The confrontation would have been amusing if it hadn't involved our costliest articles of association. Finally he looked up and said quietly, "I imagine you'd like me to lose no time about it, sir."

The ship sailed without incident and nothing in the signal log in the months that followed indicated that she had experienced trouble aboard or at the hands of the enemy. Neither the vessel nor her mate returned to Halifax as long as I was there. They joined thousands of other memories whose names and dates were faded, but whose humour, bravery and faithfulness to duty remained with me always. But the strongest connection I felt was to that particular boarding. It had brought me the voice and the shape of the poem that up to that point had only been disorganized scribblings. For the next two years and for 20,000 words, during most of the duty-free hours I was to know, I lived inside the chief officer as he spoke:

"A brave man dies but once, I've heard,
And who am I
To doubt a poet's or a brave man's word?
We others try
To join the ragged band who share
The mortal pain
Of death repeated, yet who dare
To live again."

10

The Gatineau Conference

The Director of Trade Division and his right-hand men in the ports had laboured under intense pressure since the outbreak of war. For nearly a year and a half they had not found time to meet face-to-face and confer as a group. Despite this, they were highly interdependent, communicating with blizzards of signals. Captain Brand had repeatedly urged a general council of war, but emergencies invariably arose to pin the NCSOs to their posts.

Late in February, 1941, however, the all-important session was finally scheduled. The NCSOs had been summoned to Ottawa, and the Consular Shipping Officers were coming in from the United States. We hoped that corrective measures for crew trouble would be high on the agenda of the discussions.

A factor in the timing of the conference was the return, after eight months absence, of Dick Oland's second-in-command, Commander Leslie Banyard, RCNR. Former captain of the luxury liner *Monarch of Bermuda*, "Spunyarn" had been returned to his ship when she began trooping. She had sailed with a Canadian army contingent on the day I first reported to Oland's office. I'd watched through binoculars as Banyard stood on the bridge, waving his cap in response to a farewell flutter of secretarial handkerchiefs in Oland's window. Now he was back, deeply bronzed from months of trooping to Africa. It meant Oland would be free to attend the Ottawa meeting.

During the pre-conference days, I was frequently in Dick's office, going over with him a number of the points he intended to raise in Ottawa and refreshing his memory of the most relevant case histories that had developed on the harbour. I was available myself because Officers' Appointments had just surrendered another officer for boarding duties, Sub-Lieutenant A.C.A. Baker, RCNVR. Baker had proven a winner. Back of his schoolboy's face was a shrewd mind and an eagerness for new ideas. After a few days' indoctrination he was ready to take charge of a party.

Working with the Commander as he prepared for Ottawa was the most relaxed period I had known since reaching Halifax. The demands of being the party's only officer were a thing of the past and I was able to take full part in the process of presenting our point of view.

I had no way of knowing that this was to be the beginning of the end for the hard, happy, intimate days when, with Oxner and "the originals", I had encountered nothing more complicated than a sitdown strike. I still had no intimation of this when Oland, on the morning before he was to leave for Ottawa, greeted me with, "It's lucky your shop's in good order. Captain Brand figures you'd better come along to the conference with me."

Though no one could recall so naming it, the meeting became known as the Gatineau Conference, a title given to a series of similar sessions which followed annually. The conference was the setting for developments of the first magnitude, which transformed the Canadian merchant marine.

On March 3, the day after the NCSOs came together, Captain Brand led us up Elgin Street to Parliament Hill for a session with the Interdepartmental Committee on Questions of Discipline and Treatment of Merchant Seamen. Chaired by Norman Robertson, Under-Secretary of State for External Affairs, that group had already met in January to consider the alarming reports of Oland and the other NCSOs plagued by crew trouble. The East Block setting strongly suggested that the situation had reached the point where action could be expected. The Cabinet Room was just down the corridor.

We were present at the meeting to offer first-hand information on the ships and the waterfront. What we had experienced was drawn out by committee members whose responsibilities touched every aspect of the subject. H.L. Keenlyside and Saul E. Rae were there from External Affairs; P.M. Anderson represented Justice; Captain J.W. Kerr, Transport; A.L.W. McCallum, the Shipping Board; Inspector A. Drysdale, the RCMP. Brand and his close friend and ally, Commissioner A.J. Joliffe of Immigration, completed the group.

Two days later there was a second meeting. Encouraged by Norman Robertson's conviction that the issue had to be tackled forcefully and positively, a plan very similar to one Brand and Oland had been discussing for months was approved. At its core was provision for a Director of Merchant Seamen. Brand already had a candidate standing in the wings—Arthur Randles, Cunard's general passenger agent in Montreal.

Other decisions were taken. Merchant seamen manning pools should be immediately established, and training schools should be set up to keep them at strength; more drastic and far-reaching legislation should be passed to deal with disciplinary problems; and the efforts of agencies promoting Merchant Navy welfare would be realistically coordinated.

These are all spelled out in the History of Trade Division. That document reads in part:

> "An opportunity was provided to discuss with NCSO, Halifax, the crew trouble situation which he had experienced. As a result Headquarters was able to see the picture and its possible remedies more clearly. Com-

> mander Oland also reported on the success of his local boarding service, which had developed from the original Admiralty request to search ships in convoy.... It was immediately decided to set up the boarding service in all Canadian ports, taking officers and men from Halifax as soon as they could be trained."

The last was a logical decision. Had the fo'c's'le touch of Oxner & Co. been common to the other east coast ports, trouble in certain ships would have been more effectively dealt with. This was acknowledged by all present. Nor did anyone question that Halifax was the natural training centre for future parties. What would happen to those parties when they reached the ports to which they were drafted, however, was the subject of disagreement.

Lt. Cdr. R.B. Mitchell, RCNR, pointed out that, as NCSO, Sydney, he had has own distinct conditions and problems. He wanted no boarding personnel sent to him through some Halifax umbilical cord. They must be *his* men, absolutely.

Oland coldly reminded him that Naval Orders demanded no less, but hoped that continuity between what the boarders had learned in Halifax and their duties elsewhere would be maintained. It was intended as a rebuke and Mitchell, bristling, accepted it as such. Previously controlled tensions between Brand's two senior NCSOs were in danger of a serious outbreak.

Since 1939 Oland and Mitchell had shared responsibilities which would have tested the most compatible of partners—and, except for their common dedication to the convoy effort, the two were far from compatible. Earlier in the war this had been of no great consequence. Sydney's importance had rested principally on its being the mainland terminus of ore boats from Newfoundland's great Wabana iron mine. The cargoes of red ore were made into steel in Sydney's mills. Since the North American coast was still beyond operational range of German submarines, ore carriers could ply the coastal ports independently, much as they had done in peacetime.

The ships exchanged between Mitchell and Oland were usually coasters or deep-sea vessels that dropped into Sydney only for emergency attention while on passage between St. Lawrence ports and Halifax. Inter-port irritations were minor until, in the summer of 1940, Sydney was named Canada's second convoy assembly centre.

Several hundred miles of steaming could be saved if ships loaded in St. Lawrence ports were brought together higher up the coast—at Sydney. Timed to rendezvous with the main HX movement out of Halifax, Mitchell's SHX convoys merged with HX east of Newfoundland for the long passage to Britain.

Sydney had barely adjusted to these stepped-up demands when it gained further importance, as Admiralty came to grips with the nagging problem of low-powered cargo carriers.

From the beginning, the speed of the Atlantic convoys had been set at nine knots, economical for the average ocean workhorse. Almost invariably, though, the movements were slowed down by ships incapable of even that minimal performance. When the submarine zone was reached, these stragglers were easy pickings for the waiting enemy. They affected the whole convoy's manoeuverability and caused problems for the escorts trying to protect them.

Admiralty's answer was to raise the HX speed to a minimum ten knots and to establish the SC (Slow Convoy) for everything incapable of maintaining it. Sydney became the port of departure for slow convoys.

Mitchell shouldered the new responsibility with vigour, well aware that it presented two major challenges. One was that the SC convoys would include a disproportionate number of crocks and hard cases. Old age or indifferent upkeep was often responsible for their lack of speed. The other was that, while his port offered a magnificent anchorage, its installations had never been intended for such heavy traffic. Halifax, while overtaxed, had much better services available.

Each NCSO was naturally anxious to see the facilities of his harbour put to the fullest use in maintaining the sea-readiness of the ships he would be responsible for sailing. Yet exchanges from one port to the other of candidates for repair were inevitable, since each port offered distinctive services. The suspicion arose all too frequently that one port was trying to fob off long-term cripples on the other.

Moreover, Mitchell had had little time to adjust to his increasing burden. The early complications of the slow convoys were still being worked out when *Admiral Scheer*'s ravaging of the *Jervis Bay* convoy sent its surviving vessels steaming for the nearest shelter, causing eastbound movements to be suspended. Overnight, Sydney's anchorages were crowded with more than a hundred ships, each requiring some measure of attention before returning to sea. Mitchell had met the test well, but it added to the tension of his relationship with Oland.

I was not completely unaware of the strains on the Halifax-Sydney connection. It was occasionally discernible in bad-tempered exchanges in the signal log. Until I found myself caught in the verbal crossfire of the personalities involved, however, I had not been unduly disturbed by it.

At the conference, up to that moment, I had been simply the fascinated observer of Brand's spirited orchestration of events. All the participants were names with which I had become increasingly familiar in the past year. Seeing them face to face for the first time at the Ottawa sessions, I compared the actual personalities with those I'd imagined from afar.

Captain Brand himself was the natural centre of my attention. He was a brusque, medium-sized man with a dry wit who wore the ribbon of the 1914 Star, which told me he had been at least a midshipman at the start of World War I. I learned that he had specialized as a navigator, and it was easy to associate him with the precision of sextants, chronometers and tide tables.

Stating crisply where he believed the conference needed to go, Brand had offered full opportunity of expression to anyone with ideas about how it could get there. A wealth of ideas and opinions were put forth, not all of which met with general agreement; but none had given rise to the blunt antagonism that suddenly flared between Mitchell and Oland.

Before the situation could get any worse, Brand firmly put his foot on it.

"There will, naturally, be details of the boarding service

to work out when the new hands are trained," he said curtly. "It's important that we realize its full potential. Each of you will be carrying responsibility for that. Now, to the next point—"

That night, instead of taking the train back to the Maritimes, I found myself on one heading west. Brand had decided that, since I was already part way across the continent, it would be practical for me to visit his people on the Pacific coast. He wanted me to discuss with them the desirability of extending the Naval Boarding Service—as it was now officially called—to that part of the country.

Vancouver Island's greenness was a happy contrast to Ottawa's snowdrifts and the iced-up miseries of Halifax harbour. In that time, before Pearl Harbor, the atmosphere of navy installations on the West coast compared to those on the East was the very difference between peace and war.

Lieutenant Commander Ivan Day, S.O. (Intelligence), agreed that the Pacific ports did not have the same urgent need for a boarding service as those on the Atlantic. Nevertheless, he put in a bid for an NBS unit as soon as the pool of trained boarders was large enough.

Four days spent on the train back to Halifax gave me time to grasp how thoroughly the Ottawa meeting had ended my innocence. Life had been simple before that tense moment at the conference table when I ceased to be a spectator at a gathering of supermen and realized I was working with people as human and fallible as myself.

Attempting to get my bearings, I went over the course of events. In the first place, chance had made me a link between the experience, perception and conviction of Oxner & Co., and the officers in a position to implement their findings. I had tried to do my best with what I was caught up in, and had taken on unfamiliar situations, always with Dick Oland in the background ready to pick up the pieces if I fumbled. I'd never really risked my own reputation, nor been burdened with lonely decisions. But as the train rumbled eastward I knew in my guts that those carefree days were over.

My reunion with Oland in Halifax confirmed this suspicion. He was unusually serious when he told me about the Intelligence briefing he and the other NCSOs had been given before leaving Ottawa.

"It's really coming," he said. "So far there's been nothing to prevent the U-boats from pushing beyond Forty West except American public opinion. But those days are finished. Roosevelt's in the war already, and the country won't be far behind. The Germans know it. We'll be hearing 'Action Stations' in the Halifax approaches before the year's out. It won't make your job any easier. How soon can we promise parties for the other ports?"

"How soon can we get them from the drafting office?" I parried, with memories of our long fight for bodies fresh in my mind.

"Oxner's already whipping some new hands into shape," Dick announced, "and the rest have been waiting your return." He looked at me hard. "You no longer have to justify your existence, you know."

"Could you tell me exactly what you mean by that?"

"I mean that there are some people who are still unconvinced that there is anything to learn from experience," he said grimly. "They've got to have it by the book or it can't be done—even if it *has* been done. Their philosophy and yours won't always coincide. You'll be all right, though, if you stay within the personal authority you've established."

"Are you telling me I'm getting a Headquarters appointment to coordinate the NBS operation?"

"If I could tell you that," said Dick, "I would have spared you the speech. Fact is, you're still on my staff. DNI would like you to drop in on the other ports from time to time, though. Continuity, you know."

It was incredible.

"It can't work," I said flatly. "I can just see myself arriving in Sydney as a member of your staff and announcing, 'This is the way we do it in Halifax, sir.'"

"If that was the sort of thing you'd be likely to do, I can't see Brand giving you the chance," responded Dick. "Get this straight: he knows his people, he knows just what he can get out of us, and he knows what's got to be done."

"But surely there will be something in writing that will give me some status outside this port!"

"Your terms of reference are exactly what they were before we went to Ottawa."

"It doesn't make sense," I protested.

"You haven't had as long to think about it as I have," Oland replied patiently, a crooked smile slowly asserting itself. "When you do I think you'll see that—all things considered—it does make sense. Actually, a Headquarters appointment for you was discussed. In the end Brand decided you needed to remain close to the ships—that Halifax is where the greatest amount of trouble will come and where there will be the most to learn."

"As a top organizer, he must realize—"

"In this case," Dick cut me off, "he is concerned about an organism." He gave me time to absorb the remark before he continued. "I'll do what I can for you here with Officers Appointments and the drafting office. Brand has already talked to their bosses at NSHQ and the right sort of personnel should be forthcoming. I think, too, I can get a general memorandum from the Admiral supporting the basic idea of NBS in this Command. All you have to do is make it work."

11

"Expect the unexpected..."

My tension gradually eased as I absorbed Brand's plans for the expanded boarding service and my place in it. Actually, as I had realized on my long train journey, I would have been unhappy about being separated from the daily company of the men in the launches.

Dick, momentarily forgotten, broke in on my musings with a demand to know what I was grinning about.

"I was just dreaming up a slogan for NBS," I confessed. "'*Esprit de corps* but something more.'"

"Perfect!" he roared. "You know, I can still quote some of those foul pieces you wrote for the Esquimalt Hot Box. How is the magnum opus of the convoys coming?"

"I'm just letting it have its way."

"I'd like to read it sometime."

"You will," I said, "when it says what it needs to say."

That morning we had a memorable bull session in the standby room. I was able to tell the men how the ripples had gone out from their work, and could give them some idea of the broadened framework their new duties would have when the newly created Director of Merchant Seamen got his act together. I told them about the forthcoming Order in Council that would close the gaps in 4751. The boarders took it quietly, but none missed its significance and none denied himself his moment of pride.

Oxner's granitic countenance developed fissures. When I had finished he seemed, for once, at a loss for a suitable comment, though he muttered something about how he would have liked to have heard the Commander putting those people in Ottawa straight.

I had a further talk with him after Green and Baker took their parties off on the day's operations, seeking his opinion on the forthcoming allocation of the most seasoned hands. We were committed, I explained, to turning over trained parties to Montreal and Saint John within the month. Sydney must follow shortly after. These were priorities. St. John's, Quebec and the West coast ports must take their turns as personnel became available.

"Aye, aye, sir," said Oxner. "It can be done—that is if we get the bodies handily and the drafting office doesn't empty the cell block to find them. We can give them the drill and the old hands can show them how to make it work but—"he eyed me speculatively—"it would be good if each of them had something down in writing. A sort of boarder's Ten Commandments, like—"

"You're the sort of Moses to produce such tablets of stone, Oxner," I suggested.

"I'm ready to climb the mountain for them," he replied, eyes twinkling, "but you're as close to the Almighty as we're likely to get to carve them, sir."

I thanked him for the promotion and said I hoped I could return the favour. The need to have our non-commissioned leadership uprated was something I had long since taken up with Oland. The degree of responsibility they carried, measured against the ranks they held, was ridiculously out of proportion.

Many of them were skilled seamen with a sense of initiative that would have made them outstanding in any company, but Naval promotion had been based for generations on the performance of certain tasks *at sea* over a specific period. The Royal Canadian Navy's rule book contained no reference to the specialized duties for which the boarders had fitted themselves. They were simply listed as being on shore duty, though they constantly bucketed their way outbound between the anchored gateships whose crews were accumulating sea time. They were shore-based and that was that. Technically, they did not qualify for advancement.

Oland, doubtless with some help from DNI, had managed to get Oxner and the other senior hands the chance to take their Leading Seaman examinations. They had passed them with no difficulty, but that was as far as they could go. Though I wished otherwise, the men were not promoted for over a year after that. It was a distressing situation, but we had no option except to push ahead with our work.

For all the joshing, Oxner's idea about a list of "Commandments" was dead on. That night I began working on them. There were two long pages, single-spaced, when I finished several days later.

> "Nothing is playing a more important part in the winning of the war," they began, "than the quality of cooperation between the Navy and the Merchant Marine. Naval Control Service is at the heart of that teamwork. From the first, its aim has been to win and deserve the confidence of the officers and men of the Merchant Service.
>
> "This we now possess, but it was not automatically created nor will it be automatically retained. Impatience, indiscipline or irresponsibility on the part of one boarding rating can seriously damage what has been created by the sustained effort of many men. There are no rear rankers in Naval Control. Each man carries a personal responsibility."

A detailed description of duties, depending on which part of a ship a rating was assigned to during a search, followed. I added an easily memorized reminder:

> "Remember the most dangerous spot
> Is that which stays neglected.

> Before your eyes, as like as not,
> Expect the unexpected."

Further paragraphs covered the philosophy of operation:

> "Where it is necessary for a party to remain on board a ship for a considerable period, every opportunity for giving leadership by example should be utilized. Trouble-makers are usually men of ability and frequently their influence can be redirected into constructive channels."

As they first appeared, the Commandments—officially the "Standing Orders"—were the fruits of our bull sessions. We continued to add to them, following discussions in which everyone had a voice.

There were certain Commandments which, though unwritten, were made verbally explicit. The major one had to do with drinking while a search was underway. Since booze was at the bottom of half the crew trouble we encountered, the boarders were under strict instructions to avoid liquid hospitality while on duty. Officers were encouraged to set them a good example, though they were permitted to exercise their own judgement. Navy tradition assumed that the wardroom could be trusted with a bar while the fo'c's'le couldn't—something about which I had my doubts.

There were no written Commandments, either, about pilfering or smuggling. Opportunities were plentiful to distributors of seamen's comforts in daily contact with ships carrying duty-free tobacco and liquor.

That such corner-cutting was slight could be credited to the senior hands. Discreet in their own minor infractions, shrewd in the ways of the lower deck, sensitive to their men and jealous of the Service's reputation, they exercised a control such as no printed regulations could have achieved. The faith I placed in them was justified by the fact that any dubious characters who came to us from the drafting office invariably lost interest in boarding and requested transfers to other duties.

Oxner's wartime log provided a glimpse of what happened when an unwritten law was stretched too far.

He had written in January about a new hand: "A poor example of a boarding service rating. Will observe him closely." In March was entered, "Record no good and suggested he ask for draft." The conclusion came twelve days later: "He still hung on and was slow to request draft so I did it for him and speedily cleared the air."

Though we were happily shorn of our "Contraband Control" misnomer, we still retained a souvenir of it in the International Code "C" flag which, at a ship's yard, proclaimed she had been searched. This continued to fly from the time we had boarded until the pennants indicating the vessel's number in convoy replaced it at sailing time. The red, white and blue stripes of the brightest bit of bunting in the signal locker became the battle standard of NBS.

Headquarters ordered that every ship boarded was to be more methodically reported. In the past, only those of exceptional interest had been given any written comment beyond a few statistics. Now NSHQ wanted to know about *all* the crews—those in the happy ships as well as in the unhappy ones. It also wanted all types of intelligence of interest to Trade Division forwarded weekly; before long, "weekly" was changed to "daily".

On April 24, 1941, a month to the day from the conclusion of the Gatineau Conference, Sinjun Green and his party reported to Lieutenant Commander Fred Davis, RCN, Montreal's NCSO. In the same week, Lieutenant Ted Hart, until his appointment to Oland's staff second-in-command of a corvette, became boarding officer for Lieutenant Commander Nelson Rattenbury, RCNR, at Saint John.

The Sydney party, under Lieutenant George Browne, and including Baker, remained in Halifax for two more weeks because its men needed more preparation before assuming their unusually important and demanding post. In surrendering Alan Williams to be its senior hand, we were giving of our best.

Training of new personnel followed much the same pattern as before: on-the-job, learning-while-earning on the harbour. The standby room lectures and discussions, however, became more substantial, thanks to recent developments in Ottawa which had provided positive focus for the service.

With the new Director of Merchant Seamen in his post, action began on many of the recommendations that took shape in the Ottawa sessions. The buildings for a manning pool began to rise on North Street Hill, and a training school was being added to the Lunenberg skyline. Both were urgently needed if crews were to be trained for the numerous Canadian-built freighters nearing completion in the shipyards of both coasts and on the Great Lakes—the mass-produced 10,000 ton *Park* boats and their 4,700 ton sisters.

Another development was the improved teamwork between the voluntary agencies dedicated to merchant seamen's welfare. The Navy League and the Red Cross worked to provide decent accommodation ashore between voyages, recreation that would send the men back to sea refreshed, and additional comforts to make life afloat less grim.

Dick Oland had shown me the plans of a Merchant Seamen's Club which would shortly rise on Hollis Street, handy to the docks. Built in response to a pressing need, the club would also have value for boarders in last minute searches for missing seamen at sailing time.

These developments could not help but contribute to the atmosphere of goodwill we wanted to create for visiting ships.

There was also the new instrument for encouraging discipline. Any ambiguity about the Boarding Service's place in enforcing discipline among the crews was removed by the April 2 proclamation of PC 2385 — the Merchant Seamen Order.

Captain Brand and the Judge Advocate General had been patiently working out this legislation from the time it became clear that the earlier PC 4751 was not only an indifferent deterrent to refusal of duty but, in some cases, actually assisted troublemakers in widening their influence. When all they had to do after arrest and conviction was to volunteer to join another ship, the previous legislation could be used by the hard-core agitator and the subversively inclined as a ticket to new and previously healthy pastures.

There was no such fooling about the Merchant Seamen Order. Under it, any sailor on a merchant ship under Allied control, whatever his nationality, was answerable for a delaying action. The Board of Enquiry represented the Navy, the Department of Immigration, and the Department of Transport. A man convicted under it could be sentenced to six months in prison.

While this seemed a mild deterrent to anyone who happened to be an enemy agent, there was a joker in the deck. Anyone who appeared to qualify for indefinite incarceration could find himself having his case reviewed after serving his term. If the evidence suggested it was desirable, six-month extensions could be repeatedly added to the sentence.

Before a case was referred to the Board, a master's complaint was first examined by a Committee of Investigation which conducted a hearing on the ship where the offense allegedly had been committed. If, in their judgement, an incident rated prosecution, the offenders were taken into custody.

All the Naval Boarding Service officers were gazetted members of the Committees of Investigation, and their ratings served as its police force. This was logical. In the great majority of cases where a master had laid a charge under the Order, the boarding officer was already well aware of the trouble. In the course of his regular duties he had usually explored every avenue for a peaceful solution. The Order was used as a last resort.

One of the Judge Advocate's officers, Lieutenant R.W. Curran, was his expert on the Order and during the training of the new parties he arrived to brief them on its use. The likelihood that irresponsible captains might attempt to exploit the Order to get rid of undesirables or punish crew members was fully considered. It was agreed that the Order's reputation for fairness should be absolute. The indicator of our effective use of it would be the limited number of times we were forced to do so.

In relinquishing George Browne to command the Sydney party, Oland had denied himself an officer for whom he had already planned an important job on his office staff. Having laboured amid the cut and thrust of the pre-war

Montreal Stock Exchange, George was capable of keeping his cool when the market's bottom threatened to drop out. He was no less calm when a ship was threatened with the same misfortune.

Browne's charming lack of self-importance earned him equal respect from resentful stokers and dogmatic shipmasters. When he boarded the train for Cape Breton with Baker, Williams, and their party, we all felt reassured.

For those of us in Halifax, the departures meant abrupt change. During training days there had been manpower to spare; now, we were back almost to our numbers before the expansion. Most of our veterans had gone to fill out the new parties.

Oxner wanted us to keep Gould, arguing that the quiet New Brunswicker had developed an uncanny ability to locate the diaries of sailors who shouldn't have been keeping them. (They were the sort of thing that U-boat boarding parties were interested in when they searched an abandoned ship before administering the *coup de grace.*) I accepted Oxner's recommendation. He and Gould had been the first two men drafted as the nucleus of the boarding party and it seemed right that they remain together; they did so until war's end.

At that time, Lieutenant J.C. Conkey and I were the only commissioned Halifax boarders. It occurred to me that there was enough of Jack to handle both parties. He was as tall as the Commander: in fact, he probably topped him on the rare occasions when he was startled out of his boyish slouch. Good-natured and convivial, he mixed easily both on duty and ashore. But he could be formidable if a situation turned ugly.

Until the new boarding officers had shaken down in their own ports the only official contact I had with them was, properly, by signal from NCSO to NCSO. On occasion the immediate recipient of a message was too preoccupied to refer it to the man concerned, but during these first weeks, general beachheads of communication were established. With time, letters between myself and the senior boarding officers in other ports became the most valuable means of contact.

I was still impatient with my unofficial overall responsibility for the Naval Boarding Service; but after my first visit to the units I realized there was a certain value in the absence of specific authority—one which Captain Brand had doubtless foreseen. While I could be father-confessor to the discouraged or the disgruntled, I could remind them that we were all tackling something that overrode the importance of individuals, and that everyone had to rely on inner resources rather than looking to outside authority. The sense of duty we couldn't compel we might encourage by behaviour that demonstrated the value of our working philosophy.

A memorandum from the Commanding Officer, Atlantic Coast, went to all his NCSOs on April 8, 1941:

> "These boarding officers and boarding parties have been carefully trained in their duties. It is of the utmost importance that they should remain together and be used as boarding parties. They should only be required for other duties when they have no particular duties of their own to perform and also, of course, in case of real emergency."

This was a concise description of the principle followed in Halifax. What constituted a "real emergency" left loopholes for local interpretation, but we were all glad that our status was clarified for all to see.

Sometime after the parties had gone to their ports, Dick Oland sent word that he wanted to talk to me. There had been all too many such summonses recently. At nearly every meeting I learned of some new setback in the war at sea. This morning, though, Oland looked as though he had been contemplating an unbroken weekend at Blue Wing.

"Did you know that DNI, Admiralty, flew over for a couple of days at Headquarters just after we left there?" he asked innocently.

"Should I be expected to?"

"No, I suppose not. You pick up quite a lot though, that you're not expected to."

"I couldn't tell you who DNI, Admiralty is," I said, "much less what he's been up to."

"His name," offered Oland, "is Admiral J.H. Godfrey."

"Never heard of him."

"That's all right," said Dick. "He's heard of you."

I answered in the same spirit.

"So he came from London to investigate a subversive VR two-striper?"

"Oh, he had other things to do, like briefing the Naval Staff on the state of the war, but he was obviously sniffing around for items of interest as well as passing them out. Take a look at this."

He tossed me a copy of a memorandum from Admiral Godfrey to the Commanders in Chief of the Royal Navy around the world. It drew attention to a noteworthy development in Canada. He went on to describe the Naval Boarding Service and to quote the full text of the Commandments. Selected samples of boarding forms were included. The one covering the Dutch vessel *Breedijk* was typical:

> "There was crew trouble aboard this ship in New York due to the crew members having been promised berths in ships of the same company sailing to the Dutch East Indies. This promise had not been implemented. The captain reports that Nazi agents got to the crew in their unsettled state of mind and intensified the difficulty. He believes the U.S. government is dealing drastically with these agents.
>
> "Explosives in 1 and 2 were, generally speaking, well stowed but in each instance the last cases appeared to have been stowed hurriedly. While heavy weather might not have caused major shifting of cargo, it unquestionably would have set cases of bombs rolling freely in each hold. Obtained dunnage and tools from the ship's carpenter and had the weak spots shored up."

Dick was smiling blandly when I looked up from my reading.

"Captain Brand is very pleased about it," he said. "I wouldn't be surprised if the boarders would be, too. Why don't you drop the other parties a line?"

"Won't their NCSOs get copies from Headquarters like you have?"

"I'm sure they will," he chuckled, "but write your fellows anyway. It's the sort of news they can afford to hear twice."

12

Horatius at the gangway

At the end of 1940, the mood of the war was bleak. Admiralty sent Canadian Headquarters a message singularly lacking in Christmas cheer:

> "There is still considerable suspicion among Allied crews that we are using their ships for our own ends. As a result instructions from British control officers are sometimes resented and not obeyed. It is believed the situation would be assisted if Allied shipping committees in London could instruct their ships through their consulates that, notwithstanding any previous orders, they must obey the orders of British NCSOs and Consular Shipping Officers, since these officers are kept completely up to date on the general situation and, as part of a world organization, are in the best position to interpret and transmit the wishes of the various national shipping committees."

Despite anything the committees or consulates had

done to spread the word, the loss of merchant crew strength in the first half of 1941 was unusually heavy. Of the three major factors responsible—death, defiance, and desertion—the last was to reach its peak that year. Our involvement with the desertion problem was often indirect.

The U.S. was the haven of choice for deserting seamen. They usually made their moves in the ports of that still-neutral country, and the main burden of dealing with them fell on the local Consular Shipping Advisors. Later in 1941, Sir William Stephenson, "The Man Called Intrepid", would begin to send agents of his British Security Coordination to join the struggle to keep the ships moving, but until he did the situation was desperate.

The Italian invasion of their homeland had made the Greek sailors our allies and their government-in-exile had finally put them on wages comparable to the British level. That this was likely to add to the demands on the Naval Boarding Service was suggested in a letter from Sir Edward Beatty to Admiral Nelles: "It is considered that the reduction of the very high wages now paid may lead to crew difficulties and consequently it will be endeavoured to keep Greek ships in trade between U.K. and Canadian and other British ports."

In other words, the Greeks would be denied the convenience of U.S. ports in which to desert and we could expect to have more of our share of the trouble. This was confirmed by a signal from Headquarters to the NCSOs on March 18: "Greek government has decided to reduce wages on Greek ships to approximately British level ... Crew trouble may therefore be expected."

Every Canadian port had its trials, but Montreal was the most dramatically affected. The size of the city and its Greek community offered hope of sanctuary for pierhead jumpers. In addition, some enterprising members of the colony developed an underground for moving fugitives to the States. Word that two or three hundred dollars would guarantee a man a quick crossing of the international border spread among the merchant seamen and, with almost equal speed, to the ears of the boarding parties.

In Montreal, Sinjun Green, up to his ears in it, reported that too many masters were throwing the responsibility for getting their ships to sea on the naval authorities. The general tone of his letter was positive, however: "NCSO is efficiency plus and very keen on our outfit. Coffey is of invaluable help and always keen to unearth centres of propaganda."

The operators of the human pipelines from Montreal to the U.S. eventually assisted the RCMP and Immigration people by abusing a good thing. Having collected their fee from a carload of deserters, they then abandoned them, short of the American side of the border, rather than risk the increasingly watchful authorities of both countries. The deserters, blundering into the hands of the waiting authorities, were ready witnesses when the law descended on their erstwhile benefactors. With the July, 1941 conviction of Lebris Mehalacopopoulis, Theodore Srykos, and Pendalis Bouboulis, one drain of the supply of Greek seamen was plugged.

Browne, at Sydney, was also having his bad moments with deserters, but, like Green, he was pleased with things generally. His June 7 letter contained one particularly heartening sentence: "Commander Mitchell has been backing any request or suggestion we have made."

Saint John and Quebec City were not spared the disturbing trend. One group of malcontents launched a writ of *habeas corpus* to challenge Canadian disciplinary legislation. It was the first of a number of attacks on the Merchant Seamen Order, some of which reached Parliament to test the tenacity of the Judge Advocate General. Even a year later (September 5, 1942) he was reminding the Commissioner of the RCMP:

> "As you can appreciate, situations have arisen which it was not possible to foresee because, so far as I am aware, it (the Order) has no counterpart in the Empire. It has been necessary, therefore, for the parties in charge of the Order to more or less feel their way along, making alterations in its administration which were considered to be necessary to carry out its intent and purpose of keeping the ships sailing."

Oland's suggestion that a representative of the Greek government be appointed as a naval contact in Halifax was quickly taken up at Headquarters. Chief of Naval Staff, in touch with the Royal Consul General of Greece in Montreal, had his reply quickly. Mr. Tserepis wasn't too encouraging:

> "As far as the provision of a really good man at Halifax to assist with the difficulties experienced in such matters is concerned, I have to advise that, aside from the difficulty of finding a good and dependable person with experience in naval matters, knowing the Greek laws and being in a position to exercise some authority, I have no right by the jurisdiction of our law to nominate any such person, especially since I can make no arrangement for his remuneration."

Despite Mr. Tserepis's doubts, such a representative was shortly found. Captain Mastrandreas was courageous, patriotic, decisive, and had a sense of humour which he frequently needed. As we had hoped, it was useful to have Greek meet Greek and get results when our own efforts failed to find the right wavelength.

Had there been the normal flow of Greek ships to the United States at this time, large-scale trouble would have erupted. The suborning there of disgruntled crews was constant. A steady stream of alleged welfare workers, clergymen, charitably-minded citizens and compassionate "ladies" visited Allied seamen and caused scores of them to disappear. Ship after ship suffered crippling crew shortages when the time came to sail. The missing men had not only been encouraged to remain ashore; many had been spirited away to jobs in places where they were unlikely to be discovered and brought back.

British ships were not immune. Following word that *S.S. Maplewood* had been held up by desertions, I visited her when she finally reached Halifax on May 16. Oland wanted a report on whether the disappearance of the men had been a defection of disgruntled workers—or whether a definite enemy system was at work to empty the fo'c's'les. All I could offer was the following:

> "British merchant seamen have little difficulty cadging

> drinks in U.S. ports, where there is prevailing goodwill towards the British cause. It is unlikely, though, that those well disposed towards Britain would be inclined to lure British seamen to jobs Americans could use. It is even less likely that they would finance these seamen to go to other parts of the country."

Three days earlier I had been reporting,

> "It is evident from contact with Dutch ships here that there is a steady and effective sabotaging of their crews in New York. The tanker *Odina*, which lost twenty-three of her Chinese seamen there, is an example.
>
> "Men like the bos'n, cook, chief steward and carpenter made no attempt to remove their considerable possessions before going ashore. It is unlikely that they should have done so had it been their original intention not to return."

Later, when the Oriental exodus hit American Immigration on a sensitive nerve, such nationals were allowed ashore only when accompanied by guards. But by that time, even escorted Chinese had a way of fading into the walls with the skill of men who knew exactly where they were going.

Their officers were not overlooked, but here subversion most often encountered loyalty. A trio of New York charmers, credited with considerable success in dampening men's love of the sea, were pinpointed by an officer on the Dutch *Edam* when interviewed during a Halifax boarding. Photos he had taken of the ladies were most helpful in curtailing their activities. It was necessary, of course, to sternly instruct this officer to henceforth observe the regulations by which his camera should be left in his captain's charge, but the reprimand was softened by a warm expression of unofficial gratitude from Security.

★ ★ ★

On June 22, 1941, the global background against which we worked took on a tremendously altered shape. Hitler's thrust into the Soviet Union not only ended the hypocrisy of his non-aggression pact with Stalin but, since the Fuhrer needed divisions in Russia, any possibility of Germany invading Britain also ended. In its place came an all-out attempt to starve her by a ruthless new submarine campaign. For every U-boat sunk, eight new ones emerged from the Nazi fitting basins.

This was preceded by a deadly flareup of surface action, which brought NBS several unusually grim days. Germany's super-battleship *Bismarck* broke for the open sea and on May 24, in Denmark Strait, destroyed Britain's largest fighting ship, *Hood*, and badly damaged the new battleship, *Prince of Wales*. Word that a Royal Navy force was in pursuit was thin comfort for merchantmen poised to cross the ocean where *Bismarck* was running loose.

A large convoy was scheduled to clear Halifax on the morning of May 27 and, after what had happened when *Admiral Scheer* was abroad following the *Jervis Bay* disaster, it seemed logical that sailing orders would be postponed. There was no such reprieve, though. At the appointed hour we found ourselves going through the customary routine, distributing final papers to the outgoing ships.

Meeting each master was like confronting a condemned man. When we informed them no commutation of sentence had been granted, some made a hard joke of it, and some were tight-lipped. But either way, the job was a tough one. By the time I had delivered the last orders I was heart-sick. I kept looking anxiously towards the naval signal station on the roof of the Federal Building, from which cancellation of the movement might be expected if such a last-minute decision was made. But there was no flicker from its large signal lamp.

Then, suddenly, above the murmur of harbour and dockside, came the penetrating voice of a newsboy on shore, shouting his wares with unprecedented spirit. I ordered the launch to the nearest jetty and sent a couple of hands fanning into the streets.

"If that's good news," I instructed, "I want you back at the double with at least forty copies."

The Extra couldn't have brought better news. *Bismarck* was sunk. The paper told how *Rodney* and her consorts overtook the enemy giant and sent the battleship to the bottom. As we read, we could see the Commodore's ship underway up the harbour with the long, single line of convoy vessels falling in astern. We had just time to reach George's Island as the Commodore slid past. Swinging alongside, we passed a copy of the paper to her.

The sailor who grabbed it scrambled excitedly to the bridge and, a moment later, a grizzled figure appeared on its wing and waved an exultant brass hat. We waved back, then positioned ourselves for the vessel astern. Ship by ship we went through the same happy drill as the convoy passed through the gates and began to assume formation on an ocean where the shadow of the *Bismarck* no longer glowered. There was particular joy for me in glimpses of certain faces looking down from their bridges, certain voices raised to hail us. They belonged to the men I had miserably confronted earlier that morning.

This was the same week that Oxner held the bridge—or, more properly, the gangway—of the *S.S. Nariva*. She was a big, rather old, British refrigerator ship—a "reefer" in seamen's parlance, and her cargo of beef was badly needed overseas. We had been warned from Buenos Aires that there was trouble on board and that it was going to get worse. The crew had announced bluntly that unless certain demands were met by the time they reached Halifax they intended to go over the side.

Nariva made port twenty-four hours before her convoy was due to sail. The normal means of confining her crew on board would have been to anchor her well clear of the shore, but she was a coal burner and her voyage from South America had already been a long one. There was nothing for it but to bring her under the tips to restore her bunkers for the Atlantic crossing. That meant her crew would have ready access to the shore.

Oxner and I were over the gangway the moment it was dropped on the coal dock; five ratings, looking their burliest, remained on the shore end to check the passes of anyone heading for the beach. The glances we drew from the large and rather scruffy-looking crew were less than fraternal.

A session with the master, then with the leader of the dissidents, made two points fairly clear. The first was that the impasse between captain and crew was such that there was small chance of *Nariva*'s joining the next day's movement. The other was that, while we could refuse the sit-downers access to the shore, the chances were good that they would make it with our assistance—as prisoners under the Merchant Seamen Order.

Their leader, a red-headed Australian, was obviously an old hand at bearding shipmasters. The *Nariva* gave him plenty to work with. The poor condition of her living quarters strongly suggested that men who signed on her would be unlikely to return for a second voyage. Moreover, as many crews coming north after the fleshpots of Buenos Aires had found, the comfortless, perilous North Atlantic was a harsh, depressing contrast.

The captain was prepared to lay a charge under the Merchant Seamen Order on the strength of the disobedience he had already been faced with, but I suggested that there was nothing to lose by keeping the situation open until the convoy had departed. It was possible that Oxner and his mates might, in the meantime, be able to exert some friendly persuasion in their conversations with members of the ship's company.

Before leaving I made a second attempt to reason with the Australian, giving him the assurance that his complaint would receive consideration at the right moment and in the right place. This earned me the caustic edge of his tongue. No owner's catspaw, he declared, even one wearing a Naval uniform, was going to keep him and his companions bottled up for long in this flea-ridden hulk.

I told him we'd talk again in the morning. When I left evening was falling, darkened prematurely by black clouds rising from the avalanches of coal that thundered into the vessel's bunkers. It was high tide and Oxner had moved his party to the inboard end of the steeply slanting gangway.

Around midnight I was called to the phone and Oxner's voice, more tense than usual, announced there had been a spot of trouble on the reefer. It seemed to have settled down, but he thought he should report it.

A staff car hurtled me to the dock. Nothing much had changed since I had last seen *Nariva* except that she was deeper in the water and the floodlights on the tips were painting the clouds of coal dust in hellish patterns. Instead of the two ratings who had been on the end of the gangway when I had left, the full party had been positioned there. Oxner, his twenty-four hour growth of beard and his eyebrows dark with coal dust, had a Mephistophelian air.

"Well," I said, "It looks peaceful enough."

"Peace ends at the fo'c's'le hatch," he answered. "Last time I stuck my nose in someone hurled a seaboot at it."

"What happened?"

"Well, sir," he rumbled, "things seemed as quiet as they are now until just before I called you. Stevens and I were on the gangway, agreeing it had been a great mistake to bring in coal burners while there was still wind and sails, when bang—the whole crew comes storming out on deck. That Australian wild man was yelling, 'All ashore that's going ashore!' I've got to hand it to him. He had the guts to lead the rush himself and got to the brow ahead of the others. That gave Stevens and me a chance to grab him and heave him against the engine room casing. He must have hit quite a wallop. Knocked him on his beam ends.

"That seemed to take the steam out of the others. They picked up their glorious leader and lugged him back to the fo'c's'le. Mind, what they said wasn't pretty but no one seemed to want to take his place at the head of parade ashore. You might say we were like those Romans my old teacher in eighth grade used to get all choked up about—you know, the one that blocked the gangway over the Tiber. Not that Stevens and I weren't glad when the rest of our boys came running out from amidships. Then I figured I'd better call you."

The master appeared, half dressed; his face was strained and angry. The one light in his darkness was that violence had befallen the Australian. He told me the coaling was expected to be completed by five a.m. and that tugs would be standing by to tow him to an anchorage when the last bunker cover had clanged into place. He also upbraided me for not having applied the Merchant Seamen Order the moment the ship had docked.

"I'll be out in the morning after I've had time to collect a Mountie for a Committee of Investigation," I promised.

"There's no great rush. It's plain you're not going to make the convoy."

Oxner remained with the party, now reinforced by the standby hands, who were under instructions to return to their beds only when there was a lane of water between ship and shore wide enough to drown anyone who decided to jump her. As reward for the night's work the boarders were to be allowed an extra hour's sleep before reporting to the Yard in the morning.

Nariva was anchored well clear of the land when, earlier than usual, I reached the office. When I asked after Oxner, I got the surprising information that he was still in the *Nariva*. I grabbed a fast launch and charged down the harbour. At the top of the reefer's ladder I was met by an obviously bewildered chief officer.

"How goes the revolution?" I asked.

The mate scratched his head.

"I can't fathom it," he muttered. "You never know what's coming with that damned Aussie. This morning, for the first time since we escaped from South America, the crew turned out like a bunch of cadets on their first training ship voyage. It was easy to see who was encouraging them. What in God's name he's up to this time is beyond me."

"You've still got one of my men on board, I gather?"

"Yes," said the mate. "He told me he was going forward for a shave. He needed it."

Oxner was gripped by embarrassment when I ran him down, not because he had overstepped his orders but because I caught him submitting his jaw to an exotic after-shave lotion. It had been a gift, he explained, from a South American lady to the sailor who had loaned him his straight razor. It was a sort of mixture of pansies and violets.

"Wasn't it enough to play Horatius last night without taking on Daniel in the lion's den?" I demanded. "What's happened to your friend from down under?"

"He's a great fellow," said Oxner solemnly. "A great fellow, sir."

"Easy on," I said. "The last time I saw you, you had just knocked him silly."

"True, sir, true," he admitted, borrowing a sweat rag and applying it vigorously to his fragrant jaw, "but that was just to get his attention, as you might say. After things got a bit quieter in the fo'c's'le I stuck my head in. When no one took it off, I told our friend I was sorry about the rough stuff—that I hated to discourage leadership even when it was off-course. You know—the sort of thing we put in the Commandments."

Oxner looked at me expectantly but I said nothing. So he sighed and continued.

"This seemed to interest him and we got to talking. I told him it took a good deal more to keep a ship moving than to tie one up, but that anyone who could do it would be the one to improve conditions on board. He said I was balmy. Maybe so, I said, but I could give him chapter and verse on some ships I'd known where it was smart to be crazy.

"Come time to pull the ship into the stream we were still nattering and the man was getting excited about this new idea. So I thought I ought to carry on after I sent the party ashore." He looked at me from an angle. "I thought you'd want me to."

"It looks as though your judgement was pretty good," I conceded.

"Anyway," Oxner said briskly, "it's settled."

"What's settled?"

"Everything, sir—that my idea was better than his—that they'll heave in at sailing time—that they'll get a square deal when they reach the U.K."

"I see," I said, doing my best to sound matter-of-fact. "So that's why he turned out the crew this morning?"

"That's right." Oxner confirmed. "He'll make it stick, too." His face lighted with a new thought. "Perhaps we could grab him for the Boarding Service after he's served his articles."

The movement got underway at 11 a.m. *Nariva* was among the first to run up her pennants. We were still in the lower harbour in the launch, all hands slightly groggy from lack of sleep, when she slid past in the wake of the Commodore's ship. I ordered the coxswain to close and to hold a parallel course for a few minutes, long enough for the reefer's crew to crowd the rail and to exchange profane pleasantries with the men who had held the bridge the previous evening. Among them a commanding figure with a mop of red hair raised an arm in salute and Oxner, strangely silent, raised his in return.

At the bottom of my report to Oland I noted, "It was significant, according to the chief officer, that the discipline on board the ship today was higher than at any time since the crew had been shipped. The military gunners, who had been backing the seamen in their disturbance, were again acting like soldiers. Oxner, both as a man of brawn and a diplomat, deserves highest credit."

13

"Something to live up to..."

While the destruction of the *Bismarck* in May had ended the serious threat of surface attack on the convoys, there was terrible evidence of a new and deadly submarine force hard on its heels. The U-boats' hunting ground was swiftly becoming global. Of more than 600,000 tons of shipping lost in June, a dozen victims were torpedoed within eight hundred miles of Halifax. It was plain that the North American coastline would shortly be the western boundary or even the centre of the Battle.

The situation drastically affected the men in Canada's fighting ships. The increased need for close escort of convoys across the Atlantic brought about the creation of a mid-ocean anti-submarine force based in Newfoundland. Many of the destroyers and corvettes previously familiar to us in Halifax moved to St. John's and we lost sight of them except when they returned for refit or the repair of battle or weather damage. Some never returned.

The war's new phase had a psychological effect on the boarders. I became adept at recognizing what was coming when Oxner, naming one of the ratings we could least afford to lose, would announce, "He's requested a personal interview, sir."

It was always the same—the man would express his appreciation of the importance of the Boarding Service's work, and of the mates with whom he had been serving; but he'd go on to say he felt he should be back afloat. Sometimes I'd decide these petitioners just needed reassurance, or perhaps wanted me to make up their minds for them. Other times it was plain the individual felt obliged to tell me of his intention before putting in an official request for sea duty. I could offer my understanding of how the man felt and my own reasons for resisting the same impulse. No one, I would add, could be expected to put his best into a job where the motivation was anything but his own high regard for what he was doing.

In spite of these crises, the only key ratings who left, other than those invalided out, did so through promotion. Two studied for and earned their merchant officers' tickets and one was commissioned in the Navy.

In July, the carnage at sea fell off to some extent. There was official recognition of Dick Oland's leadership, in the form of a promotion to Captain and the awarding of an O.B.E. Nevertheless, we had an oppressive sense of foreboding as the U-boats pressed steadily westward. Our service had completed a year's seven-days-a-week working regimen, and I had the suspicion that the men were losing some of their edge.

Situations that had earlier been taken in stride began to provoke short tempers. Harbour crises that had once seemed opportunities to work out better solutions seemed merely exhausting. Hunting out trouble was our *raison d'etre*, and it made no sense to resent it when it turned up.

I felt we were slipping.

Oland dealt crisply with the situation.

"Look," he said, when we were discussing a shipboard uprising that was not responding to our efforts, "when are you due for leave?"

"I'm overdue," I replied, "but with things the way they are—"

"How about next month?"

"It will probably be worse than this month," I countered.

"I'm sure it will be—and the one after that will be even worse. There'll be submarines in the harbour approaches by then. Take off while you can. Put on some fat you can live on next winter."

I was about to tell him he needed rest more than I did. But I didn't get the chance. Dick straightened up.

"Choose your ETD and make it fast," he ordered, "then wire your wife."

★ ★ ★

September was at its loveliest in the ravine on Edmonton's outskirts, where we'd rented a house. The spruce trees whispered peacefully. I was with my family. I should have been able to forget, for the time being, what waited back on the East Coast. But my mind wouldn't rest. I knew I had to try to sort it out, or my leave would be useless. One evening, talking with Ernestine, I remembered Paddy Dove.

My friendship with Paddy dated from as dismal a day as I had ever experienced in Halifax. A chill rain, carried on a gusty nor'easter, had been whipping the Yard when Dick Oland sent for me. A pile of printed notices were on the desk before him. Prepared by the Security people, they declared that, in future, the lowering of ships' boats in harbour, other than for lifeboat drill, would be strictly forbidden.

"I want you to personally deliver one of these to every captain at anchor in the Basin," Dick said. "Sorry I can't spread the load among more people, but there's bound to be plenty of negative reaction, and handling this sort of thing is your cup of tea."

He didn't need to elaborate. There had been a stink over three ships' boats that had broken the security regulations by landing men at remote points on the Basin rather than through King's Wharf, where passes could be checked. It was the sort of thing that had happened occasionally in the past, resulting in nothing more serious than a stiff warning. Recently, however, security had tightened. Even the licensed bumboatmen had found themselves under rigid control.

The new printed instruction was no surprise, but it had disturbing implications. While it would certainly inconvenience anyone planning illegal landings, its main impact would be felt by honest seamen who were already under enough strain. On a good day the Basin danced with the sails of small craft that had been lowered for windjamming. It was the one outlet for the frustration of hundreds of men whose vessels were awaiting replacement or repair of bombed docksides in the U.K. Some had spent weeks at anchor, long enough to have worked up morale-raising sailing competitions with other ships fighting boredom in the same fashion. Banning small boats in the Basin was tantamount to confining the already restive sailors to barracks.

Delivering the new instructions would be simple enough; absorbing the reaction and attempting to redirect it would be something else again. There'd be some shrill sounding-off, and it was important that the fact of the situation should not become obscured. The men needed to be reminded that the ban on sailing had become necessary for the ships' own protection—and that the need for it had been brought about by thoughtless or ill-intentioned merchantmen themselves.

Dick had no need to spell this out. He simply said, "I don't envy you."

It was a horrible day, a match for the ugly weather. The captains who accepted the order with melancholy resignation were worse than those who protested it. After the first dozen ships, my presentation was well practised and I became inured to the highly charged atmosphere the order produced, but the physical fatigue of climbing endless side-ladders, the soggy air that seemed to soak right through my oilskins, and a miserable mental fatigue had produced an acute case of self-pity by the time I headed, well after dark, for the last gangway.

I had come to the right place. The ship was the *Gold Shell* and her master was Paddy Dove, as amusing a fellow as ever captured a man's imagination within sixty seconds. Naval legend had already acquainted me with him. As captain of the *Africa Shell* he had been the first master captured by *Graf Spee* during the pocket battleship's devastation of merchant shipping in the early stages of the war.

As a prisoner he had come close to the status of guest. His quick mind and irrepressible optimism had provided *Graf Spee*'s Captain Langsdorf with the relaxation his lonely and dangerous post normally denied him. Over Langsdorf's dinner table the two wartime enemies had become friends.

The German's eventual suicide, after being ordered by Hitler to scuttle his ship when it was cornered in the River Plate, left Paddy with a sense of loss. (After the war a movie was built around Langsdorf and the *Graf Spee*; Dove was written into the script and acted as a technical advisor.)

On the evening when, soaked and resentful, I boarded the *Gold Shell*, Paddy Dove was the only captain I had faced all day who seemed glad to see me. His ship was scheduled for immediate departure, so the sports sailing proscription was of little consequence to him. What did concern him was my appearance of having been dragged up from the bottom of the Basin. When he found that my unhappy work for the day was completed, he insisted on putting me into dry clothes, then sat me down to dinner and the first of a number of fascinating conversations we would enjoy in the years that followed.

His cabin was snug—the rattle of the rain against the scuttles made it even more cosy—and his cook was a good one. Dove was that happy combination: a good sailor and an unabashed romantic. His experiences were colourfully told, and we yarned, careless of the time.

When he issued an invitation to sample his liquor cabinet, I accepted. Eight years had passed since I'd found it necessary to go on the wagon, but the circumstances in Paddy's cabin that night made it seem the most natural thing in the world to declare a moratorium.

When I finally left I had no difficulty making it to the launch as it bucketed alongside in the gale. And the following days, to my own surprise, I found I had suffered no ill-effects from breaking one of my own unwritten "commandments".

Discovering that I could usually stop at one or two slugs made me over-confident. I decided that it would make little difference if I quietly reneged on my conviction about officers holding to the same drinking standards on duty that were demanded of the men. Some, I knew, granted themselves judicious leeway, maintaining that there was certain information that was more readily forthcoming over a tot. The ratings, while in a position to be well aware of this, exhibited no apparent rancor.

Self-justification, I realized during my conversation with my wife, had blinded me to my abuse of a sensitive working relationship—one that had been built on a principle I'd laid down myself. No one had questioned my making myself an exception to the principle, but I saw my hypocrisy at last.

This truth overtook me mercilessly. Sharing it with my wife, I found myself making the most of the remaining days of my leave. My eagerness to restore what I had withdrawn from the boarding operation gave richness to the limited days of being a husband and father again. I wrote Dick Oland, giving him a rundown of my self-discovery and promising to make good what I had lost.

★ ★ ★

On September 7, a name caught my eye on the front page of the Edmonton Journal. Captain R.H. Oland, O.B.E., the distinguished Naval Control Service Officer in Halifax, had died in his sleep.

It helped to learn that it had happened at Blue Wing. He'd felt very tired and thought it would be a good idea to leave the port and the midnight calls to Banyard for twenty-four hours. At Blue Wing he had watched the daylight fade over the Atlantic and the twin lights wink into life on Devil's Island, then had gone to bed early. In the night his wife had heard him sigh deeply. And that was it.

A week had passed since the funeral when I reported back, but it was as though everyone had just returned from the service. Commander Banyard was established in the glassed-in office. He told me that things could never be the same again, but that we all had something to live up to.

He was right. It never *could* be the same again. Dick's

carte blanche, "O.K. Watto, take it from here—", was constitutionally different from his successor's chain-of-command instinct for detailed control. Banyard was no less convinced of the Boarding Service's value, but the degree of communication was not as great.

The bull session on my return to the standby room wasn't easy but it was more a relief than an ordeal. Crumpled pride was turned to profit.

"I've been beefing about our having recently lost our edge," I said, "and held certain of you responsible. But my judgement couldn't be trusted. How could it when I was sidestepping instructions I expected *you* to observe?

"I'm sure I didn't fool anyone but myself when I decided I could drink in the ships. I'm sorry for it. We need to stay sober on duty. We need to be as alert as possible, and that's only before the first tot. That's how I'm playing it from here on in. Any questions?"

It was good to be able to look them in the eye again. Finally Oxner said, "No questions, sir."

Three months earlier, as though sensing my need for a happy warrior, Officers Appointments had produced a gem called Joe Dwyer. A long friendship already existed between us, rooted in the newsroom of the Edmonton *Journal* and the wardroom of *Nonsuch*, the Edmonton RCNVR division. Bringing to his lieutenant's commission the competence that had made him a crackerjack reporter, resilient as only a natural humourist can be, Joe was quick to savour the unorthodox atmosphere and intentions of Naval Boarding Service. His reports were astute and extremely readable. To hear him in discussion with Oxner was to discover how colourful the English language can be.

With Dick gone, Joe became a doubly appreciated friend. In matters of crew morale his insight and humanity were invaluable. I had other reasons to be grateful for him. The urge to finish my narrative poem was still strong, but doubt had set in. Joe put an end to that after his first reading of what I'd written so far.

"Get on with it," he said, with rare seriousness. "What you're after is coming through."

The Knights of Columbus Recreation Hut (St. Mary's Hall) on Barrington St. (interior on next page, top). Used both by Armed Forces and Merchant Marine personnel to escape the rigours of North Atlantic crossings. Such off-duty facilities were in short supply in wartime Halifax. Public Archives of Nova Scotia/E.A. Bollinger Collection/#464A

Public Archives of Nova Scotia/E.A. Bollinger Collection/#464C

Public Archives of Nova Scotia/E.A. Bollinger Collection/#428

Downtown Halifax, circa 1941. Along these quiet streets, on VE Day, military personnel and civilians took part in the infamous Halifax riots.

Public Archives of Nova Scotia/E.A. Bollinger Collection/#311-E

Memories of the 1917 explosion, following an in-harbour collision, of the munitions carrier "Mont Blanc," which killed 1650, led to increased precautionary measures to prevent the recurrence of such a tragedy. Still, fires did occur in Halifax during World War II. Fireboats such as the *Rouille* helped keep them under control.

Commander Watt checking the cargo plan of a Greek freighter with its officers prior to a NBS inspection. Public Archives Canada/H-659

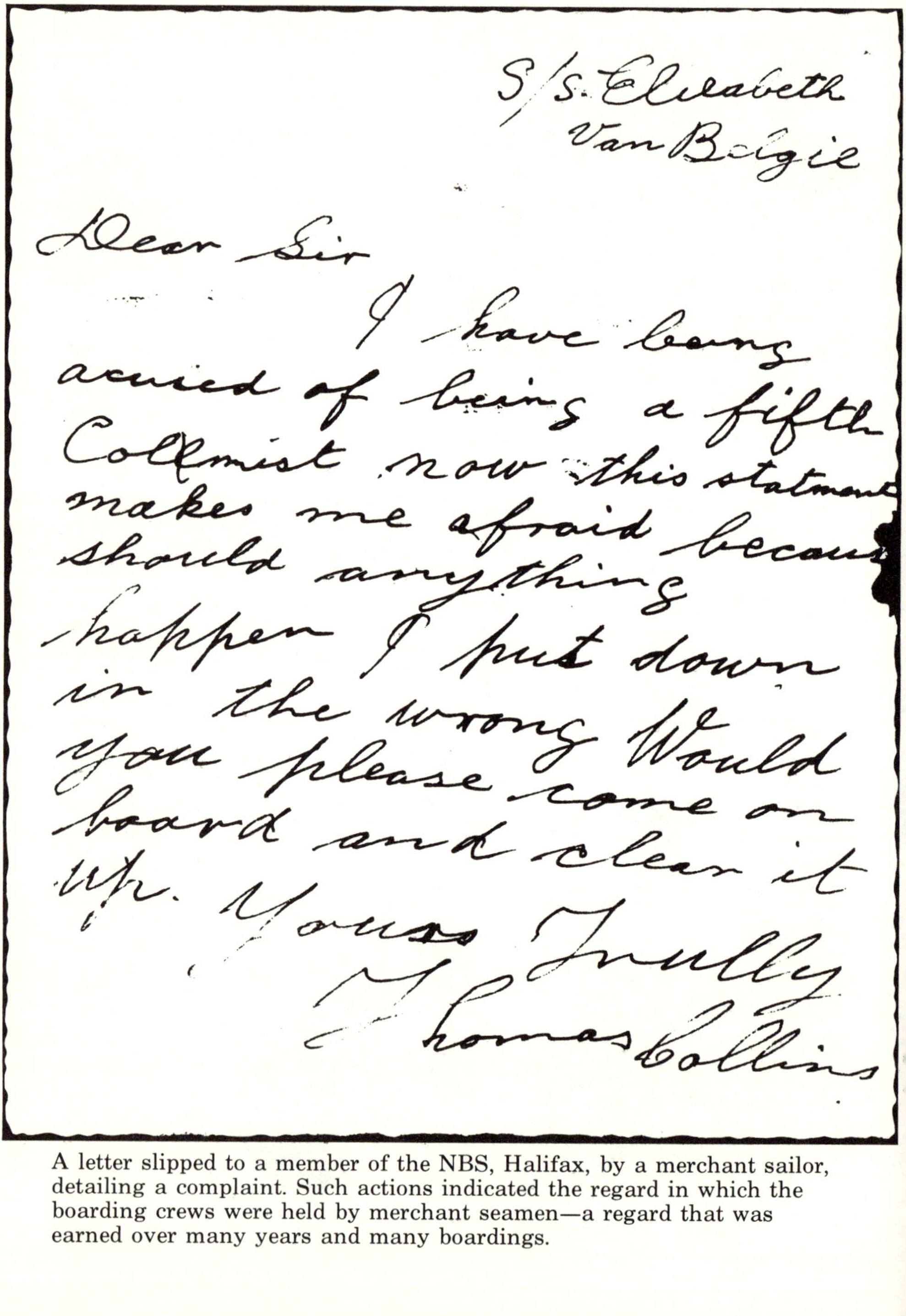

S/S. Elizabeth
Van Belgie

Dear Sir

I have beng acuied of being a fifth Collmist now this statment makes me afraid becaus should anything happen I put down in the wrong Would you please come on board and clear it up. Yours Trully
Thomas Collins

A letter slipped to a member of the NBS, Halifax, by a merchant sailor, detailing a complaint. Such actions indicated the regard in which the boarding crews were held by merchant seamen—a regard that was earned over many years and many boardings.

H.H. "Rocky" Wolfe, Stoker first class, who accompanied Commander Watt to London in 1942, when the author met Charles Jarman, Secretary of the British Union of Seamen, in an attempt to ease the difficult situations encountered on merchant ships. **Author's collection**

A hit munitions ship explodes in mid-convoy. Merchant sailors had only a 50 percent chance of surviving enemy attacks.

Maritime Museum of British Columbia

Landfall— convoy ships safely at anchor, awaiting the dangers of the North Atlantic crossing. Maritime Museum of British Columbia

Chief Petty Officer A.V. Oxner, B.E.M. "... with the smile of a satisfied mind." May 1945.

Author's collection

1944—The last meeting of senior port officers (Trade Division) before the end of the war. Lower right; Capt. E.S. Brand, Director of Trade Division. Seventh from left (seated), Commander Watt. Standing, third from left, Ansten Anstensen, Senior Boarding Officer, Halifax. This ended the series of conferences that, beginning with the Gatineau Conference of 1941, sought to remedy the adverse conditions that plagued merchant convoys. Public Archives Canada/0-80-1

Public Archives Canada/0-295-1

V.E. Day, 1945—Trade Division N.S.H.Q. Front row, fourth from left, Capt. E.S. Brand. Back row, extreme right, Commander Watt.

14

The 'persuader'

In mid August Oland had forwarded to Captain Brand what turned out to be his last observation on the work of the Naval Boarding Service. Typically, he had let the perceptive eye and forthright voice of Oxner demonstrate the sort of responsibility the ratings had become capable of shouldering.

> "To amuse you and also to demonstrate the thoroughness of the training of the boarding parties," Dick had written, "enclosed you will find the report to Lieutenant Watt of the leading hand of the party. The 'persuader' was a rather large fist at the end of the brawny arm of Oxner! Joking aside, however, the last two lines of Para. 2. and the whole of Para. 3 are rather serious."

Oxner's account of his experience on the British vessel *S.S. Empire Defiance* was appended:

> "Boarded at 2:30 p.m. Obtained names, ratings, etc. of crew members to be confined on board, then held smoke

talk forward to feel out true conditions of trouble. Results as follows:

"Not much harmony between deck and engine officers. Captain's first command and he hasn't the power of discipline. Both he and mate disliked by junior officers (deck and below) and bos'n. Bos'n drunk but, after a persuader, retired. No further trouble with him. Collected his shore pass and liquor. Collected all shore passes of firemen on board and of each fireman ashore as he returned to the ship.

"At 10:30 had some trouble with Petersen in taking his pass and, with some force, collected same. At 10:40 Green came aboard, accompanied by a female companion. Told me she was ship's stewardess. She was armed with a pass belonging to S. Williams, who was still ashore. I collected both passes and turned her over to dock constable and put Green, who gave me some trouble, in his bunk. At 1:15 Williams came aboard with a lot of noise but, with some persuasion, speedily turned in. At 2 a.m. all firemen were below except Kok, Oirjan, and Frances, who were in the calaboose ashore due to a fracas the night before. Steward, chief mate, gunners and Old Man treated boarding party fine, with plenty of food and cooperation at all times.

"Two of the firemen, Williams and O'Ryan, refused to work from Capetown to Halifax. The rest had to do their work along with their regular duties. Upon arriving in Halifax these two strikers received the same money as the workers. This doesn't go over well with the firemen.

"Another report here is that these men are on six months articles. After about five months conditions are made unbearable so the crew will rebel or desert. Their back money will remain with the captain, owners, etc. This is firemen's report. Cannot obtain much on authenticity.

"Seized all liquor in crew's possession and placed under Old Man's control.

"Leaders of this situation among firemen were noisy at first but after a bit of persuasion gave no further trouble. On the whole, a fine crew to reason with, I've found.

"Class distinction, bad boilers, poor discipline and bad quarters seem to be the trouble. I had my stoker look over the boilers to see what kind of firing job she is. Would suggest a visit from the naval engineer officer, as she's reported a tough firer. Chief engineer curses black gang and generally under the influence of spirits according to the Mohammedans who are, to all reports, honest firemen.

"Fo'c's'le alive with roaches and other vermin. Leaks in deckhead and, in bad weather, floor covered with a foot of water. Very poor crew accommodation forward and firemen's food not so good. It is reported that former crews were Lascars and officers could handle them as they pleased, with no kickbacks, but this crew resents that attitude towards them."

★ ★ ★

The Battle on the High Seas was not going well. The crew trouble we were finding in the harbour showed just how thin the thread was. If significant numbers refused to sail, Britain's lifeline, and the war, would be lost. What we read in the eyes of convoy survivors we interrogated was even more chilling. The horror of the torpedoings was bad enough. But the freezing North Atlantic was as merciless as the enemy.

An officers' steward with whom I talked prior to his vessel's sailing was one of a handful of survivors brought back a week or two later by a rescue ship.

"You'll remember," he said impassively, "we were carrying steel—great, blasted billets of it. The day after the gale began to hammer us on the beam, I heard the Old Man say to the mate, 'God help us if that cargo ever shifts. We wouldn't have carried it in those tender 'tweendecks if it had been peacetime.' We waited for the blow to ease but there was no mercy in it and it seemed the ship was taking a list. You couldn't be sure and you kept telling yourself you were imagining it, but anything could have been happening the way we were rolling—long, deep, and slow—with that great heap of metal in our guts.

"When it came it was over so fast you couldn't believe it. I had just come into the companionway under the bridge with a mug-up for the officers when she rolled heavier than before and hung there shuddering. Then all hell broke loose below as the 'tween-decks began to go. She went on her beam-ends as the cargo shifted. I dropped the mugs and froze to the companion rail with both hands as my feet went out from under me.

"Then, believe it or not, sir, I saw the sea move in at the end of the passage where my feet were pointing and it shot me out of the door at the other end like I was a cork in a champagne bottle. Don't remember much after that until they were pouring rum into me in the corvette that picked me up."

★ ★ ★

Fluctuations in Allied fortunes made it difficult for us to project optimism during our talks with the crews. Early on we had used General Wavell's brilliant campaign in North Africa as an example of what was possible where there was a will to win. If, with his thin resources, he had been able to drive a superior force of Italians out of Cyrenaica, we argued, what would he be capable of when he was re-equipped with the tanks and planes the Merchant Navy was getting to him! Certainly it would shorten the days before the Atlantic was again open to ships of every flag.

But in March, 1941, Germany's new general in Africa, Rommel, shredded our talking point almost as badly as he did the Allied desert forces. Large quantities of arms and munitions, delivered by the Merchant Navy at great cost, fell into enemy hands. Not until an Allied counter-offensive was launched in June could hope again be fanned in the men who were doing the re-arming. But the offensive stalled, and with it our attempts at boosting morale.

Compensating for the bad news from practically everywhere else was the good news developing in Washington. President Roosevelt's increasingly open support of the Allies was taking practical shape.

Feeling our way down harbour one misty morning we were confronted by a dim silhouette that hadn't been there the night before. I hadn't seen one like it since the First War, but there was no mistaking the U.S. four stacker! Roosevelt's exchange of fifty overage destroyers for Newfoundland bases had already been publicized but to actually see one, guns at the ready, was electrifying. When the mist rose, we saw the lower harbour crowded with the precious escorts.

Modern American destroyers were also accompanying the convoys. This toyed with the rules of the game, it was true. They were there, Washington claimed, to keep a protective eye on any U.S. merchant vessel that happened to be handy to a convoy, and were prepared to attack anything that threatened it. Germany's tolerance of such carryings-on would end soon. An open declaration of war would bring with it the full force of the U.S. Navy to ease the burden under which the Royal Navy, Canada's navy, and their allies were staggering.

The Naval Control Officer at Halifax hurriedly found office space for a pair of U.S. naval observers. On December 7, 1941, I stuck my head in the Americans' door to have a word with Lt. Commander Stanley, whose interest in the Boarding Service frequently brought us together. He and his captain were crouched over their radio.

"It's a gag," insisted Stanley angrily. "More of that crazy War of the Worlds stuff."

"I hope to God you're right," answered his iron-faced superior.

Stanley saw me and explained. "Some cockeyed broadcast about the Japanese bombing Pearl Harbor."

The weeks that followed were nerve-wracking. Instead of our receiving massive support from the U.S. Atlantic fleet, ship after ship that had been helping under one pretext or another was withdrawn through the Panama Canal to bolster the Pacific fleet decimated by the Pearl Harbor disaster. On top of these setbacks came the destruction of the Canadian battalions in Hong Kong and the beginnings of the swift Japanese conquest of other bastions in the Far East—the Philippines, the Dutch East Indies, Malaysia, Burma.

A month after Pearl Harbor the awaited blow fell in the Atlantic. The British freighter *Cyclops* was torpedoed only 160 miles away from Halifax. By January, 1942, thirty-nine ships had been sunk along the North American coast, many of them within sight of land. A large force of U-boats, operating almost at will in the thinly protected waters, made the previously safe passage from the Caribbean oil fields to Halifax a thing of flaming horror. Tankers became torches thrown contemptuously on our doorstep. The charred stern half of the British tanker *Kars* was towed to the inner end of McNab's Island and beached. There she lay until war's end, a melancholy monument to the crew who had died in her within sight of Sambro Head.

It was at this time that my request that small parties of boarders be given practical convoy experience was granted. Winter's paralyzing grip on the St. Lawrence made it possible. Sealing off Montreal, it caused Halifax to become the assembly point for slow convoys until the next open season. The idled Montreal and Sydney parties returned to help handle the increased Halifax traffic and, combined with the men already on the scene, they formed a force large enough to allow overdue leaves to be taken, and make possible the program of seagoing experience.

Headquarters authorized an advance group of one officer and two ratings, specifying that I should be the officer. We were to be routed to Liverpool, major terminus of the transatlantic convoys and of the other maritime lifelines between Britain and her farflung battlelines. Liverpool's NCSO was asked to arrange return passage for us in an appropriate merchantman.

I had no difficulty in making my initial choice of a travelling companion—though it would have been interesting to have watched Oxner's reaction had I suggested that he wait for a later expedition. Since an engine room rating was to be included, Beaman would have been my second choice, but risking two such valuable hands at once seemed unwise. Oxner agreed that H.H. "Rocky" Wolfe, Stoker First Class, would be a good second pick. Built like a hogshead and sporting a knife scar from his rum-running days, Wolfe had experience as a trade unionist.

On February 13, 1942, we boarded the motor tanker *Andrea Brovig*, this time bringing our seabags along. Instead of watching HX 175 lose itself in the haze off Sambro, we watched the Head and Halifax fade astern.

I already knew Captain Pedersen and his scrupulously maintained Norwegian tanker, and blessed Banyard for his choice of her for our voyage. She was a new ship and her accommodation was planned to keep her crew happy during long charters which could last for up to a couple of years. Her bridge structure contained not only the captain's quarters, but an owner's suite as well. Complete with potted plants, the latter could have looked the Ritz in the eye without flinching. When I was told it was mine, I felt like I was launched on a luxury cruise instead of a survival course.

Pedersen, in his late fifties, was a heavily built man who exuded firm authority. I never once heard him raise his voice, yet his crew always responded to orders with alacrity. Most had grown up within the Brovig company. Respect for the seagoing profession and for one another was bred in them.

For twenty-four hours we newcomers were clearly there on approval, and were treated hospitably but with watchful reserve. But by the end of that time, we had been accepted as shipmates. Oxner and Wolfe, delighted to find themselves in a spotless fo'c's'le, had assumed regular watches on the gun platform—a more than perfunctory duty once we were into the danger zone that began at the Halifax gate ships. Within a couple of days, Oxner's offer to also stand his trick at the wheel was taken up and Wolfe was making himself useful in the engine room. As part of the ship's team they escaped being regarded as observers—and were better observers because of it.

We met in my quarters at the start of each day to compare notes, not simply on the life and conduct of the *Andrea Brovig*, but on everything that we saw happen in the convoy. The undue smoking of inefficient stokeholds, the unbelievable distances light carried at night because of faulty blackout baffles, the garbage tossed overside to offer hunting U-boats a trail to follow—all were hazards we were experiencing first-hand after lecturing crews in Halifax about them for months. Our present direct involvement would add credence to future briefings. It also set our minds working on possible improvements to the security regulations.

When I asked Captain Pedersen if there was some practical task to which I could be assigned, he smiled and said, "Yes, you can provide company for a lonely man. Commander Banyard explained why you are on board. Just make yourself at home."

The hours I spent with Pedersen, both on the bridge and at meals in his cabin, allowed me a close-up view of a master mariner going about his everyday business in wartime.

In one respect I would have preferred a less admirable man in a less well-found ship. It was unlikely that the *Andrea Brovig* would ever be a source of trouble in a Canadian port, and her captain was typical of the inner core of dedicated seamen around whom the weaker strands of the profession are woven. Thoroughly seasoned in all aspects of his craft, from the traditional to the most up-to-date, he was also well-read, thoughtful and articulate. When he learned of the narrative poem I was trying to write, he asked if he might see what I already had. From then on he was not only a useful critic but an inspiration. Each forenoon watch, as long as there was nothing untoward happening in the convoy, we would have coffee in his cabin and go over what I had written during the previous twenty-four hours.

In the two years during which the poem took shape, this was the most productive period. Not only was I free to indulge the writing urge when it came, but I was no longer totally dependent on experiencing the subject through the senses of others.

One time I never put pen to paper was the hour preceding sunset. The gray of the surrounding ships would begin to blur against the black of the Atlantic. If there were U-boats shadowing, they could use the cover of gathering darkness to close. I spent this time on the bridge. Pedersen appreciated my company and in the event of an attack it was the place to be. More importantly, the bridge was the place where I could best confront the fear that unvariably took hold of me at this ominous hour.

As the light drained from the sickly horizon, my courage seemed to retreat with it. I had an insistent urge to seek refuge in the owner's suite, where there was a reassuring sense of order amid handsome fittings, and photos of my wife and boys smiled their encouragement; where there was nothing of the darkening menace outside. In the cabin the threat was only half an inch of steel away, but at least it was mercifully unseen.

This uncomfortable self-knowledge made me realize that I had to force myself to stay on the bridge beside the captain, peering into the thickening murk until the blue pinpoint of sternlight on the vessel ahead was our last link with the visible world. Total darkness ended the fear. Whatever it hid was as perilous as ever, but my instinct to retreat to the false security of the cabin was under control.

All of Pedersen's officers had grown up in the company and many were like members of his family. The fact that even the Chief Officer, when he came to speak to the captain in his cabin, did so from the far side of the coaming and with cap in hand, didn't alter the essential intimacy of the relationship. It was the same on the bridge. Discussions over a chart or a visual signal from the Commodore were unforced and natural. Yet the officer of the watch was always respectfully aware of the authoritative presence of the man who, eighteen hours a day, stood beside him at the wheel or sat with one leg propped on the chartroom table in the shadows just behind him.

The captain needed to take the weight from his leg because of painful circulatory trouble. The ship's owners had suggested he take up duties ashore, where he was genuinely needed, but Pedersen was respected enough to win support for his argument that he had more to give afloat. The pain in his leg, he reasoned, was really a seagoing advantage. It kept him wakeful much of the time—which, after all, he needed to be.

War had scattered Captain Pedersen's family, leaving him in a state of emotional suspension which seldom failed to touch our conversations. He told me his eldest son had recently escaped Norway in a fishing boat and was now serving as engineer officer in a lend-lease four-stacker manned by his country's government-in-exile. His wife and younger son were still in enemy hands.

"I worry more about the youngster than I do about the one at sea," he said. "The one may die for what we both believe in but it is wrong ideas that frighten me, not torpedoes. The young are so susceptible to ideas! All those young Germans—. My boy is only fourteen and it's two years since I've been able to talk to him."

The fact that I had a Norwegian-Canadian wife and a sixteen-year-old son named Erik unquestionably worked in my favour, but I like to think that my rewarding relationship with Pedersen would have developed in any case.

Our morning sessions over the latest rough of my poem were animated by his trenchant criticism, and led to close examination of convoy procedures, crew issues, the use of special gear issued for a ship's protection, and other topics I was on board to explore. The very proximity of the action going on around us as we talked gave substance to our discussions—and to the verse.

On one occasion my literary advisor proved less than infallible when he took issue with a new passage I had submitted.

"Too sentimental," he pronounced. "No mature shipmaster would express himself so."

I accepted the verdict, but with a half concealed grin.

"You are not convinced?" Pedersen challenged.

"I'm just trying to get my bearings," I explained. "What I just read you is almost word for word what you said on the bridge yesterday."

The captain frowned and I suffered a bad moment or two. But his innate good grace won out, and he acknowledged the point with a smile.

★ ★ ★

The weather our convoy faced was not overly bad, considering the time of year. We were almost equally fortunate in evading the silent threat beneath the ocean's surface. Not until we were three days out from Ireland was there evidence of the enemy's presence. As darkness fell, we heard the sound, a couple of miles off, of a depth-charge attack by an escorting destroyer. The next two days were punctuated by the thump of further explosions. From our position at the centre of the convoy, we couldn't tell what was happening on its fringes, but we were more sharply alerted as, an hour before daylight on February 25, the underwater reverberations were joined by the flash and crack of gunfire. In spite of these skirmishes, the convoy was still intact when, next day, it broke into sections and headed, under aircover, for various destinations.

We made several abrupt changes of course during those few days, and I became aware of just how ponderously a tanker moved in evasive action, of how big a broadside it presented to enemy fire. My previous naval experience had been in agile, speedy warcraft, and the turning circle of the *Andrea Brovig* had a nightmarish deliberation. I was thankful she was carrying bunker oil and not high test aviation fuel, though my sympathy deepened for the men whose ships did carry highly volatile cargo.

Andrea Brovig was originally routed to the Clyde, but Pedersen found himself decoding a signal that sent him northward through the Minches, en route to Scapa Flow to fuel the fleet anchored there. At Loch Ewe, a lonely Scottish coastal convoy assembly port, he dropped anchor long enough to be picked up by a coastal escort and to land his supercargo.

When a drifter came alongside to take us ashore and Oxner and Wolfe had been jovially seen over the side by their shipmates of the past two weeks, the captain walked with me to the sideladder in a silence I had no wish to interrupt. We had said all that two men who had found friendship needed to say. At the break in the rail we shook hands. Pedersen regarded me steadily, as he might one of his own under-officers.

"God bless you," he said.

We never met again. The *Andrea Brovig* was sunk that spring in the Caribbean, fortunately without loss of any of our friends. Pedersen accepted a shore job and our contact was reduced to greetings carried by masters with whom we both had business. But to this day, I have only to read the passages of *Who Dare To Live* that are pure Pedersen to restore the gift of his companionship.

★ ★ ★

Aultbea, where the drifter landed us, was an obscure fishing port to which war had brought the bustle of a naval base.

To this could be attributed the attention it received from hostile bombers that otherwise would have passed it by.

Its NCSO was a bearded Royal Navy commander whose staff gave forth with yarns about the many brilliant eccentricities which had stood between him and the Admirals' List. One had to do with his allegedly having kicked in the bass drum at a Salvation Army meeting, and pleading in self-defence that he had suffered temporary religious fanaticism!

There was suspicion that his act had sprung from musical rather than religious passions: he was an accomplished flautist, who made his own instruments. The gift was encouraged at Aultbea since one of NCSO's duties was to distribute anti-aircraft kites to the merchant ships. These great toys, flown from a vessel's mainmast on a strong wire, were supposed to cut the wings off anything making a low-level air attack. Their bamboo frames, with struts just the right diameter for flutemaking, had aroused both the craftsman and the musician in the NCSO. The unremitting moan of wind that swept between Loch Ewe's crags was frequently sweetened by passages of Mozart drifting from his office.

The NCSO's cultural interests were not allowed to overshadow our discussion of Trade Division business during the two days before a staff car carried us across the wildly beautiful Highlands to Auchnasheen, the nearest railway point. Arriving in Gourock, on the Clyde, we found that its NCSO had been well briefed by Aultbea. The great Scottish waterway, birthplace of the *Queens*, Mary and Elizabeth, was well acquainted with crew trouble; our experience of it was thoroughly plumbed before we were routed overland to Liverpool.

Not only was Liverpool the port most closely linked with Halifax; it was the terminus of most of the North Atlantic convoy movements. Troops, munitions and supplies moved in and out of the Mersey's broad stream and crowded her docks in endless parade. Here, too, was the headquarters of the Commander in Chief, Western Approaches—the man responsible for the entire Battle of the Atlantic. His fleet of overworked warships slipped in and out with the merchantmen, whose vital work they made possible.

Liverpool was hurting and drab from heavy bombing and the snow that covered its battered buildings was soot-stained. But behind the blackout curtains were bright rooms filled with dedicated men and women. Nowhere was this more evident than in the Liver Building, dominating the waterfront and housing NCSO. Here a remarkable Royal Navy Reserve lieutenant commander took us in hand.

His name was Rankin. He had duties in NCS commensurate with the gold braid on his sleeve, and made himself useful in uncounted other ways. A well-to-do businessman in peacetime, he took personal care of the convoy commodores. After their glowing accounts of Rankin's thoughtfulness, I greeted him as a friend from the first.

Rankin was well aware of our mission in Liverpool. He'd been alerted by Halifax, Aultbea and Gourock; but more important was his own concern for the morale issue. His knowledge of our Boarding Service was already established through daily dealings with shipmasters who had sailed from Canadian ports. Apparently tireless and always cheerful, he supplied Oxner and Wolfe with the necessary credentials for free movement through dockland and the ships alongside. Then he began piloting me through a series of offices, starting with that of Rear Admiral Ritchie, the Flag Officer in Command.

At convoy conferences and in discussion with the men behind the great movements originating in Liverpool, I was given in two days what no reading of reports could have communicated in a month. It was, moreover, a two way exchange.

Canada had managed to coordinate its merchant navy morale-building and disciplinary measures more successfully than the U.K. had done; this was acknowledged in practically every discussion. Lacking any counterpart to the Merchant Seamen Order, disciplinary action in Britain was supported only by the civil courts, with wide divergences in the quality of justice. Inconsistencies abounded. What could be expected of a Glasgow magistrate might be quite different from what officials in Newcastle would do. And there was a tendency toward extremes. In the matter of seamen's welfare, the agencies involved lacked overall coordination and tended to be competitive.

Many officers with whom I spoke were in favour of simplifying the approach to crew trouble by putting the merchant navy under regular naval discipline. The situation had reached such a critical point, they argued, that there was no time to create a system like the Canadian one. They admitted, however, that the likelihood of their government's accepting their solution was slight.

Expecting each morning to be alerted to the ship chosen for our return passage, we suddenly found events taking an unexpected turn. Rankin informed me that Admiral Ritchie had decided we should visit London before we left for home. He was sure Oxner and Wolfe could usefully duplicate along the Thames the useful days they had been spending along the Mersey. He felt, too, that I should bring my story at first hand to someone of sufficient rank at Admiralty.

"So," announced Rankin, looking very pleased, "you have an appointment with the Deputy Director of Naval Intelligence next Tuesday."

This was exciting but it raised a question.

"Why not Trade Division?"

"That would be the natural place to route you," admitted Rankin, "but I'm sure the Admiral has his reasons for doing it this way. He has probably recalled the rave notices about NBS that Admiral Godfrey distributed when he was DNI. Godfrey has gone to another appointment but Intelligence will still be well briefed on you. Doubtless DDNI will pass you along to Trade Division when he's through with you."

A sudden hope took hold of me.

"Could he introduce me to Charlie Jarman?"

This was one man I had been anxious to meet for more than a year. Jarman was secretary of the National Union of Seamen, the body that represented the greatest number of sailors with whom we dealt. His officials in America and his ships' delegates had always shown superior leadership, and not a few of them had told me, "I'll take that up with Charlie," or "You and Charlie Jarman would see eye to eye on *that*. You should get together."

Rankin, quick to appreciate my eagerness, smiled.

"Meeting Jarman should be no problem with the right man opening the door. DDNI is one of the right men."

Admiralty, as I crossed its ancient courtyard, was holy ground. My boyhood heroes—Drake, Nelson, Franklin, Scott—seemed to hover at my elbow as I passed deep into its creaking corridors and found the office where DDNI awaited me.

The Deputy turned out to be a Royal Navy captain of the type disgruntled Colonials claimed was standard for the breed—fearless, fastidious and frigid. Having served a couple of First War years in the RN, I knew the generalization was unjust. My experience had been that inside even the most arrogant senior officer there had usually been a human being. I was prepared to give the unsmiling man who received me the benefit of the doubt.

He remained seated as he acknowledged my entrance. His offer of a chair was icily patronizing. However, I had been treated with as little initial friendliness by a number of merchant captains and was undismayed.

"Well," he said abruptly, "what do you wish to do in London?"

I told him how keen I was to meet Jarman, explaining how important it would be to Canadian rapport with the merchant seamen.

When I had finished he said, "I can't see that any useful purpose can be served by what you have in mind."

"But, sir—" I gasped, unable to believe I had heard him correctly.

"Good day." He dismissed me, turning his attention to the papers on his desk.

With one stroke he had cut the "Service channels" on which I was dependent for everything I had hoped to accomplish in London.

15

Derby House

I wandered down Whitehall, filled with my own disappointment and scarcely seeing the faces of the Londoners I passed. They might have been reflections of my own, except that their distress was caused by the loss that day of Singapore—which Whitehall had long assured them was impregnable.

I turned into the sanctuary of Westminster Abbey. Near Poets' Corner I discovered a small and ancient chapel. It was untenanted, but tapers were burning on the altar. I sat for a while on one of the rush-bottomed chairs, and finally I knelt at the rail.

In that chapel, a name entered my mind and stayed there. I left the Abbey and stopped at the first pay phone. It was several years since I had been in touch with George Light, who I had met at a Moral Re-Armament assembly in London in 1937, but I had reason to hope he would still be active in labour circles. The stuff that had made him a leader of the unemployed during the Depression was not likely to have diminished in his country's present crisis.

He was in town and, shortly, on the line.

"What in the world are you doing here?" he exclaimed.

"I've come for a talk with Charlie Jarman," I explained.

"Good man!" said George. "When?"

"That's for you to say," I answered, and told him my story.

"Let's have lunch tomorrow," suggested Light.

By wartime standards it was a good lunch, but George Light's news was better: Jarman had scheduled me a fifteen-minute interview the following week. Confident that Liverpool would authorize my remaining in England long enough to keep the date, I accepted it. I was due to return to the Mersey and a security conference chaired by Vice Admiral Osborne.

As I had anticipated, Liverpool was as anxious as I that the meeting with Jarman should take place and extended our U.K. stay to make it possible. That, in turn, led to more unexpected events.

It started with Ridley Weymouth, a Royal Navy commander and signals specialist I had known in peacetime. He was now Staff Officer, Signals, for the Commander in Chief, Western Approaches. We had dinner and talked shop for as long as he could absent himself from his demanding post, then we agreed to dine again two days later if circumstances allowed.

This time he brought along a colleague who wore the same wavy gold stripes I did, with the addition of shoulder fittings for a flag lieutenant's aeglettes. He was, he confessed, "flags" to Admiral Sir Percy Noble. Guy Welby had been a fashionable London jeweller before the war. He had the relaxed manner of one whose social world had no ceiling.

But Welby was not interested in Burke's Peerage on this particular evening. He wanted to talk about the Canadian boarding service and its relationship to the morale of merchant seamen. Sir Percy, he explained, was worried about the suborning of those who laboured in the cargo carriers and along the docks. Totally responsible for the

Battle of the Atlantic, Noble was sharply aware that erosion at the civilian base of his military operations could impair them as fatally as enemy action could. Welby was certain Noble would be interested in the Canadian experience; He intended to discuss the details with him when the opportunity arose.

"Why not let the Commander in Chief get these stories first hand?" suggested Weymouth.

The flag lieutenant was thoughtful.

"Sir Percy sees practically no one except the convoy commodores these days," he said, "but why not? I'll try him out with that story about Oxner and see what happens. Wouldn't be surprised if he let me slip you in for five minutes or so. Don't tie yourself up for tomorrow morning."

Rankin, still enthusiastically filling my days with appointments, cancelled those for next morning even before there was word from Welby.

"We've got to be ready to jump as long as *this* possibility exists," he declared. "Commander in Chief has been known to keep flag officers waiting, cap in hand, for days. I've a staff car on standby in case it comes off."

Welby's call proved the wisdom of Rankin's state of alert.

"You've got twenty minutes to get here and five minutes to spend with him!"

Rankin, shoving me into the car, said, "I'm counting on you to tell me what it looks like in Derby House. Cracking the Bank of England should be a cinch for you after this."

Derby House, headquarters for Western Approaches, was an ordinary enough business block from the outside, but became more interesting as you penetrated its closely guarded interior. Eventually, I found myself with Welby in a huge underground operations room at least two storeys high. One wall was occupied by a magnetic chart of the Atlantic on which, under the guidance of Wren officers, models of convoys, escorts, hunting groups, air cover and U-boats were in constant movement in response to wireless signals taken from adjacent alcoves.

High on the opposite wall a large picture window faced

the chart and behind it sat a graying but still youthful man in the uniform of a full admiral. Even at a distance, I could sense the naturalness with which he wore his authority. Except for one brief phone call, his eyes stayed steadily on the battle model, representing the tens of thousands of men and the millions of tons of shipping under his direction.

Welby, glancing at his wrist watch like a race timer, announced, "Five minutes to go." The wait was long enough for the jitters to get to me and when he finally ordered, "Come along," I was in bad shape. Climbing the narrow stairs to the eagle's nest did nothing to ease my apprehension. Welby, noticing my nervousness, became a bit tight-lipped himself.

Courteously but crisply, Sir Percy offered me a chair.

"Welby tells me you have had some experience with trouble on the waterfront," he advanced.

My carefully rehearsed rundown evaporated. Stumbling and incoherent, I was close to panic within thirty seconds. The admiral gave Welby an edged, quizzical glance, then excused himself to follow something that had happened on the giant chart. It gave me a couple of minutes to recover and by the time he directed his attention my way again I had remembered an anecdote Welby had said would definitely interest him.

It was hard to tell how I was doing, for Noble's eyes were more frequently on the operations plot than on me, but when I had finished he said, "Good. How is your relationship with the longshoremen?"

I was pleased to be able to tell him they were harmonious. We had had some trouble in Halifax, where the boarding parties had encountered carelessness regarding fire regulations on the part of some of the men who worked the cargoes, but the incident had taken me to Jimmy Campbell, leader of their union, and his door had always been open after our first talk. This was a handy illustration of the new cooperation being fostered by the Boarding Service and Sir Percy began giving me almost his full attention.

Finally he rose and, rising with him, I awaited dismissal. Instead, however, he suggested it was time for a cup of tea; that we could talk with fewer diversions in his apartment. On the way to the elevator he paused at the office of his Chief of Staff and invited him to join us. The lift carried us to the top of Derby House.

The Chief of Staff, Commodore Mansfield, was another link in my chain of lucky breaks. He quickly recognized me as the author of a set of jingles that had recently been finding their way into several naval publications. Written originally for our merchant navy audience in the hope of getting across in verse what sometimes grated in prose, they had reached Mansfield by way of his old shipmate, Captain Brand. The Commodore had had them printed in the Western Approaches Bulletin and promptly recited his favourite:

> "Ole Cap Cole was a merry old soul
> And a merry old soul stayed he;
> For the only time he would call for his bowl
> Was when he was in from sea."

For at least half an hour I tried to give these two leaders a detailed, low-level view of the fo'c's'le and dockside, and to suggest anything which, demonstrated there, might strengthen the war effort. The questions they asked were brief and incisive. There was no suggestion that they came from questioners who thought they already knew the answers. In most instances I had a practical case history for the point raised. Their gifts as listeners cut through my nervous awareness of rank, to the point that I had a sudden fear I was monopolizing the conversation. This faded as I realized that I was at centre stage because that was where they wanted me. The information and ideas they extracted came readily and with as much accuracy as I was capable of.

There was no abrupt termination of the interview. Unhurriedly, Sir Percy finished his second cup of tea, sighed and suggested that we had all better get back to our jobs. We descended to Derby House's depths, where he thanked me and returned me to Welby.

My hosts at the Liver Building, obviously delighted by the Derby House development, were equally happy about the forthcoming appointment with Jarman. Influenced by

Rocky's familiarity with trade union offices, they advised me to take him along. On the train to London the two of us carefully plotted the details of what we would attempt to cover in the fifteen minutes granted us.

Clapham Common, on which faced the offices of the National Union of Seamen, was about as salty as Queen's Park, Toronto. The promise of spring was evident in its flowerbeds. There was comparative relief from the roar of the city's traffic, and the man to whom we were led seemed completely at home in the setting. Jarman had some of the ruggedness one might have expected of the boss of the largest group of merchant seamen in the world; but his features were notable for their openness, and there was a quietness in the way he spoke.

Accustomed to dockside labour offices, with the jostling of the rougher elements of the profession and the pervasiveness of marine smells, we were impressed with the orderly atmosphere with which Charles Jarman had surrounded himself. Wolfe, with a heightened pride in his profession, developed a crisper stance. My impression was that Jarman had the same gift as Admiral Noble for encouraging a man to assume his best trim.

I gave him a quick sketch of our job and the reason we had been anxious to meet him. A section of his memory bank clicked into place.

"Ah, yes," he said. "Thompson and some of our people over there have written of you."

He pressed a buzzer, and spoke to his secretary. We were joined by two of his lieutenants and tea was served.

An hour and a half later we excused ourselves. The conversation, under the encouragement of our host, had never lagged. At one stage Charlie (he was happier with that that "Mr. Jarman") phoned introductions to some shipping magnates he felt would be the better for the information and assessments Rocky and I had offered.

The spirit of the Merchant Seamen's Order, the implications of the new manning pools, the possible post-war complications that might accompany the output of Canadian shipyards and training establishments, had all come up for discussion. Jarman had named those of his officials in America with whom, he hoped, I could maintain close touch.

We left thoroughly pleased with the communication we'd achieved.

We were encouraged to remain longer in Britain and to visit other assembly ports, but the second Gatineau Conference was due to begin in Ottawa. We stayed in London just long enough to greet Joe Dwyer, Leading Seaman Wick and one of the ratings who made up the second overseas NBS party. We briefed them on the ground we had covered. Some of it could be usefully retraced, and new opportunities were pointed out.

Back in Liverpool, as a final goodwill offering, Oxner and Wolfe were given a tour of Derby House by Commander Weymouth. Rankin sent me with his wife to see a young ballerina named Fonteyn who was bringing colour to the drab and battered city. Then, in the shadow of the Liver Building, we boarded the British factory ship *Sourabaya*, Halifax-bound.

The big vessel, still pervaded by the rancid smell of the mountains of whale blubber that had until recently come over her open stern, was British in name only. Her dour captain was Norwegian, as were most of the crew. On eastbound voyages her storage tanks, once filled with whale oil, carried less aromatic petroleum from Lake Maracaibo and other South American fields. What made her doubly useful now was her extensive crew accommodation.

The *Sourabaya* was bringing out crews for three new ships being completed in Canada. We had an opportunity to study the merchant navy in an inactive state.

Oxner and Wolfe, living among the three ships' companies, spotted the emergence of leadership in each group. Some of it was good, and some bad—with the bad, as usual, the more vigorous and articulate. The situation, of course, favoured negative influences. A hundred seamen with absolutely nothing to do for two weeks presented fallow ground for troublemakers.

We also gained useful convoy experience. A submarine attack was repelled off the north of Ireland, but later, in 41 west, the *Imperial Transport* was torpedoed. The victim, a tanker riding light, was on our starboard quarter—like ourselves occupying an inside position. Yet despite our proximity, the blackness of midnight prevented our seeing what happened after the explosion. All we knew for sure was that the tanker was missing when the bleak light of dawn filtered over the Atlantic.

Had we had night vision, we would have seen one of the merriest men in the RCNR winning himself a Distinguished Service Cross. Lieutenant Commander George Stephens brought his corvette in close enough to determine that *Imperial Transport* still had sufficient unholed tanks to keep her afloat. Passing a line, he took her in tow. By daylight, he and the *Transport* had the ocean to themselves. Stephens dragged the cripple across the rest of the perilous course to a Canadian drydock which, in time, returned her to the Battle.

16

"the eye of the whirlwind..."

The *Sourabaya* was still feeling her way towards a harbour anchorage when Jack Conkey's launch bumped alongside to take us ashore. Heading for the Yard, he laughed, "You certainly picked the right time to be out of the country. If you'd been home you'd have been accused of running an election campaign."

What he was getting at came quickly when Banyard, after greeting me, produced copies of three memoranda.

The first, dated the day I had left for England, was from Brand to the NCSOs:

> "In surveying the year's work I have noted the very considerable assistance the work of the boarding parties has been, not only to this Department, but to the whole war effort as well. I would like you to pass on to all the officers and men comprising the Boarding Service my appreciation of their faithful and untiring work. Not only have they made a substantial improvement to the morale of all seamen landing at your port, the boarding form has been invaluable to us."

Giving specific examples of how the forms had been the starting places for corrective Headquarters action, he continued:

> "The boarding form was enthusiastically received by a number of senior officers of Admiralty on their visits to Headquarters and, as a result, this system has been recommended by Admiralty for use throughout the world."

Apparently sensing what was in the wind, NCSO, Sydney, acknowledging the memorandum, had commented:

> "While it is fully understood that the morale idea originated in Halifax.... and while the closest cooperation and exchange of information between the various parties is essential, no one of these officers should be placed in a position whereby he can dictate policy or issue orders to boarding officers and crews in another port."

This hadn't headed off what Headquarters had in mind. On March 6, the Secretary of the Naval Board had sent this message to the Commanding Officer, Atlantic Coast:

> "It is suggested for consideration that Lieutenant Watt should be appointed directly to your staff rather than under NCSO, Halifax, so that he would be in a better position to coordinate the work of NBS throughout your entire command and would thus be in a position to oversee ratings employed in the NBS at Sydney and elsewhere. Your remarks are requested."

The knowledge that one word, "Concur", penned on the memorandum by Admiral Jones, would end the subtle handicap that had accompanied me on my visits to the ports beyond Halifax, was heady stuff.

"Perfect!" I exclaimed.

"I don't think so," said Banyard.

"But—?"

"You belong on my staff," he said firmly. "I need you there and it will be the best thing for the Service. I have put that as strongly as I can to the Admiral. However, the final decision will be made at Headquarters when we go up next week to the Gatineau Conference. Captain Brand would like you to come along again this year."

Whatever *his* reasoning, Admiral Jones failed to concur. Whatever *its* reasoning, Naval Board decided not to press its suggestion further. I returned from Ottawa in the same appointment I had carried there.

Across four decades it would be difficult to trust to memory the emotions that accompanied me to Halifax, but fortunately my wife retained the letter in which I attempted to record them:

> "I think Banyard was wrong and unfair—not so much to me as to Trade Division, including his own branch of it, but that is no reason for my failing to serve him to the best of my ability as long as he remains my NCSO."

Shortly after my return, Admiral Jones dropped into my office to congratulate me on having been promoted to lieutenant commander at a time of year when promotions were not usually made. Smiling crookedly he said, "Should have happened long ago," and left as abruptly as he had appeared.

At the Gatineau Conference, NBS itself was fully recognized. Its first authorized complement of fourteen officers and seventy ratings was approved. St. John's and the port of Quebec had been added to the list for active servicing. I was also told to hold myself in readiness for another survey of the West Coast situation.

My stiff-upper-lip relationship with Banyard was a far cry from the one I had enjoyed with Dick Oland, but I found a useful outlet in the work I did on my narrative poem. In that summer of 1942, as the Battle of the Atlantic moved towards the climax of its blackest year, the poem was reaching completion.

Three people shared its progress. Joe Dwyer, who had once urged me to stay with it, was one. The others were Commander Peter Gow and his wife, Jean.

The Gows had been friends since the carefree days of

the early Twenties when, with others like Dick Oland, they had been part of the tightly knit naval establishment at Esquimalt, B.C. Nearly two decades later, their apartment in Halifax was a snug harbour for a weatherbeaten boarding officer turned after-hours poet. Peter had a keen literary mind, and Jean was a writer and artist who had worked for Macmillan Publishing. Both were stimulating listeners and critics.

Jean voluntarily tackled a problem I had not considered—what to do with the poem when the last line had been written. She asked if she might have samples to get a reaction from Macmillan's.

When it came, the response was highly encouraging. Their reader had recommended the work, provided the whole lived up to the parts he had seen. Unknown to us at the time, the reader was E.J. Pratt, the noted Canadian poet.

Following on the heels of this good news was Joe Dwyer's announcement that he had been appointed to the *Iroquois*, a new Canadian Tribal class destroyer completing in a British yard. Not wanting to lose him, I told Joe I was sure, in view of his now-proven gifts as a boarding officer, that Officer's Appointments could be persuaded to change the assignment. But Joe told me he had requested a seagoing appointment, and that he knew I would understand.

I did understand. But Banyard, equally conscious of Dwyer's value to his staff, was less flexible. He had the seagoing appointment stopped. Joe, however, was a match for him. How he worked it I never knew, but one day he reported to the British destroyer *Veteran* for passage overseas and his berth in *Iroquois*.

Veteran, along with a sister ship, *Vanoc*, sailed from St. John's on September 21 as escorts for the strangest convoy that had ever dared the North Atlantic crossing. It consisted of eight American river boats that had been shored up for passage over seas they had not been built for. Four days out, the first two were torpedoed. *Veteran*, dropping astern, plucked more than seventy-five crewmen from the icy waters. At thirty-eight minutes after midnight, steaming at sixteen knots to overtake the convoy, she was speaking to *Vanoc* when the radioman's earphones suddenly went silent. It was the last anyone heard of *Veteran* until, with the war a memory, the log of *Korvettenkatain* Otto von Buelow of U-404 gave details of the destroyer's sinking.

★ ★ ★

In November, before setting out for my first visit to the boarding party shaking down in St. John's, I dropped in on the Gows. I told them the poem had been accepted for publication, and that I'd received a contract to sign.

The time had come to select a title for it. It was Peter who chose *Who Dare to Live.*

Peter had a further suggestion. He, too, was heading for Newfoundland and there would be an extra seat in the Air Force plane: why not go along with him? But I preferred the opportunity for further time afloat in a combat area, which the entire Eastern seaboard had become.

I was the senior military officer aboard the liner *Fort Amherst.* Shipboard responsibility for its passenger complement of soldiers, airmen and naval reservists on leave was a valuable new experience. On the return passage from St. John's, a hurricane scattered our convoy and I encountered for the first time the uncanny dead space at the eye of the whirlwind.

Emerging from it into the smother again, we heard the distress call of a merchantman not far distant. Unbelievably, a submarine had managed to send a torpedo to its mark, when it should have been deeply submerged, waiting out the tremendous, swells that were clubbing everything on top. There was no hope for the sinking freighter; every other ship in the area was fighting for its life against the elements. Our helplessness in the face of repeated S.O.S. signals was as cruel as the sledgehammer waves thudding against our hull.

Halifax harbour, when at last we reached it, never looked better, but my relief was short-lived. I came ashore to hear that Peter Gow's plane had been lost with all hands. A few days later I said goodbye to a heartbroken Jean as she boarded a train to a less haunted place.

My acute sense of personal loss was complicated by a

growing feeling that such deaths were buying no more than time in a losing struggle. In 1941, forty million tons of cargo had run the North Atlantic gauntlet, enough to keep Britain fighting for her life and to ward off total disaster farther afield. Seventy-five of the merchant ships we had seen on their way had failed to make it, but—painful though the losses had been—they could be tolerated if it meant better times to come.

In 1942 a buildup was envisioned—one that would put the Allies on the offensive. But that dream faded in the harsh reality of a calamitous year. At a cost of twice as many ships—one hundred and forty nine of them—the supplies reaching the other side had actually dwindled to five million fewer tons than in 1941.

There could only be one conclusion to a battle that exacted such a price. If it continued much longer, no miracle of the spirit could be expected to indefinitely survive the physical toll.

True, there was some promise of relief. Escorts were more numerous and coastal convoys replaced independent sailings along the North American rim and reduced some of the carnage there. Very Long Range aircraft were thrusting out from both sides of the Atlantic to shrink the size of the killing ground between.

In spite of these improvements the wolf packs, increased in strength and range, were striking almost at will in mid-ocean.

The unbroken intensity of the ordeal, which had deepened with the Pearl Harbor disaster, tested to the limit human fortitude that had once seemed unexhaustible. The day I was sent to bring ashore the master of a British freighter who had cracked up on the western passage is burned into my memory.

"It's a bad one," Banyard told me. "The captain went so crazy on the bottle halfway across that the mate had to take command after he and the chief engineer decided there was no other choice. This will finish the master. The owners have instructed their agent to remove him but he won't leave—says he'll knock off anyone who tries to take his ship from him. He's anchored near George's Island. Get him ashore quietly. We don't want the story to get to the press."

Even in peacetime a ship's master usually has a weapon in his cabin. Such things as sub-machine guns had become common with the war. For the first time since I had joined Naval Control, I belted on a revolver and took a picked, armed crew with me when I shoved off for the freighter.

This method of handling things went against my instinct and experience. The example of unarmed and effective London bobbies had always appealed to me. So far, our version of this had paid off. The lone pistol that usually went aboard ships with our inspection parties was carried by the leading hand, and had never been needed except for show. On the rare occasions we'd encountered physical resistance, the unarmed boarders had been quite up to meeting the demands of the situation.

Judging by the agent's report, however, the holed-up shipmaster presented a serious danger.

Between shore and ship I realized that the gun I carried might be a liability, rather than an asset. It was creating certain expectations, far out of line with those I'd previously carried with me into trouble spots.

I made my decision.

Before boarding I unbuckled the holster and left the weapon in the launch. I left the ratings there too. I told them to lose no time in covering me if they heard any shots from the vessel.

The mate and chief engineer met me at the gangway. They seemed to be under great strain—but they also expressed sadness at the situation.

"Never sailed with a finer man," said the Chief. "Not much of a one for the bottle either, but suddenly in mid-ocean, he comes storming out of his cabin like a maniac. Damning and blasting everyone from Hitler to the King to the cabinboy. The mate and I got him back behind his own door, but there was no choice except to take over from him. He's been raving away in there ever since. The steward's been leaving food outside his door and he's been picking it up in the night—like some hunted animal. Man, it would break your heart if you knew him as well as we do."

"How has he been since the agent was on board?"

"He might be dead for all the sound he's made," said the Mate. The man's expression was tragic. "God knows I've always wanted my own command, but not this way."

The captain's cabin was on the upper deck under the bridge and its door stared at the end of the companionway from which the other officers' accommodation opened. Moving cautiously down the dimly lit passage, I made myself as slim a target as possible.

I tried to make my rap on the door sound friendly, but it seemed hollow and menacing, and brought no response. After about sixty silent seconds I knocked again. This time there was a faint stirring inside and a hoarse voice demanded to know who the hell was there.

I told him my name.

Again there was a long silence; then, "What do you want?"

"I understand you have some business ashore, captain," I said. "I'm heading for King's Wharf. Could I give you a lift?"

The silence stretched even longer this time. I was about to rap again when the master's voice halted my raised knuckles.

"That's good of you. If you can wait little, I'll be along."

It was more than "a little" before the door opened, but I waited patiently. The middle-aged mariner who eventually appeared was fresh-shaven and his packed bags stood behind him. The ravages of the past few days marked his features, but I thought I could recognize the man of whom the Chief and the Mate had spoken with such affection and respect.

"I'm ready," he said, reaching for his bags.

"Let me send a hand for them," I suggested.

At the gangway his officers gathered around him, their faces reflecting the controlled agony of his own. There was a silent shaking of hands; the bos'n, donkeyman, steward and other crewmen on deck joined the lineup. Finally the Chief spoke—with difficulty.

"You understand, don't you?"

"I understand," the master answered.

On the run ashore the men in the launch talked quietly among themselves. At the dock two were quick to take the captain's bags and we walked unhurriedly to the agent's office. There he turned and offered me his hand.

"Thank you," he said, "and goodbye."

★ ★ ★

On one other occasion I carried a gun, and this time it stayed with me to do the job in hand. I needed it to deal with the greatest concentration of hard cases we had ever encountered.

Originally there had been three hundred of them, as unprepossessing a mob as was ever scraped from the British waterfront. They had come to America to crew the trooper *George Washington*, once a large German liner that had been included in the U.S. share of World War I reparations. If the Americans had immediately sailed her to the breaker's yard they would have been ahead of the game. German engineers were the only ones who had ever run her economically.

After being laid up for years she was resurrected by the desperate need for shipping in World War II. The Americans turned her over to the British and she managed to sail to Halifax, where she was filled up with Canadian soldiers. Then her boilers collapsed. The damage was irreparable and *George Washington* was junked.

The need to return her now-surplus crew to England resulted in a secondary disaster. It had been simple enough to bring them out in half-empty westbound troopers, but the same ships heading back to Britain were so tight-packed with military personnel that many were sleeping in the companionways.

Taken ashore until shipboard room could somehow be found for them, the nasty lot of *Washingtonians* became nastier still. Denied the immediate repatriation they demanded, the crew wrecked their shore accommodation. Broken up into three groups of a hundred each as a result, they continued to tax the resources of those looking after them. One brilliant plan resulted in a group being shunted to a siding in the Nova Scotia wilderness on board a special train. They simply wrecked the train.

At last a partial solution became available. The trooper *Letitia* was about to sail with a cargo of soldiers from Halifax and room was made for a hundred of the *Washington*'s crew in a lower mess deck. Far from showing gratitude, they protested that the accommodation fell short of their fastidious tastes and continued their riotous ways. Though there were a couple of thousand soldiers fit for battle in the ship, the Army whistled up legalities to prove that the agitating seamen were not *their* pigeons. *Letitia*'s captain insisted that as long as he lay in harbour the troublesome men were not his responsibility.

Since they were not members of *Letitia*'s crew refusing duty, NCSO decided they couldn't be prosecuted under the Merchant Seamen Order. They seemed to slip neatly between the jurisdictions of every authority.

My instructions were limited to supplying NCSO with the latest shipboard word on the mounting debacle. I was not included in the councils of war considering the matter, but my involvement deepened inexorably when I was summoned by Captain Creery, the Admiral's Chief of Staff. He asked if I thought the Boarding Service could do anything about the *Letitia* if given a free hand. I told him I thought we could give it a good try.

"It wouldn't do to have anyone killed," observed Creery.

I sincerely agreed.

"Very well," he said. "We'll be keeping an eye on you. Have a signalman standing by if you need help."

Oxner was on leave, so Leading Seaman Jim Crosson was in charge of the fourteen men we could muster. He was a mature Naval Reservist from the west coast whose trustworthiness and intelligence were well established. Most important, he had a calmness under pressure which was contagious. Our operational plan was clear in our minds as, with the entire party armed, we took off for the troubled liner.

At the gangway the duty officer reported that the bulk of the unwelcome passengers were raising hell in the lower messdeck, but that a strong delegation had just besieged the purser's office to demand a better quantity and quality of soap than had so far been offered them. Considering the state in which they had left all their previous quarters, this sudden passion for cleanliness was touching.

I told Crosson I would take on the purser's callers while he and the party pursued our plan of establishing seaman-to-seaman communication with the *Washingtonians* below. We had settled on a simple theme, which went like this: if the troublemakers were so all-fired anxious to get home, they were damned fools to be tying up the boat that would get them there. We planned to remind them that, while they might not be going first class, they were doing as well as, if not better than, many of their battledressed fellow-passengers.

The last was an implied threat. If there was one thing that seemed to disturb recalcitrant merchant seamen, it was the possibility that misbehaviour might lead to their being conscripted into the army. There had been considerable discussion in the United Kingdom about making such action automatic.

My own negotiations didn't go smoothly. Descending the grand staircase from the upper deck, I found the harrassed purser barricaded behind his wicket, fighting to be heard above the strident shouts of the toughs occupying the flat. Making the tactical error of moving down to the fringe of the crowd before attempting to get some of them into intelligent debate, I not only drew their verbal fire but found myself being jostled.

Breaking free, I managed to make it to the landing halfway up the staircase before turning to face them. By dropping my hand to the butt of my holstered revolver, I managed to produce silence long enough to be heard when I shouted "They tell me you want to get back to Britain."

This produced a loud wave of invective, but gradually there was a suggestion that rationality was winning a tenuous toehold. It became possible to advance the boarding party's argument, but it was hard going. The ringleader of the gang declared—with some accuracy—that I was talking down to them from a high altitude and maintaining my position by force of arms.

How long this went on I was never sure, but the interminable verbal backing and filling suddenly ended with the appearance of a couple of the ringleader's companions from below. Crosson and his boys had done well there. The men on the messdeck had bought the boarders' argument and had decided to withhold their beefs until they were back in England. It took a very short time for the men in the purser's flat to make it unanimous.

★ ★ ★

These minor victories paled in the face of continued reversals at sea. The inexorable working of the law of diminishing returns haunted hours when I should have been sleeping, and incidents by day grated on my nerves.

This became sharply obvious once when I was accompanying the investigator of deliberate sabotage on board a recently completed 10,000-ton freighter. The ship's steering gear had been crippled by the puncturing of a copper pipe deep in her stern, allowing the escape of vital fluid. The site of the damage was accessible only through the long tunnel down which the propeller shaft stretched from the engine-room to its exit through the stern.

There was just room enough for a stooping man to move. I hadn't previously encountered anything quite so confined, or so seemingly endless. But anxiety to get on with the investigation made me forget that I had emerged from a First World War explosion with a bad case of claustrophobia. The passage of years had freed me from its horrors, but I had always avoided situations which might cause any recurrence.

Halfway down the tunnel the unreasoning fear returned, seizing me as abruptly as a pair of hands at my throat. Sweat broke out from every pore and I knew that in another few seconds I would have to smother a scream. Trembling, I leaned against the steel of the shaft, and muttered, "Oh God, oh God."

It was a cry of despair, and of supplication.

Whether I had somehow been heard or not, the attack passed almost as suddenly as it had struck. I was able to move again, and continued towards the site of the sabotage.

Overcoming the phobia was a reassuring experience, but the fact that the attack had happened at all warned me that I walked a narrow line.

17

"Fire!"

Among the officers appointed to the enlarged Naval Boarding Service were several young enough to be reclaimed after seasoning for warship service. We returned none gladly for without exception they learned quickly and served with spirit. As the war went on, however, lieutenants around my own age arrived and, like the older non-commissioned ratings, became the unchanging framework of the force. Most had the stamp of Captain Brand on them. At Headquarters he had the means of spotting particularly well-suited prospects, and took full advantage of this.

Lieutenant Ansten Anstensen, RCNVR, was one of the new officers. The Norwegian-born head of the German department at the University of Saskatchewan was tailor-made for his new duties. He had a background of experience in the training ships of his native land and had worked in a Brooklyn dockyard while financing his academic climb in America. Oxner hailed him with unfeigned respect when he learned that some of Ansten's seagoing experience had been under sail.

A university dropout myself, I at first experienced a bit of nervousness at being responsible for a mature full professor, but I quickly found reason only for gratitude. Ansten gave me a better understanding of why higher education is referred to as a discipline. His teacher's instinct for clearly stating ideas and for drawing the best from lively young men were particularly instructive to me, and our friendship continued until his death forty years later.

Reporting with Anstensen was another of brand's hand-picked and inspired choices—Mate T.L. Arnold, RCNR. Lately of the Merchant Navy, he possessed an austere sense of humour (which was quickly and frequently tested) and his command of his native Dutch added to our ability to communicate with merchant crews.

From the day the first munitions ship had reached Halifax for convoy in 1939, memory of the *Mount Blanc* holocaust of 1917 had spurred the enforcement of strict fire prevention measures aboard ships in harbour. Despite this, fires did break out on vessels with explosive cargoes. Arnold was involved with one of these in an unusual way.

With Wick as his leading seaman, he boarded the British ship *Lautaro* in the Basin, not far from where the *Mont Blanc* explosion had occurred, devastating the city and harbour. Normally *Lautaro* would have been in the special munitions-ship anchorage, since her No. 2 hold was heavy with thousand-pound bombs consigned to the air force overseas. Because the cargo had shifted on her passage from the States, a more sheltered berth had been assigned her until restowage could be accomplished. The upper 'tween-decks of No. 2 were filled with sacked sugar, which was being unloaded into a lighter alongside when Arnold and his party arrived.

He had barely begun conversation with the duty officer when the heartstopping cry of "Fire!" sounded. Stevedores erupted from No. 2 hold faster than the smoke curled skyward. The cargo workers streamed to the sideladder where their launch was secured, their mates on deck at their heels.

As Oxner later described it, "they came down that Jacob's ladder four abreast." With its throttle wide open the packed motorboat headed for the nearest shore.

Arnold didn't wait to see what *Lautaro*'s crew would do. With remarkable speed for men in a strange ship, he and his party rigged a hose, plunged into the hold and directed a column of water at what appeared to be the seat of the blaze. Gradually the smoke thinned. They kept the hose going until the last wisp had dissolved.

The fireboat, Corporal Bryan, and I arrived almost simultaneously in response to a message flashed from the Turple Head signal station. Arnold and his party, sweaty but triumphant, were just climbing out of the hold. Stolidly, he told us what had happened.

I mentally filed the account away as copy for the citation which would go with the decoration the boarding officer would surely be awarded. The men had acted with extreme courage. No one could have had any illusions about what would have happened had the flames reached the high explosives stored just ahead of the hose stream.

Eventually the stevedores were lured back to continue the transfer of sugar sacks to the barge. With some urgency, the work was concentrated on the area of the fire. As it proceeded, the RCMP corporal filled his notebook with the testimony of the men who had been in the hold when the alarm had sounded. All agreed the outburst of flame and smoke had come almost without warning. None, they admitted, had remained in the hold long enough to make any detailed assessment of the fire's cause or extent.

The tunnel into the cargo went deeper and deeper as the stevedores worked. Each sodden bag of sugar was examined for charring as it was hoisted out. With increasing disbelief we found all of them unmarked. This was still the case when the workers reached the deck plates on which the cargo had rested.

The Mountie went doggedly back to his interrogations. He was a tough and patient man. Eventually he turned up the heart of the affair. The story was unfolded by a red-faced stevedore who had been on deck when the alarm sounded.

"It's this way," he confessed sheepishly. "I was working the winch on No. 2 when something jammed on the cargo boom. When I came back I gave her the steam again. Then the fire—well, anyway, the excitement—broke out down below. Mister, there were some scared men down there, but not as scared as this one. That wasn't smoke, it was steam—steam from the steam-smothering system. Some stupid clot had turned the wrong valve.

"When I ducked back to the winch I knew for sure. Why in Christ they had to put the smothering valve where a new operator could confuse it with the winch throttle beats me. Anyway, I lost my head—shut off the steam, and ran for the launch with the rest of them."

The "fire" that had so terrified the crew was really the untimely functioning of the very safeguard built into the vessel to extinguish such a blaze.

Arnold and his party, who had acted as if a real fire existed, were no less brave because they had fought an illusion, but there were no medals for them. They took a lot of good-natured joshing, and took it in the spirit it was offered. Still, we knew they were brave men indeed.

In most cases shipboard fires were far from imaginary, and the potential for disaster could be terrifying. One blaze we encountered might well have blasted the *Mont Blanc* explosion into a secondary place in history.

The degree to which word of this scare was suppressed at the time was a triumph of security. Years later, when I sought documents to embellish this account, none existed.

For me the incident began when a phone call informed me there had been a small fire on the Yugo-Slav vessel *Dubrovnik*, lying at a dock in the centre of the city. I assumed we had another case of careless cargo handlers.

Precautions against fire, like so many other measures for protecting the ships, had become something the boarding parties were expected to take a hand in. Smoking in proscribed areas was by long odds the most worrisome risk factor, and infractions by stevedores, often working in surroundings where the danger was greatest, presented a major problem.

I got there as fast as a launch could carry me, but when I boarded *Dubrovnik* the blaze itself was extinguished. We concentrated on finding out how the fire had started. The first deadly link in the chain of events was all too easily pinpointed.

A lighted cigarette, laid on the inner lip of a forward hatch by one of the men working it, was the culprit. Normally the cigarette would have burned itself out harmlessly on the steel ledge but instead it had taken its place in a series of coincidences.

The most remarkable of these was the nature of the *Dubrovnik*'s previous cargoes. One had been wheat, one nitrate, another sulphur. The accumulation of dust ringing the inside of the coaming added up to what was almost a low-grade gunpowder! No one could guess how long it had taken the smouldering cigarette to ignite it—least of all the fool who had laid it there—but, once going, the mixture had blazed merrily, running around the coaming and dropping viscous gobs of ignited material on the cargo below.

The hold was topped with heavy rubber tires, nasty stuff when alight under any conditions. The situation was saved because the burly mate of the *Dubrovnik* had ordered a hose run out before loading had started—probably because he knew what lay beneath the tires. The hose was stretched on the offshore side of the foredeck, locked to its standard and ready for instant use. When fire broke out, the mate was ready for action; he and his crew had the blaze out by the time the last of the stevedores had hit the deck.

I congratulated the men on their quick action, but nearly choked on my words when I learned that under the rubber cargo was a lower hold *solid with bulk explosive*.

What in the name of every security precaution had a munitions ship been doing at a dock in the heart of Halifax?

I completed my investigation, hurried back to Banyard's office, and gave him a factual rundown on what I had found.

"My God!" he exclaimed. "Where were CXO and the Harbourmaster and the RCMP?"

"I'm glad I'm not the one who has to find out," I said.

I had never seen NCSO so shaken.

"Give me a written report in ten minutes," he ordered.

"Just the bare details of what you found."

Various responsibilities for the movement and location of munitions ships, which involved the Chief Examination Officer, the Harbourmaster, and the Port Security Officer, had been foolproof until that day, but obviously a final set of coincidences had permitted the *Dubrovnik* to move about with the freedom of a ship carrying general cargo. The harrowing possibilities for a disaster on the scale of the 1917 explosion came inevitably to mind, and I was grateful that the responsibility for finding out how the *Dubrovnik* had been allowed to berth where she did belonged to someone more senior than myself. Amicable working relationships with the harbour officials who would be the storm centre of any investigation were important to my job, and I hoped fervently that the brief factual account of what I had found on the *Dubrovnik* would simply be a starting place for others to go to the source of the incident.

There was one relationship in particular which I was anxious not to have disturbed, for it had been established with considerable difficulty. The Port Security Officer was the Commanding Officer of the RCMP, Superintendant Alex Eames, an unbending disciplinarian with a limited sense of humour. He was not the easiest of men to deal with. Somehow you got the impression that Eames had gone through his long career without ever having made a mistake.

In my newspaper days he had once loomed large. As the RCMP inspector in charge at Aklavik in the depths of the Arctic winter of 1932, Eames had headed the manhunt for the legendary Mad Trapper of Rat River, Albert Johnson. After several bloody battles, he had brought the killer's body back to the wilderness settlement. The North was my newspaper beat then, and Eames' scrapbook—if he kept one—would have several columns of his exploits under my byline.

When I first arrived in Halifax to join the boarding service under Dick Oland, I found that Eames was cool and distant towards NCSO and his command. I suggested to Dick that I might be able to use the old connection to improve relations. Dick laughed and said, "Eames has been on the warpath with the press here, so I wouldn't count too much on working your reporter's pass with him. Anything's worth trying, though."

The link with the Mad Trapper in fact worked pretty well. Oland was the first to acknowledge my success, though he threatened to put a private detective on my trail to find independent evidence of my claim that I'd become a dinner guest at Eames' home.

The Mountie's basic character didn't change, but we got to understand one another. To the extent possible between serious bridge rivals, we relaxed together off duty. Our on-the-job communication was reserved, but very useful, and I realized this rapport could be endangered by the *Dubrovnik* affair. As Port Security Officer, Eames bore some of the responsibility for the foul-up.

I knew the worst had happened when I was called to the office of the Chief of Staff, Captain Cuthbert Taylor. Prematurely gray, with a bulldog jaw, Taylor already looked like the gruff admiral he eventually became. He paced the room, pausing impatiently to growl out a sentence or two, then resumed his restless stalking back and forth. In contrast, the lanky figure by his desk stood very still. Superintendent Eames stared at me with eyes as hard as they must have been the time he drew bead along his rifle sights on the Mad Trapper of Rat River.

Taylor came to one of his brief halts.

"What's all this about a report you turned in on the *Dubrovnik*, Watt?"

"It was routine, sir."

"It was an attempt to put me on the spot," rasped Eames, his face parchment-coloured.

Had we been alone I would probably have said, "Take it easy, Alex," or something similar, but under the circumstances I could only reply, "I mentioned no names, Superintendent—only what I found."

The Chief of Staff demanded bluntly, "Have you two ever collided before?" He resumed his pacing.

"On the contrary, sir, we have been friends," I said.

"There's nothing in this report that would suggest otherwise," Taylor told Eames.

"Any fool could see who it's aimed at," snapped Alex.

Taylor came to a halt and his irritation showed briefly. Gradually, though, his glance became one of rough compassion and his voice became almost gentle.

"Think it over again, Alex," he said. Then turned to me. "Thank you, Watt. That's all."

I was glad of Taylor's support, but otherwise the incident had unfortunate results. The C.O.'s door at RCMP headquarters was no longer open to me and there was no more bridge. The door opened again soon after, though, when Eames became Assistant Commissioner and a less rigid man, Superintendent Forrest, took over the Halifax detachment.

★ ★ ★

Dangerous cargo seemed to invite fire. The *Trongate*, a scruffy British tramp that first came to our attention because of a sitdown strike, was a case in point. She was lying alongside in the Shipyards, requiring attention to her engineroom before she could move on. The reasons for the strike were entirely understandable. With her fires drawn, *Trongate*'s boilers held no heat: it was winter, and the fo'c's'le was like a refrigerator. What steam could be piped from shore was completely inadequate and conditions in the living quarters, miserable at the best of times, made one shiver at the thought of actually having to stay there.

Negotiations with the captain and the owners, along with the willingness of the crew to more than meet them halfway, provided a satisfying example of how sitdowns could be solved by conviction and patience. The crew were provided with comfortable quarters ashore, and the vessel, while no luxury liner when the Shipyards finished, was made habitable. But all this went for nought when *Trongate*, loaded with munitions and ready for convoy, caught fire in the harbour one night.

The conflagration was deep-seated before it was noticed. Hoses directed through a ventilator had little effect, and when the fireboat *Rouille* surged alongside and added her powerful jets to the attack, the inferno shrugged them aside.

Wallace Creery, Captain in Charge, immediately sent a naval tug, *Pugwash*, to bring her portable pumps into play. Still the deck plates near No. 4 hold glowed, turning from red to white-hot. While the greater part of the explosives cargo was in the forward holds, No. 4 held its share of volatile goods. At five minutes after midnight, the master admitted that the ship was doomed. He had to turn his efforts to saving surrounding vessels and the shore from a devastating explosion. He signalled that he was evacuating his crew and intended to scuttle. When the Chief Engineer went below to open the seacocks, however, he was driven back by the smoke.

Creery had ordered the minesweeper *Chedabucto* to stand by and sent a party of demolition experts by launch to guarantee the scuttling, but the charges they detonated at 2:30 a.m. produced only a slight list. Fifteen minutes later, directing the race with time from the *Chedabucto*, Captain Creery decided the freighter was sinking far too slowly and ordered the minesweeper to sink her by gunfire.

Conscious of the hazards of a bombardment within the narrow confines of the harbour, Creery called for practice rounds using shells filled with sand rather than high explosives. The holes punched in *Trongate*'s waterline abaft the bridge increased her speed of descent, but it was still maddeningly slow. When the six practice rounds in the *Chedabucto*'s locker had been expended, the tough old freighter still wallowed, a lurid promise of disaster.

Creery ordered all ships anchored in the vicinity to be cleared of their crews and took his chance with armour-piercing shells. Three ripped into *Trongate*'s vitals. Still the ship refused to be hurried; the minesweeper's crew waited in painful suspense as the sea inched up its beam. At 3:25 a.m., the tramp slowly rolled over at last, and sank to the bottom where she lay a harmless hulk instead of a lighted bomb.

Naval records solemnly record that there was a price to pay beyond the loss of the vessel and her cargo. One of the practice shells had landed on Bisset's Wharf in Halifax and it cost the Navy twenty seven dollars to repair the damage.

Not until 1956 was the difficult job of exhuming *Trongate*'s remains completed. In the fourteen-year interval she served a useful purpose: her topmast and yard, stabbing up alongside the wreck buoy at low water, were constant reminders of the need to prevent shipboard fires.

★ ★ ★

The U.S. freighter *Volunteer* blazed her way to fame of a sort on the morning of November 3, 1943. Oxner and I were just setting out on our routine duties when a messenger panted up with word that a ship was burning in the Basin. He gave us her position, but when we rounded Turple Head in a losing race with the fireboat, *Rouille, Volunteer* readily identified herself with an impressive pillar of smoke.

Drawing close, we discovered another fireboat, the *James Battle*, already alongside. Once on board, we encountered the Commander of the Dockyard, Commander O.C.S. Robertson, RCNR, directing hoses in the engine room and the adjacent forward hold. "Robbie" Robertson seemed glad to see us, and filled us in on events.

"The damn ship has been burning since about 5:30 when a fireman tried to flash up a boiler and set alight the stokehold instead," he explained. "There was an all-night party going on and nobody's quite clear about anything—including the balled-up signals that didn't get through to me until 7:30. If we'd had half a chance, the fire could have been held to the stokehold but now it's eaten into No. 3 hold and God only knows what's stowed there."

"From the cordite fumes and the popcorn noise, I'd guess it was small arms ammunitions," I offered.

"*That* doesn't bother me," said Robertson. "It's what we *haven't* heard that does. Some of the crew have gibbered about heavy explosives but I haven't been able to locate a cargo plan. The officers are drunk and the captain is drunker. Not only are they no help, they're obstructing us. You may have to restrain them while I fight the fire."

I suggested signalling for Lieutenant Commander Stanley, the U.S. naval observer. We already had our difficulties with Americans, particularly seamen's union officials, who were very touchy in matters of jurisdiction on their ships. Stanley had been an ever-present friend in time of trouble. A visual signal for him through Turple Head station brought word that he was already on his way. Robbie and I decided to call on Captain Peterman and his officers.

It was a weird scene. Drifting through the cabin door were the sounds of the fiercely burning ship and the fight to save her. The acrid mist of exploding cordite hung in gauzy swirls around the solemn gathering at the captain's table. Peterman was at that advanced stage of intoxication where an exaggerated sobriety accompanied even the act of pouring another tumbler of whisky. There was no sense of crisis.

Robertson was still trying to identify the cargo he was dealing with in the inferno below and controlled his rage with obvious effort. He was also remarkably restrained in his eventual report:

> "The engine room fire was extinguished by foamite from the *Rouille* but was stubborn in No. 3 lower 'tween-decks, where ammunition was exploding. CDY (Robertson) asked for the cargo plans and for officers who had seen the cargo stowed but the captain said no plan existed and no officers had been present. The Chief produced a plan finally but it didn't show the disposition of the cargo. As soon as the presence of magnesium barrels was noted, orders were given to flood No. 3. The captain and officers objected and gave no cooperation.
>
> "They then held a council as to the best method of putting out the fire, assisted by two bottles of whisky. On its conclusion the Master, accompanied by the Chief Engineer and 1st Assistant Engineer, decided to make their way to the engine room and thence to the stokehold. CDY had just left this space, where he had found it extremely difficult, even with the aid of an oxygen mask, to survey the area. The Master and officers were only equipped with gas masks and if they had been allowed to venture into this area it would have been necessary to dispatch badly needed firemen to rescue them. I therefore gave orders that, if necessary, the Master and officers were to be forcibly detained from enter-

> ing the engine room or stokehold. These orders were carried out by officers and ratings of NBS.
>
> "At this time Lieutenant Commander Stanley arrived and removed the commanding officer from the scene of the fire. He gave orders to the ship's officers that they were to obey implicitly any instructions given by CDY relative to the safety of the ship.
>
> "By this time the fire had spread to No. 2 hold. It was recognized that water from the engine room would find its ways to No.'s 4 and 5, leaving only No. 1 dry."

Signals were flashed to the Admiral and Robbie's decision that the vessel should be beached before it sank in the Basin was approved. McNab's Cove, near the harbour entrance, had the right sort of bottom for the purpose. Shortly the tugs *Bansaga, Marten* and *Security* bustled into the Basin to take *Volunteer* in tow. Since the crew couldn't be mustered, a naval party took over the securing of the lines and the buoying of the anchor which, there being no steam to heave it in, had to be burned free. Lieutenant Commander Cassivi, Robbie's assistant, and Anstensen, who joined us after spotting the fire on his way to less exciting duties, were responsible for the operation. Oxner and other boarding ratings supplied the skilled hands.

Robertson asked for a civilian pilot to take the bridge while he himself continued to direct the fire fighting. It was three o'clock in the afternoon when Captain Bracken arrived and signalled the tugs to take the strain. Slowly the *Volunteer* began to move towards the Narrows, then down the fairway. During the next hour Halifax, accustomed to maritime drama but not so blasé as to ignore a cloud of smoke with a ship at its centre, watched nervously. As *Volunteer* dragged its way along the harbour's entire length, there were doubtless many others who shared our anxiety about what might be in the vessel's holds.

One of my own lasting memories of the journey was the abrupt discovery that I was hungry. I had breakfasted early and it had become a long day. Oxner admitted he was also feeling the pangs. I suggested that since he was so well acquainted with galleys, he might scout that of the

Volunteer. He disappeared in the smother of cordite fumes and eventually returned in triumph with two pork chops. Greasy, cold pork isn't the greatest delicacy, particularly if it has been treated with cordite fumes for ten hours, but we wolfed his loot. I could taste mine three days later, and Oxner swore, after a year had passed, that he could still feel the cold, hard lump in his innards.

Again taking up Robbie's report of the trip down harbour:

> "Some half hour after the ship was under way, the Master made his way to the bridge and ordered the Second Officer, who was one of the few sober, to send a man to the wheel and to give him a megaphone. In order to humour the Master he did so. The captain placed himself in the end of the flying bridge and ordered a non-existent crew on the fo'c's'le to 'heave in, when ready.' He stayed on the bridge without taking further action, then returned to his cabin.
>
> "Somewhere in the region of 16:00 the ship was berthed in McNab's Cove and all efforts were concentrated on flooding her with the exception of No. 1 hold.
>
> "An hour after the beaching the Master came on the bridge and informed the chief officer, who with other officers were now cooperating with the naval fire party, that there was no hope of saving the ship and she would have to be beached."

Even though her hull was mostly submerged, the *Volunteer* continued to burn stubbornly for several days. The worst came, in fact, after she was beached and the magnesium cargo had been located in No. 3. One of the fire party, Stoker W.S. Carson, courageously clearing away bags of phosphate in an attempt to vent the highly sensitive magnesium beyond, was blown out of the hatch when the first barrel exploded. Carson was among several men to be hospitalized as more explosions followed and the fire smouldered on.

Narrow escapes were frequent. The Naval Fire Marshall, Lieutenant Spinney, and Lieutenant Buxton were trapped by smoke and fumes in the starboard bunker hatch with two of their men. Buxton and Stoker Green managed to make it into the open but when Buxton found he had not been followed by the others he returned below and found Spinney attempting to rescue Stoker Munt, down with smoke suffocation. Together they finally made it but, as Robertson reported, "it was only by the greatest of good fortune that these men were not lost."

As long as it was necessary for the hoses to be kept going, NBS parties, relieving Oxner and his men at the end of the first day, continued the twenty-four hour watch. As the Master painfully returned to the realities of his situation there was no further need to enforce his cooperation, but there was a job of policing to do when it became clear that there would be no major explosion.

A procession of small boats bringing civilian shore parties for various clean-up tasks included certain members anxious to return to the beach with "souvenirs" of the *Volunteer*. "Wrecking" was the term used among a fraternity who for generations had considered anything salvageable from the sea to be heaven-sent and theirs by right. But these scavengers met with the stern disapproval of Oxner, on his second turn of duty. The souvenir hunting stopped.

The American authorities thoughtfully relieved us of any involvement in the investigation that followed, other than taking into evidence our written reports. Captain Peterman and his entire complement were whisked home for hearings, and the *Volunteer* was pumped out, pulled alongside a Halifax wharf, discharged and, eventually, restored to seaworthiness.

In due time Robbie was awarded the George Medal, and honours went to Spinney, Buxton and others who had fought the dangerous blaze. Some years later Robertson, as captain of the naval icebreaker *Labrador*, took her through the Northwest Passage and, as a Commodore, became an authority on the Arctic.

★ ★ ★

The ever-present menace of fire gradually turned another Boarding Service commitment into a heavy one. This dated back to a talk between Oland and the security-conscious captain of one of the troopships. As a result we were asked to put a special patrol on board during the ship's stay in Halifax, and other requests followed. It was not a popular detail. As Oxner said after the two hours it took to make his rounds of the giant *Queen Mary*: "I don't mind a long tramp if it's necessary but it's that mountain climbing that leaves me with collapsed ankles."

In the early days when we were short of manpower most of the troopers did without our services. It was a matter of pride for many of the liners that their own security measures were perfectly adequate. However, the thoroughness of the boarding parties that *were* called on spelled an increase in such duties. The boarders discovered several minor fires and a number of situations that would have encouraged bigger and better ones. When the French liner *Normandie* burned out and capsized alongside her New York pier while being converted into a trooper, the demands on NBS mounted sharply. The word "saboteur" regained its menace overnight.

A glimpse of this aspect of the boarding operation is provided by one of Oxner's reports. The ship was the world's largest—the *Queen Elizabeth*:

> "Boarded Friday at 2 p.m., six ratings all told—two on gangway and four patrolling every part of ship. Found almost everybody smoking in spite of abundance of No Smoking signs in places easy to see. We stopped this speedily.
>
> "Things progressed in order until the crew members, consisting of Aussies, Liverpool and Glasgow fellows, started to roll aboard from 11:30 until 3:30 a.m., very much under the influence. They had been paid on Friday afternoon and were flush. Plenty of trouble started on the gangway when an Aussie called one of the Provost Corps corporals a Canadian bastard. However, after a melee lasting about an hour, in which many teeth were knocked out and features disfigured, order was restored and continued except for a hardwood box, used to contain emergency lights, being torn from its place on the boat deck and thrown by someone there down a distance of about sixty feet, to land about five

inches from an Army sentry on the dock. We investigated but found nobody who looked guilty.

"Order was kept until Saturday 2 p.m. when we were relieved by Leading Seaman Wick and five ratings.

"Boarded again on Monday p.m. to relieve Leading Seaman Burrows and party. Not much smoking in evidence and good order was kept. Ship patrolled from boat deck to engineroom shaft tunnels, and from stem to stern. We received personal praise from the Staff Captain and the visiting Lieutenant Governor this p.m."

18

The Tide Turns

The turn in the Battle of the Atlantic came with dramatic suddenness. It was preceded by a full-scale conference in Washington early in March, 1943, where convoy structure was reorganized and word passed that the time had come for the Allies to take the offensive.

The desperate holding action of the merchantmen had succeeded in buying time for an adequate military buildup. Sufficient escorts had slid down the ways to provide close escort and allow formation of hunter-killer groups capable of independent punitive action or for emergency support of sharply pressed convoys. Matching this, those responsible for developing the Very Long Range aircraft announced they were ready to close the final mid-Atlantic gap—henceforth no submarine stalking the lifeline would be safe from detection and attack from the skies.

The conference also straightened out areas of authority that had been going through a costly trial-and-error phase since the United States entered the war. The strengthened

Canadian fighting fleet, providing the bulk of the escorts in the western sector, had previously been covering HX, SC and related convoys under direction of the U.S. High Command. Now, along with ships of the Royal Navy, they took over entire responsibility for these movements and Admiral Leonard Murray, RCN, Flag Officer, Newfoundland Force, moved to Halifax as Commander in Chief, Canadian Northwest Atlantic. As such he was able to work directly with his partner at the other end of the battle line, the Commander in Chief, Western Approaches. The Royal Canadian Navy, ultimately to number nearly 100,000 men and women, had come a long way in the twenty years since its total strength had been just under five hundred.

The impact of the Washington conference and the new hardware it brought to bear was stunning. Overnight the hunting wolf packs became the hunted. They were spotted when they came up to breathe or communicate, and relentlessly attacked whether closing a convoy or shadowing it. By summer the killing of merchant shipping had been drastically reduced, and many convoys were making the passage without encountering evidence of the enemy. While the Battle of the Atlantic would have to be fought for another two years, and while its cost would be severe, its final result was no longer in doubt in the minds of those who fought it.

Losses in the St. Lawrence river, which had bothered certain Canadian politicians more than those in any other theatre of the war, turning them into instant naval experts and critics, ended once and for all. For the first time the pressures on Captain Brand relaxed enough for him to be able to leave his Ottawa post and take a personal look at the perimeter of his responsibilities. These, largely due to the vast expansion of Canada's mercantile fleet, had increased to the point where Trade Division occupied four-fifths of his time. Brand handed over Intelligence to his close associate, Lieutenant Commander H.M. Little, RCNVR.

Now simply D.T.D. (Director of Trade Division), his tour of inspection carried him to the West Coast, which had become a good deal less peaceful since Japan's entry into the war. Changes followed in his wake. Boarding units were established in Vancouver, Victoria and Prince Rupert, bulwarked by veteran officers and senior ratings from the Atlantic.

The improving situation on the eastern seaboard was allowing previously bypassed issues to be tackled with the vigour they demanded. One was the unfairness of the long-delayed promotion of senior hands. After his gruelling years of outstanding service, Oxner was still a Leading Seaman—a relatively insignificant step up from the rating at which he had begun the war.

On May 5, 1943, Captain Brand informed me that a solution of sorts lay within Naval Order 2434, Para 3(c). The RCN had a Shore Branch in which sea time wasn't a requisite of promotion. Certain clerical and other personnel not required for service afloat had their own yardstick for advancement. The Chief of Naval Personnel had agreed that those men in NBS who applied for transfer to Shore Branch and were recommended by their commanding officers would receive favourable consideration.

The men concerned were disappointed. They had long denied the sailor's instinct to be at sea. As compensation they had the knowledge that their proven qualities as mariners were indispensible to their shorebased activities. To ask for transfer to Shore Branch, where seafaring skills were of no account, cut cruelly at their fierce pride of profession—a pride that had given the boarding parties their motivation and worth.

Had there ever been a favourable moment for anyone who wished to leave the Boarding Service this was it. Merchant seamen were no longer as severely tested as they had been in the past, though there were still dangers. Naval Personnel was encouraging any man who wished to get ahead to do so in a warship. Shore Branch was the last service with which any self-respecting deepwater mariner wished to be labelled.

The senior hands had to consider their futures now. They hammered out the issue as a group, but each certainly had his lonely inner war to fight. Some came to me for advice, but I could only tell them that where a man's honest pride is threatened, he is himself best fitted to pilot it through the shoals.

Each in his own time, those ratings I was prepared to recommend let their intentions be known. Without exception they decided to stay with the Boarding Service. If going Shore Branch was inescapable, so be it, was the attitude. But the melancholy of their decision could be sensed long after it had produced Petty Officers and Chief Petty Officers.

If the men under my command had problems because of a lack of recognition, I was faced with virtually the opposite situation. In the context of Navy tradition, it seemed just as hard to handle.

In March, 1943, *Who Dare to Live* was published. Initial public reaction was enthusiastic, and the first reviews were barely coming in when second editions were announced in both Canada and Britain. The Canadian Broadcasting Corporation and NBC in New York both dramatized it on their national networks.

To a freelance writer who had known the crumbs of the Depression, this was a heady experience. I had been spared even the gruelling search for a publisher. The Gows and Joe Dwyer had taken over—along with Anstensen and his wife, Edna, whose skills as proofreaders had seen the book through final production stages.

From the time my publishers announced their intention of publishing the poem, their promotional people found themselves with powerful allies. Not only were naval information officers there to help, but the Navy League of Canada—always anxious to develop a greater awareness of the merchant seaman's critical role—had alerted its national contacts with the media. The resulting wave of public interest was substantial.

David Gibson, president of the Navy League, was also vice president of a large national retail chain. An invitation to autograph copies at the firm's Halifax outlet brought the first warning of what lay ahead to challenge my concentration on strictly Naval responsibilities.

It was simple enough to decline commercial invitations as conflicts of interest, but requests to speak to patriotically motivated organizations or appear on radio broadcasts were not within my authority to answer. Uneasily, I routed them to my immediate commanding officer—the recently promoted Captain Banyard.

The Navy had proudly called itself "The Silent Service" for a good many generations and my indoctrination in the tradition had been at the impressionable age of fifteen. Naval information officers were a phenomenon as recent as the present war and, while they were slowly being accepted by the Executive Branch as a necessary evil, the role grudgingly granted them was that of softening the impact of bad publicity, rather than drawing attention to the Service itself.

It was almost with a sense of guilt that I referred the first request for a public appearance to Captain Banyard, who said he would pass it on to the Admiral's office, his own disapproval silently implicit.

But Lieutenant Commander George Lawrence, the Command information officer, was unabashedly pleased. The appearance was quickly approved by the Admiral, and word was passed that such opportunities should be exploited. This was an opportunity for the Fighting navy to pay tribute to a blood-bought fellowship with the merchant marine.

I was instructed to use my own judgement with direct invitations that followed, but others, reaching the Department through official channels, were accepted for me. All were kept meticulously within the framework of Naval regulations, but the spotlight of publicity which followed as a result was anything but helpful in my working relationship with my immediate superior.

There were no open clashes. It was just that our ability to talk out situations to a point of common acceptance, already difficult, grew more so. Since the final decisions were inevitably Banyard's, my frustration deepened to cold resentment.

As so frequently happens when personalities cloud issues, a matter of no great importance brought the situation to a head.

Rebuilding of the Yard had provided vastly improved quarters for the boarders in a new warehouse some distance from the Administration Building. The Chief of Staff, walking by one morning, spotted Oxner & Co. paraded outside the new quarters for the inspection that preceded their march to the launches. They were so close to being a precision squad that the Chief of Staff decided the ceremony should take place, as in the past, in front of the Administration Building. It would provide a martial lift, he felt, for the deskbound labourers inside.

Boarding officers had always carried out inspection of their own men, but shortly after the drill was transferred to its more visible setting, Banyard decided it would be a good thing if the other officers on his staff took their turns at it.

This move might have been justified as a means of reviving the gunnery school reflexes of the long-deskbound personnel, but after a week it was obvious to me that the men's response to command slackened when they were deprived of their own officers. Seething, I did the unforgivable. I went over Banyard's head and asked Brand if he would arrange to have me appointed away from Halifax. If I had the choice, I said, it would be to go to Combined Operations, by this time flexing its muscles for the invasion of Europe. Then I wrote my wife and told her what I had done.

A few weeks earlier she had had her first close-up view of my job. Anstensen, who by some miracle had obtained a small apartment for himself and Edna in the overcrowded city, had gone on leave. The empty accommodation had made it possible for Ernestine to farm out our youngsters in Edmonton and join me for nearly a month. She had become personally acquainted with many of the boarders who had dropped in on us, and with the stresses of my duties. She would, I felt sure, grasp how untenable those responsibilities had now become.

I had no need to wait for a written reply. A long-distance phone call on the evening my letter reached her wrecked the sleep of the self-righteous at 2 a.m. Halifax time. Ernestine did not mince her words. She was strongly convinced, she said, that I had been thinking more about my personal feelings than of larger issues. I told her I was disappointed in her lack of understanding. It was a long, expensive conversation and, until I had a few hours to mull it over, one that enraged me. Only when I wearied of avoiding the real issues with myself did her truth get through.

There was a convoy to sail before I could catch Banyard alone in his office. Then I told him what I had done and apologized for it.

"I don't know what will happen," I said. "Possibly it will be disciplinary action, possibly Combined Operations, or possibly Brand'll tell me to grow up and carry on where I am. If the last happens—and you can still use me—you have my word I won't go over your head again."

I wrote Brand at the end of that day:

> "I had been asking the men under me to maintain open, fighting relationships with each other and with me—and had denied the same thing to my immediate superior. My apology has cleared the air, even if it hasn't much changed our differing attitudes towards the most efficient form of Boarding Service. Captain Banyard has been promised my frankness and loyalty in future.
>
> "Possibly by this time you have taken some action which will make that irrelevant. Captain Banyard has assured me that if I should go elsewhere nothing would make him happier than to have me ultimately return to NCS, Halifax."

A month later Brand hadn't answered either of my letters. Whether I was being allowed to sweat out my folly before the axe fell or whether a Nelsonian blind eye had been turned on me lay somewhere in the silence. The Director, given to cracking down unsparingly if he felt the situation called for it, had also been known to let well enough alone if there was promise of better things to come.

One thing was certain; there was still a war to be fought. From the moment of my cards-on-the-table meeting with Banyard, it was proceeding more favourably as far as the Boarding Service was concerned. NCSO decided it had been a mistake to interrupt the regular duties of his office staff by having them inspect the boarding parties and our previous routine resumed. While Brand continued to withhold word of my fate, he was forthcoming with more handpicked officers.

One, Lieutenant Garry Hansen, RCNVR, was a tight-lipped man with relatives still in occupied Norway. He had a background of global trading and intimate knowledge of the ships carrying it on, some of which were owned by members of his family. Another, Lieutenant Ian Ogilvie, RCNVR, was normally a Montreal newspaperman, and had many of Joe Dwyer's qualities.

In Sydney, most sensitive of the ports since the first Gatineau Conference, Commander Mitchell reacted positively to *Who Dare To Live* and wrote: "Certain parts of it may not appeal to the landsmen as to we seafarers but you have good work there, work which contains many truths and deserves study." The "we seafarers" meant a good deal to me. I had always thought Mitchell regarded me as a landlubber.

Shortly after this, Mitchell was appointed a coastal convoy commodore and Commander Bill Simpson, RCNR, took over as NCSO, Sydney. Empathy between Bill and myself had been excellent while he was Banyard's second-in-command and it continued to be so. By this time, a delightfully aggressive Irish-Canadian, Lieutenant Jack O'Neal, RCNVR, had become senior boarding officer at the Cape Breton port. His credentials included a good university degree and a first-rate record on the staff of Arthur Randles before the latter had emerged as Director of Merchant Seamen in Ottawa. Jack O'Neal and Bill Simpson became a team whose creativity was a story in itself.

And still I waited for Brand to answer my letters. It seemed out of character for him to ignore them indefinitely. Yet that, strictly speaking, was exactly what he did do. To this day he has never discussed them with me. Eventually a signal came from National Defence Headquarters to the Commander in Chief, Northwest Atlantic. Its dispassionate instruction: "Lieutenant Commander E.F.B. Watt, RCNVR, is appointed to Bytown (Ottawa) for duty as Staff Officer (Merchant Navy)."

19

Dispersal

My work at Headquarters in Ottawa was often familiar, but there were two marked differences from being stationed in Halifax. The first was that the powerful voice of the Director no longer reached me through a filter of intermediaries. It was as close as his office two doors down the corridor. The other was that instead of experiencing the waves of change among the merchant seamen affected by them, I found myself constantly in the presence of the men making the waves.

These were essentially the same people I had met in the East Block at the time of the first Gatineau Conference, with the important addition of Arthur Randles. Known simply as the Merchant Seamen's Committee, they had various extensions in the form of sub-committees, and wielded impressive clout.

There were aces in the hole which the Committee could play if absolutely necessary. The Minister of Munitions and Supply was one. Hon. C.D. Howe's primary duty was producing the tools of war, but he was acutely aware that they had to cross three thousand miles of dangerous ocean to be put into action. If obstructionism threatened Canada's maritime effectiveness, a quiet briefing of "C.D." usually ended it. His voice, next to the Prime Minister's, was the most compelling in Cabinet.

Three men, along with Brand, gave the Committee its main thrust. They were in constant touch and apparently trusted one another completely. The responsibilities they carried in their military and civilian posts spoke of powerful individual talents, but their major strength was a willingness to collectively storm barriers public servants shied away from.

Not that they were rash or brash. Brigadier "Reg" Orde, who masterminded the Merchant Seamen's Order, was a no-nonsense lawyer with a sharp awareness of political realities. He wasn't surprised when that drastic Order in Council, which had leap-frogged the civil courts, was challenged in Parliament. Nothing was left to chance when the time came for its justification. Yet in his tailoring of the legislation he was both daring and imaginative.

Joliffe, the Immigration Commissioner, was an unflappable, quiet man who had been a source of understanding and strength to Brand from the first. Joliffe's inspectors had confirmed the difficulties NCSO experienced in keeping the convoys moving. When the imperfect PC 4751 was the only instrument with which to counter sitdowns, the instructions his office sent to the Immigration stations where detainees were held were gems of reasoned flexibility. When the more clear-cut Merchant Seamen's Order replaced 4751, Joliffe's officers in the ports performed with the firmness of men sure of their Ottawa backing. Their role was a key one. As members of the Boards of Enquiry, they pressed their conviction that the Order should be used only as a last resort.

Arthur Randles' job as general passenger agent for Cunard Steamships had been sufficiently lively to absorb his endless energy until his liners were taken over by the Canadian armed forces. After that he was more than ready for the post the government offered him. His wide knowledge of ships and their personnel, his skills as a diplomat in high places, and his tireless, hard-headed effervescence were all invaluable in his role of Director of Merchant Seamen.

My own job called for regular contact with Arthur, but it was far from a routine dutifully observed. He received duplicates of boarding forms as quickly as they reached Ottawa and they touched off many spontaneous meetings between us. Not only were the boarders providing him with a shipboard view of the men emerging from his training schools, they were in constant touch with the officials of his manning pools. Equally vital to him were their observations on the distribution of comforts and other aspects of seamen's welfare. In return, he provided me with insights and foresights which were of distinct value to the men in the launches.

I encountered Orde and Joliffe less often and then, as a rule, at meetings where Brand took me along or where my discussions with their lieutenants called for top decisions. One way or another, though, I had opportunity to appreciate the rare understanding that existed between them. Each was heavily engaged in his own sensitive operation, and each was definitely an individualist; yet they brought a refreshing lack of credit-seeking to their mutual responsibilities.

When, in Halifax, I experienced their policy decisions being implemented in the ships, I had gratefully taken them for granted. Their decisions seemed logical, and in keeping with the need addressed. Seeing those decisions in the making, however, reminded me that what makes sense is not automatically acceptable to everybody concerned. The periphery of the Committee had its empire builders and obstructionists, some with a fair amount of political influence. Without the unity of conviction at its centre, delay and dilution could well have supplanted the drive and the scope that made the body so important to the war effort. As it was, the four-man core provided the balance and directional authority of a gyroscopic compass.

Brand never ceased to emphasize the need for meticulous information by which the Committee could chart its course, particularly information which revealed the mind of the merchant seamen. Shortly before I left Halifax he had written:

"Thanks so much for the notes handed in by the hands

> in charge of parties on board the troopers. They not only give a picture of conditions on board but provide a pretty insight into the way your fellows take their responsibilities and carry out their duties.
>
> "It was also a pleasure to read the genuine ways they have of expressing themselves. As you know, one gets all too little contact with the sailor himself at this desk and the mere reading of their reports conjures up memories of the days when I had more to do with that charming individual, the bluejacket."

The letter gave a "pretty insight" into the man who had written it. For all the endless organizational responsibilities he carried—the routing, diversion, convoying, independent sailing, reporting, and arming of millions of tons of shipping—Brand never failed to find time to turn his mind to the state of the individual seaman. When he said he never failed to read every boarding form, the evidence supported it.

On one occasion I had included in the report on a seriously troubled foreign ship an afterthought about a lone British fireman I had encountered there. He was the only one in the stokehold who had refused to join a sitdown strike. Already a man apart by reason of his nationality, he had drawn outright hostility from his mates. Had he been less muscular and remained less sober he might well have borne the physical brunt of the savage regard in which he was held. The fireman was a dour example of determination to stay on the job.

Whether he was moved by patriotism, a low opinion of his companions, an unwillingness to let others make up his mind for him, or the simple instincts of an obedient seafarer, I had neither the time nor the ability to establish. He volunteered nothing on his own account, except to say that he intended to stand his watch whenever it came around. Yet his presence was so noteworthy that I made passing reference to it after the crew trouble had been straightened out, the ship had sailed and the time had come to file the boarding form.

Some months later an inquiry from Admiralty was forwarded to NCSO, Halifax, for action. It asked for a detailed account of how a certain British fireman had stood his ground in the face of attempts to intimidate him into refusing duty. He was being considered for a decoration. As I recaptured the incident in retrospect, the dogged, inarticulate, unconsciously heroic figure of the man from the black gang came into proper focus. He became the embodiment of the unquenchable Merchant Navy at its best.

Perhaps I had sensed this when I had made my first comment but it was Brand who properly evaluated the situation. Buried though the item was in the detail of just another sitdown strike, he had considered it carefully enough to draw the seaman to Admiralty's attention.

★ ★ ★

Topping the "In" basket on the morning of my Headquarters arrival was the day's collection of boarding forms from both coasts. The Director's instruction was that he still wanted to scan each himself, but that I should process them first. There would be some I could expand from personal knowledge, and some from which I might extract ideas for future action which might not occur to him. The initial reading would also keep me consistently abreast of both the intelligence and the men who provided it.

My position with the boarders remained one in which nothing could be taken for granted. They were still directly responsible to their NCSOs and my function was still an advisory one. Yet the change brought about by my new appointment was significant. It could be assumed—correctly—that any advice I might offer had first been threshed out with the Director.

My stint in Ottawa was giving me some idea of Brand's full stature and the scope and significance of the organization he had created. Rear Admiral Manisty, organizing genius of the convoys in World War I, and originator of the system for their control in World War II, visited the North American ports in 1943. He reported to Admiralty that "Naval Service HQ, Ottawa, has been the basis of the organization [of merchant shipping control in North America] and has been the source from which the whole mechanism derived its impetus. This mechanism seems to have worked so smoothly it has been accepted as being almost automatic."

If I faced a hazard now it was that of complacency. But, here again, the Captain's personality protected me. For all his backing of the unorthodox, for all his openness to what others had to offer, for all the humanity in his reading of men, Brand was unsparing when he sensed self-satisfaction and awesome in his expression of it. Being on his carpet was either a healthy purgative or the beginnings of a passion for a new appointment. He ran a happy ship but a tight one.

I wasn't unacquainted with his carpet, but had no urge for a softer one. There was fairness and truth in what I heard there.

After a month's shakedown I was on my way overseas again, sailing by special dispensation in the "gray funnel line". The Bangor-class minesweeper *Guysborough*—soon to be lost in the invasion of Europe—landed me in St. John's; the corvette *Fredericton* bounced me to Londonderry. I had waited a long time to feel the heartbeat of a convoy from a warship's spray-spattered bridge, or to catch its pulse in towering geysers from depth charges dropped over the stern. My naval uniform seemed to fit me better for the experience.

On the train from Liverpool to London I found myself alone in a compartment with a Royal Navy officer who was deep in a book. He nodded and returned to his reading, but in a few moments looked up again. "Listen," he said, and read:

> "And never think, that poets want the moon;
> They want an England better than the last,
> An England using to the full its skills,"

The lines, he explained, were from the just-published *Wonderings* of John Masefield, the Poet Laureate, whose *Sea Fever* had caught my imagination when I was a land-locked prairie youth.

This incident was the first link in a chain of memorable circumstances. After my arrival in London I received a telegram from John Masefield, inviting me to spend the day with him at his home near Oxford. It transpired that he and the eloquent Leonard Brockington (at that time special assistant to Prime Minister Mackenzie King) were longtime friends. They had recently spent time together, and "Brock" had put a copy of *Who Dare to Live* in his hands.

My London superiors sent a naval photographer to record the meeting, which was an unforgettable experience for me.

I found that London was no longer a place for knocking on formidable doors. Charlie Jarman's already stood wide and the Director of Trade Division, to whom I reported, not only opened others I had in mind but had some ideas of his own about whom I should meet. Even the Marine colonel who had replaced the unhappily remembered Deputy Director of Naval Intelligence smiled at me over his long-stemmed "churchwarden's" pipe.

Trips for seasoning experience were now standard for NBS and two three-man groups arrived in London while I was there. Trade Division, Admiralty was making full use of their turnaround time, sending them to various ports for the sharing and expanding of experience with their British counterparts.

Another corvette, *Trillium*, carried me back across an Atlantic that seemed very different from the ocean I had crossed in the *Sourabaya*. There would still be casualties—*Sourabaya* among them—but the promise of ultimate victory had become unshakeable. The sense of this was particularly strong in London. At Admiralty, at Jarman's headquarters, and in every shipping office, I found much thought being given to the foundations on which a new day for the merchant seaman would be permanently built, once peace returned.

This was equally true in Ottawa, where men like Brand were contemplating the war's aftermath even as the drive to win it reached its peak. The production of Canada's shipyards was carrying the nation towards seventh rank among the world's maritime nations. The government-created Park Shipping Company alone had nearly two hundred vessels afloat or building, most of them 10,000-ton dry cargo carriers. Manning them was the immediate challenge—and no easy one—but, even as they wrestled with it, far-sighted planners were considering what the future might hold when the frantic construction ended.

Brand showed me a letter he had just received from Captain W.D. Stephens, D.T.D. Admiralty:

> "It will be interesting to see the extent to which the RCN will have a say in the post-war management and control of the Canadian Merchant Navy. I am sure that the good relations and firm trust inspired by your Boarding Service will prove a solid foundation for the post-war collaboration that will be necessary."

But there was still more than a year to go before April, 1945, when HX 348, losing two ships to German torpedoes, had the unhappy distinction of making the last payment for victory in the Battle of the Atlantic. In the interval, the boarding parties found as many headaches among the vessels sailing under the Canadian ensign as there ever had been under other flags in more dangerous times.

Competent seamen with a mature attitude towards their profession were not as readily produced as ships were. With most of Canada's experienced sailors already afloat in either the fighting or merchant services, the training schools under Arthur Randles could not perform miracles overnight. Considering the number of green hands involved, the miracle was that so many did so well. But in a number of ships that was not good enough.

There was an equally acute problem in turning out competent officers. The promotion of half-qualified candidates was the only alternative to keeping ships uselessly tied up. In the absence of seasoned people to take them to sea, the drive for global victory compelled a decision to sail every Park ship with such personnel as were available.

This nearly impossible situation in turn made things difficult for Arthur Randles in his relationships with some of the independent operators. Accustomed to selecting their ships' companies, they found the pool system—which arbitrarily assigned them personnel—not at all to their liking. Their objections to it reached a new high when the Canadian Seamen's Union was certified to represent the outpouring of new sailors. Leadership of the CSU from the moment of its creation on the Great Lakes in 1936 had been as red as the background of the hammer and sickle flag.

By the end of 1943 Canadian ships' delegates and union representatives in the ports were predominantly Communist or Communist-oriented, and the reputation for crew trouble in the ships they served had become worldwide.

Nevertheless, when Captain Brand wrote his annual report for 1944, he was able to record:

> "During the year the difficulties in Park Steamships Company in regards to the discipline and control of seamen in their ships diminished.... Though the number of Canadian ships doubled, the number of cases of crew trouble was approximately the same as the previous year."

If there was one factor above all others in the change for the better, it was the relationship which developed between Randles and Pat Sullivan, president of the CSU from the day he organized it on the Lakes.

Pat had been outwardly inactive between 1940 and 1942, since he was an internment camp guest of the Government along with other prominent Communists. Released following Hitler's invasion of Russia, he had emerged in the Canadian wave of goodwill towards its new Red ally. He returned immediately to his CSU presidential duties, and a fascinating set of circumstances shortly carried him to the secretaryship of the Canadian Congress of Labour.

In his book, *Red Sails on the Great Lakes*, Sullivan tells how his convictions as a trade unionist ultimately won out over his subservience to the Communist Party and caused his subsequent break with it. The process was well advanced during his sessions with Randles, some of which I sat in on. Because of these meetings, I was better fitted to brief Brand and the senior boarding officers who were dealing with CSU growing pains in the ships.

By 1944, the greatly improved situation in the Parks vessels provided a positive talking point for Captain Brand and others of the committee advising the Cabinet on the future of the Canadian merchant marine. Not that it produced a positive response. On December 27, 1944, the Minister of Transport made public the Government's attitude: "I see no future for Canada going into the shipping business in a big way after the war."

Much has been written of the virtual disappearance of Canadian flag ships in the post-war period. The controversy is still open-ended, but is outside the scope of this narrative. So, for that matter, is any detailed account of my subsequent years at NSHQ after Trade Division was suspended. I have set out to tell what happened between the June day in 1940 when Al Oxner, A.B., strode down North Street hill to become the first searcher for shipboard sabotage, and September 30, 1945, when I, as Staff Officer (Merchant Navy) closed my door on the record of 50,000 boardings and walked down the corridor to another appointment.

★ ★ ★

To all intents and purposes that story ended on May 9, 1945—the day conflict ceased on the Atlantic and broke out in the streets of Halifax. Of that, more later. But first, a parting glimpse of Chief Petty Officer A.V. Oxner, British Empire Medal. It is taken from a letter of his dated March 8, 1945:

> "About the time I was dropping you a line, sir. Thank God the end is in sight and people can and will become normal again. After thirty-seven years of wasted time, energy and cursing the married state, I met four months ago—and every night since—the 'one'! Her father is Captain Gerhart, who I sailed with years ago out of Lunenburg. Mother and all well pleased. Cook, ye Gods, and bake as well! She insists on keeping her job after the chapel bout. All my fangs, false and otherwise, are showing every morning with the smile of a satisfied mind."

For all the salty, pink cloud on which Oxner floated as the unsparing years moved towards V-E (Victory Europe) Day, there was no rest for the boarders until after the final hour of the war with Germany. A Headquarters "Confidential" to the boarding parties had noted:

> "These days there comes a suggestion in the boarding reports that a state of mind is developing in which wartime standards of discipline will be lowered. It can be taken for granted that NBS will be exposed to that

> influence and it is greatly to be desired that we remain up to the mark until the job is done. Should there be an emotional post-war upset and a rash of troublemakers released from wartime restrictions, we may again be challenged to become a rallying point for common sense and order."

Symptoms of relaxing discipline had been evident since the February arrival in Halifax of four Great Lakes tankers, acquired by the British Ministry of War Transport for service overseas. Taken over in harbour by British crews, the ships developed trouble early. All went well on the *Willow Branch*, but even junior officers aboard the *Oak, Cedar* and *Pine Branches* declared that the ships had been misrepresented to them by the English authorities, and that they had no intention of risking their lives on such unseaworthy tubs.

Anstensen, now a lieutenant commander, M.B.E., recognized an old acquaintance among the men around whom the storm of disobedience swirled. Bos'n Tom White was making the most of what struck him as an honest grievance. Anstensen wisely signalled Montreal to send down Charlie Jarman's man to offer White evidence of the ship's fitness to weather anything the Atlantic had to offer.

The bos'n was eventually convinced—but it was too late. Civilian restraints practised during the terrible years of uncertainty were slackening, and in a burst of sentimental concern for abused merchant seamen, the Halifax press took up the cause of the *Branch* sitdowners. The fact that White admitted he had been wrong got scant attention. With so much sensational print appearing, the Mayor of Halifax complicated matters by deciding he should be publicly recognized as a champion of the fo'c's'le underdog.

The seriousness of the mischief was all too apparent. George Thompson—Jarman's top man in America—hurried up from New York and persuaded all but five of the National Union of Seamen members that they had been led down the garden path. When the hard-core quintet were dealt with under the Merchant Seamen Order, no sympathy was wasted on them.

The *Branches* were still in Halifax, straightening odds

and ends before sailing, when Anstensen was ordered overseas to join the Allied Control Commission preparing to move into Germany when its inevitable collapse came. Garry Hansen, just back from his turn at sea, took over as senior boarding officer.

The *Branches* were scheduled for convoy on May 9. Even if the war ended in the meantime, there was the possibility of fanatical U-boat commanders refusing to surrender, and the order was for convoys to be maintained until the last of the submarines had been accounted for.

The tankers were visited from time to time and the boarders were well received. Certificates were in order, crews alert to command. Hansen and his men would have been happier had they sensed as reassuring a climate on Barrington Street or in the Yard.

On May 8, satisfied that VE Day and the sailing of the *Branches* were about to coincide, Hansen talked things over with Oxner, then stopped all leave and put his entire crew on twenty-four-hour standby. The trooper *Scythia*, alongside Pier 22, already required the usual security guard.

Next morning the lid blew off. The spontaneous celebration that greeted the Nazi surrender sent masses of civilians and Service personnel into the streets. The high-jinks degenerated into a day that Halifax remembers only less bitterly than it does the time the *Mont Blanc* blew up.

It was fun until the mobs broke into the brewery and other wholesale sources of Dutch courage. After that, the destruction and looting along the business streets got completely out of hand. The world saved for democracy could scarcely have looked less inspiring than on the day of its deliverance.

In the aftermath, the civilians blamed the men of the Forces, recalling the threats they had made against larcenous landlords and other exploiters during the years of overcrowding. The Forces put the finger on the civvies, maintaining that mobs of them had pillaged behind the cover of a negligible number of men in uniform.

In a few hours the hospitality and sacrifice, the gratitude and human warmth that had marked the life of the city for six years evaporated in a rage of violence and recrimination.

When the financial price was paid, the federal government put up the dollars. But, by a supreme irony, the cost in things that mattered was exacted from one man. He, probably more than any single Canadian, had brought the celebrants a free Atlantic as the background for their celebration. Seeking no scapegoat where there were candidates aplenty, the Commander in Chief, Canadian Northwest Atlantic, accepted final responsibility for his Service's contribution to the disgrace. Gentleman and sailor, Admiral Murray removed himself from Canada after his resignation, sparing a number of uneasy consciences the goad of his physical presence.

Garry Hansen was confronted by more than the sailing of the *Branches* on the day victory was proclaimed. *Scythia*, having contributed her contingent to the riot ashore, called for reinforcements for the security guard. The need for them was clear in Hansen's report:

> "When looting occurred in downtown Halifax, the boarding parties on duty in the *Scythia* were placed on the gangway. Loot recovered when crew members returned was passed to the Staff Captain for forwarding to police ashore. All precautions were taken with the ship, with the gangway protected by steam lines and water hoses. The use of these, fortunately, was not required."

Then the unexpected appeared from another quarter:

> "The *Cancalais*, a schooner laden with rum, was berthed alongside Cunard's wharf and the Chief Examination Officer, on orders from C. in C. CNA, instructed the agents to move the vessel to an anchorage in the stream to ensure there would be no looting. The operators refused and CXO requested our assistance. Lieutenant Hansen, accompanied by two parties, accompanied CXO in case of difficulties but, fortunately, no intervention was necessary."

His report on the *Branches* was equally terse:

> "At 1400 we were advised that the entire crew was

AWOL from the *Cedar Branch*, whose gate time was 1600. In consequence she would be unable to sail. The missing men were all found in the Merchant Seamen's Club, more or less intoxicated, and were taken back to their vessel without undue difficulty."

What would have had to happen to have earned a "difficult" classification is a good question. "Tense" would not have been overdoing a description of the passage of Hansen's station wagons through the streets choked with increasingly unruly mobs. Taut nerves were not unusual during the urgency of any last minute sailing, even with the streets under the rule of law. That day, it was a matter of edging through a sea of booze-inflamed vandals, with no certainty that the appearance of law enforcers might not spark them to greater truculence.

Years of intimacy with highly primed dissidents were invaluable to the boarders at this moment. Their instinctive use of the wisecrack rather than the crack of the billy brought them at length to the upper end of Hollis Street without serious incident. As they drew to the curb outside the Merchant Seamen's Club the roar of voices inside rolled out through open doors to further swell the clamour of the streets.

Hansen said. "I think there will be less likelihood of anyone panicking if I go in alone. Stand fast, Oxner, unless I shout for you."

The main lounge was jammed with so many singing, shouting sailors it seemed that every ship in harbour had followed the *Cedar Branch*'s example. It took Hansen some time to pick out one man he was certain had taken part in a talk he'd had on the tanker. As he moved towards the ship-jumper the latter obviously recognized him. Far from attempting to lose himself in the crowd, the seaman lurched belligerently in the officer's direction, jostling intervening drinkers aside. Holding a beer bottle, he shifted his grip to its neck as he came closer.

"And what the hell would you be wanting?" he demanded.

Hansen had to raise his voice to have it heard above the row but he kept it level and calm.

"I want you to pick up your mates and get back to your ship," he said. "You're due to cast off in an hour."

The sailor, wielding the bottle more threateningly, proclaimed his low opinion of the proposition. From there he moved to sulphurous personal abuse, loud enough that spectators close by fell silent. The quiet spread until there was an island of it in the sea of surrounding noise. All eyes were now rivetted on the fuming seaman and the officer waiting him out. The air was thick with the smell of beer and danger.

Suddenly a new voice was heard, edged enough to cut through that of the drunken sailor.

"Easy on, mate," it ordered. "Is it true what the officer says?"

The speaker, whose Tyneside accent matched that of the man from the *Cedar Branch*, had eyes that appeared more deep-set than they actually were. The stokeholds of many coal-burners had given them a permanent shading. He was of modest build, but a lifetime with the shovel had raised the sinews on the backs of his hands. His voice had equal strength and the effect on his fellow Tynesider was striking. The blusterer shook his head as though he had been clipped in the chin, then regarded the fireman more in sorrow than anger.

"You don't expect us to sail the bloody ship the bloody day the bloody war packs up!" he exclaimed.

"If the officer's been good enough to come for you," said the fireman patiently, "the least you can do is go with him. Let him down and you let us all down. You wouldn't do a thing like that on a day like this, would you?"

The seaman protested that he wasn't going to be dragged off by any copper's nark.

"You know better than that," chided his self-elected conscience. "At least you would if you'd been at sea when these boarding blokes first started coming over the side. They're our friends, man."

Several heads in the surrounding circle nodded. Others joined the fireman on his mission of reason.

From then on there actually was "no undue difficulty". The idea of getting the *Cedar Branch*'s crew back on board for sailing time swept the club, becoming an added element of the celebration. One by one the scattered absentees were located and persuaded by their companions that every man was expected to do his duty.

Finally assembled, they were given an impromptu honour guard to the station wagons. Some required physical assistance, not because of reluctance, but for the simple reason that their legs had difficulty supporting their purpose.

Their voices raised in slurred determination, the crew of the *Cedar Branch* rode through Halifax's sorry streets. They helped each other over the tanker's brow, and mustered sufficient men with their senses about them to sail her past the gate ships at 1600.

Hansen, back in the Yard, watched the section of the convoy from the Basin and upper harbour pass downstream on the day so long awaited, the day so many had been denied. As each ship came abeam of the building where the masters knew the men in Naval Control Service would be watching, ensign after ensign slowly dipped, then rose again—the Red Duster, the Stars and Stripes, the varishaded crosses of the Scandinavians, the Dutch tricolour, the pale blue and white of Greece.

"I had difficulty distinguishing them," Garry confessed a quarter of a century later. "Because to tell you the truth, I was crying."

Dispersal

The bunting breaks at the halyard
And the Commodore's word is terse,
Terse and sweet as the ships repeat
With fluttering flags, "Disperse!"
A warm wave sighs through the convoy,
Through the discipline-frozen ranks;
The chill ungrips and the floe of ships
Crumbles along its flanks.

The motor craft that was throttled
For days to a galling nine,
Starts to careen to a good fourteen
And drifts from her ordered line.
The breathless tramp on the quarter
Drops back to an easy eight,
And the tankers part from the convoy's heart
At a lumbering peacetime gait.

This is the last dispersal
(Pray God that the word is true!)
The single course of a welded force
Splays out in a freedom new.
Each to his port of choosing
And each to his favoured track—
The channel clear of its close-sown fear
And the perilous tide turned slack.

Each to his own broad fairway
As the bloody page is turned,
But the quiet dead and the seas ahead
Clamour the truth we learned:
That each ship lives by the other,
Whatever her turn of speed,
And a free world still means the selfish will
Bent to a consort's need.

F.B. Watt
May, 1945